Using the Internet for Social Science Research and Practice

EDWARD P. KARDAS
Southern Arkansas University
Magnolia

TOMMY M. MILFORD
Southern Arkansas University
Magnolia

Wadsworth Publishing Company
I(T)P® An International Thomson Publishing Company

Belmont • Albany • Bonn • Boston • Cincinnati • Detroit • London • Madrid • Melbourne
Mexico City • New York • Paris • San Francisco • Singapore • Tokyo • Toronto • Washington

Sociology Editor: Eve Howard
Assistant Editor: Susan Shook
Editorial Assistant : Carrie Kahn
Production Editor: Karen Garrison
Print Buyer: Karen Hunt
Cover: Andrew Ogus
Printer: Malloy Lithographing

For more information, contact Wadsworth Publishing Company:

Wadsworth Publishing Company
10 Davis Drive
Belmont, California 94002, USA

International Thomson Publishing Europe
Berkshire House 168-173
High Holborn
London, WC1V 7AA, England

Thomas Nelson Australia
102 Dodds Street
South Melbourne 3205
Victoria, Australia

Nelson Canada
1120 Birchmount Road
Scarborough, Ontario
Canada M1K 5G4

International Thomson Editores
Campos Eliseos 385, Piso 7
Col. Polanco
11560 México D.F. México

International Thomson Publishing GmbH
Königswinterer Strasse 418
53227 Bonn, Germany

International Thomson Publishing Asia
221 Henderson Road
#05-10 Henderson Building
Singapore 0315

International Thomson Publishing Japan
Hirakawacho Kyowa Building, 3F
2-2-1 Hirakawacho
Chiyoda-ku, Tokyo 102, Japan

Library of Congress Cataloging-in-Publication Data

Kardas, Edward P., date
        Using the Internet for social science research and practice /
Edward P. Kardas, Tommy M. Milford.
                p.   cm.
        Includes bibliographical references (p. 221).
        ISBN: 0-534-51388-3 (alk. paper)
        1. Social Sciences—Computer network resources. 2. Internet
(Computer network). I. Milford, Tommy M., date. II. Title
H61.95.K37 1996   95-44835
025.06'3--dc20

Preface

"Just about everything you could want to know is on the Internet, if you could only find it," is a common sentiment. As social science teachers, we use the Internet and believe in its potential as a teaching tool. But we have witnessed the frustration of students and colleagues attempting to find worthwhile information efficiently on the Internet. Like anyone else, students and faculty will embrace technology if it makes their work easier. Fascination with computers is not the real issue. Instead, we see computers and networks as simply another set of tools for social scientists. Like any tool, networked computers can be dangerous or can be used to create useful things. However, we believe that before long the Internet will become the major medium for teaching, research, and practice in academia.

Why did we write this text? We wrote *Using the Internet for Social Science Research and Practice* as a simple introductory manual to the Internet for undergraduate social science students. We realized that social science graduate students and teachers would comprise a significant part of our intended audience too, given the newness of the Internet. But our main target group was undergraduate students.

What courses did we target? As teachers of research and practice courses, we saw the answer clearly enough. We found ourselves teaching the skills we write about and realized the need for a text like this one. So our goal was to create a short, affordable text that could be used in a wide variety of social science departments—in short, a supplementary text. We did not see the text as an encyclopedic survey of software or resources. Since then, and thanks to a Title IV-E grant, we have begun a new course titled, aptly enough, "Computer Methods for Social Science Research and Practice." Our text will serve as a primary resource for that course. We saw the need for such a course and perhaps others will, too. Finally, we came to realize that the text could also serve as an introductory reference for both the software tools and the specific Internet addresses we list by discipline.

What is the structure of the text? The text is divided into two major parts, software tools (Chapters 2-8) and discipline-specific chapters (Chapters 9-15). This structure was based on the premise that students need two things in order to use the Internet. The first is knowledge of how to use its tools, and the second is information on where to look using those tools. Interestingly, we did not deviate much from that original structure, other than to add a discipline and a software tool along the way. Of the many software tools available to navigate the Internet, we chose to emphasize electronic mail, gopher, and Web browsers because of their ubiquity and ease of use. We believe that those same tools will remain the most used ones on the Internet, barring the arrival of the next generation of software.

What do readers need to do to benefit most from this text? Both of us are heavy readers and believe that other readers could benefit by simply reading this text. But to get the full benefit, readers should have some level of access to the Internet—the more the better. Readers with electronic mail, gopher, and a Web browser will get much from the text, we hope. We know that the distribution of computer and network assets varies widely. As time passes, those disparities in equipment and connectivity should become less pronounced. If nothing else, this text can serve as a stimulus for such expansion.

How can readers find listed resources? Following the notion of allowing readers to choose their own methods, we have provided several ways of finding those resources. First, they are listed as notes for each chapter. Second, they are indexed by discipline and by software tool in an appendix. Third, they are provided as a set of Netscape bookmarks on the enclosed disk. Another source of information is provided by OCLC and their FirstSearch™ databases. The purchase of the text enables the buyer to access those databases free of charge. Finally, there will be construction of a Web page devoted to updating the text. Readers will be able to find additional resources there.

Did we make an attempt to rate the resources listed? No, we did not. We simply found and listed them. We did, however, attempt to ensure that those sites were stable so they could be found again. The Internet is a shifting and slippery place, and we cannot guarantee that all of the sites will still be there when you go to look for them.

Did we attempt to find all of the resources possible? No, we knew better than to embark on that Herculean task. Instead, we attempted to find useful and representative resources. We expect readers to learn how to find their own resources soon after they learn the basic skills involved. We also expect and urge readers to judge for themselves the worth and utility of the materials they find. We make no claims about the academic worth of the resources listed. *Caveat emptor.*

Is the Internet the answer to all of our problems? No, it is not. We are not so naive as to believe such a foolish notion. We realize that teaching and learning is a very complicated business. All of us, teacher and student alike, need to use whatever tools we can find to make the process easier. That is how we see the Internet, as another tool in our toolbox. We still have plenty of other tools in there: books, lectures, demonstrations, field trips, quizzes, videotapes and films, tests, papers, and the like. All we are advocating is that you make some room for this tool, too.

Where should readers begin the text? In our classes, we attempt to disabuse students of the notion that the only way to read a text is from beginning to end. We will continue that practice here. If you know little or nothing about the Internet, do start at the beginning. If you believe you are reasonably well informed, you may start at the discipline-specific chapter of your choice. For those of you who are not sure, we offer the following little quiz. If you can answer the majority of these items, you probably fall into the knowledgeable group. If not, start with the first group of chapters.

Quiz:
1.   What is a URL?
2.   Do you have an e-mail address? If so, do you remember it?
3.   What is a gopher?
4.   Do the acronyms FTP, WAIS, TCP/IP, and WWW mean anything to you?
5.   Have you ever flamed someone, or been flamed?

Well, how did you do?

Did we write this text by ourselves? No, many people assisted us in the creation of this book, and we would like to thank of all them for their work and encouragement. Specifically, we thank the folks at Wadsworth, both past and present; their skill and care were evident from the start. We thank Dean Allsman, once again, for helping us academics understand the publishing world; Helga Newman, who encouraged us early on; and Eve Howard, who again played the role of midwife, assisted by Susan Shook, Karen Garrison, and their staffs. We also thank their reviewers, and our copy editor, Tom Briggs. At Southern Arkansas University, we thank our colleagues from the English department: Elizabeth Davis, who painstakingly corrected our English; Mike Belmont, who proofread the entire manuscript; our administration who offered unflagging support; and our own departmental colleagues, who put up with us these last six months; and our new colleague, Diana Watkins who used an earlier version of the text in her class. Others from SAU include Jim Ferguson and John Weber of computing services for checking our technical language and for other services, and Agricultures's Randall Adams, fellow Mac user, for loaning us 1.7 gigabytes. Our student workers—Cindy Hicks, Stephanie Bennett, Charles McCartney, Angela Leake, and Randy Hart—helped us more than they know. We know we have not named all who helped, and for that we apologize and thank them in this manner. Finally, and most importantly, we thank both of our families. They are the only reason we worked so hard. To our wives, Julie and Deebe, we cannot express in words the gratitude and the debt we owe, but we thank you anyway. To our children, we apologize for the stolen hours; they will be repaid in full.

Edward P. Kardas
Tommy M. Milford

Magnolia, Arkansas

Contents

Contents

Chapter 7 Wide Area Information Server (WAIS)   73

Chapter 8 Usenet   79

Chapter 9 Psychology   97

1

Introduction

CHAPTER PREVIEW

In this chapter we will introduce the book, tell you why we wrote it, and outline its structure. This chapter will help you decide how you should read this book or where you should start to read it.

WHO IS THIS BOOK FOR?

We are social science teachers who use the Internet every day, both academically and personally. Like many other instructors, we are trying to integrate our traditional methods of teaching with the new resources and tools available on the Internet. We teach our students (and some of our colleagues, too) how to use the Internet. For us, the Internet is a huge information source, one that grows every day. We hope that this book will help you find information for social science research and practice courses from the Internet.

   The Internet has evolved rapidly into a very large collection of on-line information. Some of that information is of little value to researchers and practitioners, but some of it is very valuable. For example, to find census information before the Internet existed, you had to go to a library and thumb through several large books. Today, using the Internet, you can search for that same information from anywhere in the world using a networked computer. The same is true for many other sources of information. Also, the Internet has given rise to new possibilities for information sharing and retrieval. For instance, not only are textual materials available, so are audio materials and both still and motion visual materials. So, your next paper or presentation could use multimedia and be an interactive demonstration using those various types of materials described above. You could have done all of that before, you may think. But could you have done it in a matter of a few hours? Could you have done it without leaving home? Or, think of the possibility of communicating with experts in your field. You could find such experts

1

and have them assist or consult with you on your project. With a little practice and your networked computer, you can do all of that and more. To us, these examples reflect the real power of the Internet in social science research and practice. With the Internet, you can transcend barriers of time and space, not only learning course materials but collecting new knowledge yourself interactively. In fact, you can even become a purveyor of knowledge by establishing your own Internet site. The Internet will help you go far beyond the places that traditional instruction can take you. This book will show you how to become a skilled Internet knowledge navigator.

FEAR AND THE INTERNET

Like many new things, the Internet can be scary. One of our prime goals is to eliminate, or at least to reduce, any fears you may have about the Internet. If you are like a lot of our students, you have not spent much time on a computer, and you have spent even less time on a networked computer. On the other hand, some of you may have spent a good deal of time on the Internet and already lost your fear of it. For those of you in the latter category, though, remember your first time? Were you not just a little apprehensive? For those of you who have little or no Internet experience, let us assure you now that what is to come will help you much more than it will hurt you. Yes, we did say hurt. It is possible to get hurt on the Internet if you are not careful. For example, your electronic mail is not private. So, do not act as if it is. Also, most of the Internet is not secure for financial transactions. So, just as you would not give out your credit card numbers over the telephone, do not give them out over the Internet.

All of us are in a time of transition with tools like computers and the Internet. Because we grew up using other tools, we may be reluctant to learn new ones. Interestingly, if you watch young children—say, two- to four- year-olds— they seem to lack any fear of computers. They don't view computers as being new and different, and computer use seems to come to them naturally. So, maybe it is best to approach computers the way your little brother or sister might, assuming that computers are just another part of your world, something to learn, explore, and use. In the end, the Internet is neither good nor bad, right nor wrong, scary nor pleasant. As with any tool, our feelings about it come from our success at using it. Once you learned to hit the nail and not your thumb, you felt more positive about hammers, didn't you?

When you are done with this book, you will see the power of the Internet; you will know what kinds of things you can and cannot do safely on it; you will have a working knowledge of the various tools that have been developed to navigate and use the Internet; and you will have learned the rules of conduct for the Internet, or netiquette. Most importantly, you will know how to access information in the social sciences.

WHAT IS THE INTERNET?

Although we will answer that question in detail in Chapter 2, a few words about the Internet are in order here. First, the **Internet** is a vast collection of networked computers. Some of those computers are very small, the kind that used to be called microcomputers or are that are now called personal computers. Others are huge supercomputers. Computers in between those two extremes (minicomputers, mainframes) also populate the Internet. Any one of those computers, even yours, can be a server. A **server** is a computer that allows some access to it from other users on the Internet. Servers may be public, accessible to all Internet users, or they may restrict access to only certain Internet users. For example, some news services require a fee before they assign you a password required for access. Other servers may not require a fee or a password but may be automatically restricted to users at the organization that houses the server. It is even possible to restrict access to a server to just one class at a school!

Computers can be servers part–time as well. In other words, a networked computer may spend part of its time distributing or serving information, and it may spend the rest of its time searching for information or doing non-networked kinds of things. Of course, some computers only distribute information, and many computers only search for it. This approach to computing is known, naturally enough, as client-server computing. So, one way to look at the Internet is as a large collection of servers and an even larger collection of clients. We are going to teach you to become a client in this client-server arrangement. One of the most exciting aspects of the Internet is that nearly anyone, even you, can set up a server. Hundreds of new servers are added to the Internet daily, and no one knows how many clients come on board every day. So, the Internet is growing very quickly, both in number of servers and in number of clients or users.

We will guide you to those parts of the Internet that have their use in social science research and practice—for example, to show you where to find specific databases relevant to particular subjects or how to find experts in various fields. We also have arranged for you to be able to perform literature searches using The Online Computer Library Center, Inc.'s (OCLC) FirstSearch™ software. When you purchased this book, you also received unlimited literature searches from over 50 specialized databases. So, you will be able to browse the contents of many of the world's libraries without ever leaving home. We hope that you will find the text and what it teaches you useful, not only in the course you are in, but also in the rest of your undergraduate experience and after.

NETIQUETTE

"Netiquette" is the name given to the rules and customs of the Internet. Obviously, the word is a contraction of "network" and "etiquette." Shea (1994) has published these rules and customs in a book. You can also get netiquette tips directly[a] from the Internet[1]. Or, like many people, you can learn them from experience. But then you risk being called a "newbie" or being "flamed." See Seabrook (1994) for a particularly harsh example of flaming. You should not expect the Internet to be any different from any other set of human interactions. However, knowing and using netiquette may keep those interactions on an even keel.

RESEARCH AND PRACTICE

We view research and practice in the social sciences broadly. Thus, we have chosen to err on the side of overinclusion of resources in the discipline-specific chapters (Chapters 9-15). We believe that it is better to include a resource and then let you decide if you can use it. In other words, we tried not to act as a filter when choosing resources. If a resource appeared to have some possible use in social science research and practice, we included it.

HYPERSPACE AND HYPERTEXT

Imagine a structure where every item is just as close as any other item. Or imagine a place where items have no inherent organization, but where they can be organized in any number of ways. Does that sound absurd or impossible? Well, it is neither. In fact, the Internet is such a place, and it is probably the first real example of a hyperspace. Exotic research in such topics as black holes, wormholes, and gravitational waves also involves hyperspace principles. However, we will not look at those complex subjects. Rather, we will restrict our focus to a subset of hyperspace, hypertext.

---

a   We will indicate pointers to Internet locations by notes at the end of each chapter. Later chapters will show you how to use these Internet pointers or hyperlinks.

In a **hypertext**—a term coined by Nelson (1965) although Bush (1945) was the first to publish a paper on what we would now call hypertext—text or other materials are encoded in such a way as to make them difficult to represent on paper. Computers make possible the creation of hypertext and other hypermedia. We found a review of the history and implementation of hypertext[2] on the Internet.

Hypertext items are hard to put on paper precisely because of the constraints that paper imposes on text items. Namely, text items have to fit on paper, they have to be fixed in place, and they cannot be moved afterwards. Text items are also linear, meaning that the author has provided them in an ordered sequence. Every book ever written, including this one, is bound by those constraints. Hypertext, in contrast, is both nonlinear and moveable, and it can be easily viewed in more than one sequence and reordered in an infinite number of ways. Further, hypertext, unlike paper-bound text, can be located anywhere in a hyperspace. All that is required is that a **hyperlink**[b] exist somewhere to take the user to a particular location in that hyperspace. That location may be hyperlinked from many other locations. Computers make the easy handling of hypertext materials possible. Without computers, we would probably still be at the stage of merely imagining hypertext. However, because of computers and the Internet, not only can we talk about hypertext, we can actually manipulate it. That manipulation is what the Internet is all about and what this text is all about. We find it just a little ironic that we are discussing hypertext using old-fashioned linear text. However, we do address that irony, in part, by providing you with hypertext additions to the text in the form of computer disks and our own location in hyper-space that contains pointers to many of the Internet resources cited in the text.[3]

BASIC STRUCTURE OF THE TEXT

Much of the first part of this book (Chapters 2-8) will focus on the various software tools that have been developed to navigate and use the Internet. The Internet is not very old (see Chapter 2 for a short history), and software tools have been developed to help users cope with the growth of information on the Internet. Those tools have also evolved in terms of their power and ease of use. Each new generation of tools has been easier to use and has enabled users to accomplish more in less time.

Below, the tools will be briefly discussed. Later, each tool will be explained in more detail in a chapter devoted to it (Chapters 9-15). You

---

b   Hyperlink: a marked location that moves a user's display from the current position to another position in hyperspace

should read each of those chapters because they will provide you with the basic skills that you will need to successfully use the Internet for social science research and practice.

The chapters that follow the tools chapters will largely consist of descriptions of Internet locations of sites containing useful, discipline-specific information. If you are an Internet novice, or newbie, you will probably not get much use from the discipline-specific chapters until you have read the tools chapters. On the other hand, if you already are fairly conversant with Internet tools, you can probably safely skip to the discipline-specific chapters. For example, if you already know what a **URL** is, you are probably ready to look at the later chapters. If you do not know what a **URL**c is, you should continue to read.

There are seven discipline-related chapters (Chapters 9–15) : psychology, sociology, social work, political science, geography, anthropology, and history. Each chapter is arranged around courses in those departments, and useful URLs for those courses are listed. Appendix A lists URLs, sorted by software tool; for each chapter. The URLs are also listed in electronic form in the accompanying floppy disks. Many of the URLs are also available on the Thomson Publications WWW Site4. We expect you, the student, to learn to use the Internet as a way of finding out new or additional material relevant to a particular course or as a way to confirm statements made in class or published in your textbooks.

INTERNET SOFTWARE TOOLS

As stated above, much of the utility of the Internet as a source of information comes from the software tools that have been developed to help users navigate and use the Internet. Those tools have evolved and improved over the Internet's brief lifespan. The newest tools incorporate many of the features of earlier tools. World Wide Web browsers, the software that interprets **HTML**d (see Chapter 6), for instance, have their own unique features, but they also can be used for electronic mail, FTP, TELNET, gopher, and other functions. But we are getting ahead of ourselves. Let us examine each of the tools briefly.

---

c   URL: Uniform Resource Locator, the "address" of an Internet site. Each type of Internet software tool has it specific type of URL.

d   HTML: Hypertext Markup Language, the language used to create World Wide Web Documents

Electronic Mail and Listservers

One of the oldest uses of the Internet, and still the biggest use by volume, is electronic mail . Chapter 3 will cover the details of electronic mail and will also discuss listservers, an automated type of electronic mail. Electronic mail is useful in social science research and practice, too. For example, electronic mail allows you to contact individuals who may have already done research similar to yours. Or, by finding a specialized listserver, you may discover a self-selected group of people interested in the same research or practice topics. Many such listservers exist, and the discipline-specific chapters each contain lists of such listservers. Finally, electronic mail and listservers can be used as quick sources of data themselves. Many people already use the Internet as a population for drawing survey samples. You could, too.

File Transfer Protocol (FTP)

File transfer protocol, or FTP, is another older Internet tool. It, along with TELNET, was one of the first tools for networking. FTP was developed as a method of transferring files from one computer to another regardless of its type or brand. Servers that allow any Internet user to log on by using the account "anonymous" are known as anonymous FTP servers. The anonymous account allows server managers to set up a public area on their server and to allow any Internet user access without managers having to assign those users their own individual accounts. FTP shows its age in that users must remember fairly arcane UNIX commands to use FTP (UNIX is a computer operating system used by many servers on the Internet). For instance, users must remember that "cd" means "change directories." FTP frightens new users (and old users, too) because of its command structure. Many newer tools have been developed on top of FTP to make it easier to use. Fetch and anarchie are two examples of such tools. They allow users to use FTP without having to remember all of the commands. Still, there are times when FTP is the tool of choice, as, for instance, when you have none of the newer software clients (e.g., gopher or WWW browsers) but do have access to FTP. You can get any of the newer tools by using FTP. Data files are available by FTP as well. Also, you should learn about FTP just in case you need to use it someday. But, realistically, you will probably use the newer tools much more than you will ever use FTP. Chapter 4 covers the use of FTP.

TELNET

Unlike FTP, TELNET is an old tool that is still widely used. TELNET allows you to use a remote computer as if it were at your physical location. TELNET is extremely useful, and it is made possible by the large number of public and restricted servers mentioned above. When you TELNET, you end up connected to a server somewhere in the world. You may find, as we did a few years ago before Southern Arkansas University upgraded its computers, that your connection to the remote computer is actually faster than your connection to your campus mainframe or other Internet provider. Other times, of course, it may be slower than your local connection, especially if the remote computer is several oceans or continents away.

The FirstSearch™ account included with this text uses TELNET. FirstSearch™ maintains restricted servers full of library data. The account included with this book allows you to access that information. Details on how to use FirstSearch™ and how to use your searches efficiently are given in Chapter 4. TELNET is also useful for checking your electronic mail when you are away from home. One of us recently attended a computer conference in West Virginia. The organizers had thoughtfully provided a room full of computers linked to the Internet. During breaks in the conference, participants checked their electronic mail by telnetting to their home servers.

Gopher Clients and Servers

To our minds, gopher (see Chapter 6 for the origin of gopher's name) software was the first breakthrough in making the Internet accessible to users who did not have a great deal of training and experience in computers. One reason that gopher was a breakthrough was its ease of use. Another reason was that gopher clients and servers were available for a wide variety of computers. That variety meant that anyone who wanted to set up a gopher server knew that the information on that server would be accessible to nearly anyone with Internet access because, once a user had the appropriate client software, it no longer mattered what kind of server the client was accessing.

Gopher is a kind of client-server software based on a file structure model. Because most computer users are already familiar that model, gopher is easy to use. Gopher is also fairly fast, even on older client computers. Another breakthrough for gopher was that it automatically or semi-automatically invoked helper applications to deal with complex file types like still and moving graphic files and audio files. Chapter 5 covers the use of gopher clients, and the various discipline-specific chapters contain numerous references to useful gopher sites.

Gopher servers may be set up on a wide variety of computers including all of the popular brands of personal computers. Although setting up such servers is beyond the scope of this text, the University of Minnesota (home of the gopher tool) provides gopher clients and servers for nearly any kind of computer.[5] Setting up gopher clients can be seen as a form of publication, and such publication is one of the advantages (or disadvantages) of the Internet. The same kind of activity e.g., serving, can also occur with the World Wide Web, our next topic.

World Wide Web Clients and Servers

The World Wide Web (WWW or Web) is the implementation of hyperspace principles in software. WWW clients and servers are written in HTML short for Hypertext Markup Language. That language creates both home pages[e] and hyperlinks, the basic features of the WWW. In the evolutionary context described above, the WWW incorporates within itself all of the basic tools, except TELNET. (TELNET can be used, but its use requires a separate TELNET application program.) Also, the newer clients automatically call helper applications for dealing with graphic and audio files.

WWW clients or browsers enable users to "surf" the Internet in a much more effortless manner than earlier tools. All of this power comes at a price, however. Most WWW clients are graphical, so users without computers that support graphical user interfaces (e.g., Macintosh or Windows) must use versions that do not support the graphical features of WWW. Also, because most WWW clients can display graphics by themselves, the amount of data they move from place to place is larger. In Internet terms, WWW requires more "bandwidth," a measure of the capacity and, thus, the potential speed, of an Internet connection (see Chapter 3 for more discussion). Finally, WWW clients are typically slower than gopher clients because they do more. However, the newest versions of WWW clients are markedly faster than the earlier versions, especially on faster PCs like Pentiums and Power Macintoshes.

Like gopher, WWW servers are also fairly easy to set up. Again, such discussion is beyond the scope of this text. CERN, the European Center for Nuclear research and the originator of WWW, provides information on how to set up WWW servers for those of you who may wish to do so[6]. Many users are setting up personal home pages using WWW server software. We can imagine a day when nearly every Internet

---

e   Home page: the basic building block of the World Wide Web. A home page can be self-contained, or it may hyperlink to other pages (including other home pages)

user will have his or her own home page. Hopefully, bandwidth problems will be solved before then.

Because of the power, ease of use, and æsthetics of WWW, we will spend a disproportionate amount of time on it and on WWW URLs. We believe that you, too, will see just how powerful and easy to use the WWW clients are. However, do not take our emphasis on WWW clients too far. One of the themes we wish to develop in this text is that you will probably need most or all of the tools mentioned above at one time or another. So, we will be emphasizing the use of the Internet in a variety of interconnected ways. For example, both of us are likely to have our WWW client, our electronic mail program, and our TELNET program all open simultaneously. Very often, we may reply to an electronic mail request by performing a FirstSearch™ search or a WWW search. Thus, those applications will all be open, and we may hop between them, hardly thinking about it.

KEY THEMES

We already mentioned one theme, using the appropriate tool at the appropriate time. Another theme we want to stress is empowerment of students (and faculty). To us, the Internet is akin to the biggest library ever created. Just as students must learn to use the library, so must they learn to use the Internet. When you learn to use the library, you learn that you can find things out for yourself. The same is true for the Internet. We want you to learn how to teach yourself how to use the Internet.

Associated with this last theme is the theme of bottom-up organization. If ever there existed an example of bottom-up organization, the Internet is it. The Internet is about as anti-hierarchical a structure as has ever been conceived or implemented. To us, that is good. It is good because it reflects the same kinds of self-organizing principles that embody natural selection, intelligence, and learning. As users put new servers on the Internet, they may add useful pieces of knowledge or skills, and others will find them. For example, one of our colleagues, James Willis, has installed a series of historical pictures of life in southwest Arkansas. Those pictures are available on the Southern Arkansas University WWW server[7]. Previously, one had to trek to Cross Hall on the campus to see those pictures. Soon, however, anyone with a WWW client will be able to see them from anywhere in the world! Think of the implications of that last statement. Of course, servers could just as easily add useless, frivolous, or nonsensical pieces of information, consuming precious bandwidth. But the latter types of information will be ignored by most users, and useful information will predominate.

Finally, the democracy of the Internet appeals to us, and we hope,

Finally, the democracy of the Internet appeals to us, and we hope it does to you, too. On the Internet, the usual trappings of power and prestige are diminished. Already we have noticed such democratizing effects. On public listservers, anyone can post an opinion, for example. On electronic mail, you can literally send a message to anyone in the world, provided you know his or her address. You can set up a gopher or WWW server with any information on it you choose.

Some of you may find these themes scary, and we are not so naive as to believe there is nothing but good on the Internet. But, in the long run, we believe, those bottom-up principles of self-organization will ensure that the cream rises. Further, the Internet is really no different from other information repositories of the past in terms of its content. For example, the recent bombing in Oklahoma City prompted concern that bomb making instructions were available on the Internet, but those same instructions have long been available in print, too. What makes the Internet different is the ease with which one can find and publish information.

USING FREQUENTLY ASKED QUESTIONS FILES

Frequently asked question files or FAQs are another invaluable resource to the Internet newcomer or "newbie." For instance, most mailing lists (see Chapter 3) and Internet tools (see Chapters 4, 5, and 6) keep and maintain one or more FAQs. As a new user, you should seek out and read those FAQs. Very often they will keep you from being "flamed" by experienced users. Flaming is when you receive abusive or insulting electronic mail. See Chapter 3 for more discussion about flaming.

SOME CAUTIONS AND SOME ADVICE

Like any complex machine, the Internet has its limits. Once you begin to use the Internet, you will quickly find that some times when it will be unavailable to you. You will often hear the words, "The Internet is down." The Internet may go down or crash for any number of reasons. The problem could be widespread, as when heavy rains recently flooded a basement at the University of Nebraska and knocked out most of the Internet connections in the Midwest. Or, the problem could be local, as when the server providing your Internet access crashes. In either case, the best you can do is to plan around the likelihood of such interruptions. If you like to put work off until near its deadline, you may find that you cannot complete that work because of an Internet problem.

experience slower response times or rejection of your connection requests. You may have to work at off-peak times to deal with such delays. Another way to deal with traffic problems is to access servers in parts of the world that are locally at an off-peak time. For instance, when it is 3:00 p.m. at our location, it is 10:00 p.m. in Rome. I may not be able to access a server easily in North America at 3:00 p.m. But I may have less trouble accessing a server storing the same information in Europe because of reduced local traffic there. Many computers come with the software that displays worldwide local times. If yours does not, time zone maps of the world are readily available.

Finally, be aware that Internet sites are maintained by human beings. Some sites mentioned in this book may well no longer exist by the time you go looking for them. Other sites may have moved. Some site managers will leave a forwarding address to the new sites, but other managers may not. So, when you do find a site you are interested in, be sure to note its address so that you can return to it. If you attempt to return to a site and find it no longer there, you may be able to find the same information elsewhere. See Chapter 6 for tips on how to search the Internet yourself. We have checked and confirmed all of the sites mentioned in this book. However, that does not ensure that you will find them when you look for them.

The Internet will become a very useful tool for you soon, we predict. But be aware that the Internet may not be available to you when you want it. Avoid the frustration caused by such unavailability by planning your access ahead of time.

NOTES

1.   http://rs6000.adm.fau.edu/rinaldi/netiquette.html

2.   http://www.isg.sfu.ca/~duchier/misc/hypertext_review/index.html

3.   http://mulerider.saumag.edu

4.   http://www.thomson.com

5.   gopher://gopher.tc.umn.edu:70/hh/Information%20About%20Gopher

6.   http://www.w3.org/hypertext/WWW/Provider/Overview.html

7.   http://mulerider.saumag.edu/history/historydocs/WalzPics.html

2

History and Technology

CHAPTER PREVIEW

One of the best features of the Internet is that you do not need to know a lot about the workings of the Internet in order to use it. This chapter will cover how the Internet came to be, how it works, and what is likely to happen to it in the future. So if you are the type who likes to understand things by looking at how they are put together, then this chapter is for you. If you are not, there are still some interesting tidbits awaiting you. For example, did you know that the ARPANET (the precursor to the Internet) was only designed for a maximum of 256 connected computers? Obviously, the designers had not foreseen the explosive growth of today's Internet. Will the Internet ever become too large for its present protocols to handle? Yes, that day is coming.

HISTORY OF THE INTERNET

The late 1960s, when the proto-Internet started, might seem ancient history to you. Further, the computer technology of that era might as well be compared to automobile technology in 1903. You may not realize just how much the concept "computer" has changed since the days before the Internet. Back then, computers were very large and expensive–so large that they filled whole rooms specially equipped with raised floors to accommodate all the required wiring and special air conditioning systems. Today, in contrast, you can buy a microcomputer the size of a pizza box for under $2000. This computer will be much more powerful than most of the computers that populated the early Internet, and you can use it nearly anywhere.

The people who originally developed the Internet had very little idea about what they were creating. They knew they wanted computers to be able to communicate with each other, but that is about all. Thus, the history of the early days of the Internet is made even more fascinating because of the founders' nearly total lack of vision of what was to come.

Don't get the idea that the founders were stupid or that they just stumbled onto the Internet as we now know it. No, quite the contrary. They knew that they wanted to connect or to network computers. Beyond that, however, they did not envision the Internet as it now exists.

Who were these people? For the most part, they were faculty and graduate students in computer science departments at large American universities who were receiving financial support for their research from ARPA (later called DARPA), the Department of Defense's Advanced Research Projects Administration. DARPA was one of the many responses to the launch of the Soviet satellite *Sputnik* in 1957. If you were not alive then, it might be hard for you to imagine the effect that *Sputnik* had on the American consciousness in general and on the scientific establishment in particular. Basically, it shook Americans out of their previous beliefs about their academic, intellectual, and technological superiority. The fact that the Soviets had been able to launch and orbit a satellite while the Americans had not was shocking to most Americans. In response, many new government programs were launched to improve science education in the United States. DARPA was one of those programs. However, unlike many of the other programs, DARPA funded pure research. Also, DARPA's mission was not specific, and its directors allowed researchers a great deal of free rein. The result was that DARPA was willing to fund projects that might not have a short-term payoff but did show long-term potential. It was DARPA's interest in connecting computer, radio, and satellite communications that led to the eventual creation of the Internet.

ARPANET

The need to construct a communications network that could survive nuclear war and other disasters was one of the driving forces at DARPA. By the late 1960s, some scientists began to see computers as part of the communications equation as well. The business community and computer manufacturers, for the most part, did not share that vision. They still saw computers as number-crunching arithmetic devices. Most saw the idea of using computers as part of a communications network as impossible or worthless.

However, some, including DARPA, did see computers as possible components in a communications network. So, in 1968, DARPA funded research in connecting packet-switching (see below) networks composed of radio, satellite, and computer components. DARPA's obvious interest in such networks lay in their utility in battlefield communication, command, and control. The creation of the ARPANET in 1969 was the main result of that funding. Construction and development of equipment began shortly after, and the first sites were connected.

The biggest start-up problem was getting all of the different computers to communicate with each other, because the computers had not been designed for networking. In fact, the very idea of networking different computers to each other was completely new. Isn't it amazing how far things have come in the world of computing? The goal of networking the various types of computers was accomplished by making each computer on the network use a new protocol, or standard system for communicating. That new protocol was called NCP, for Network Control Program. Each different brand of computer on the network required its own unique software to conform to the NCP protocol, and all of that software had to be created from scratch. Later, that protocol was modified to the current protocol, TCP/IP (Transmission Control Protocol/Internet Protocol), and nearly every computer that has been directly connected to the Internet since has had to conform to that protocol.

Do you remember that at the beginning of this chapter we said that the early ARPANET could support only 256 connected networks? That limit resulted because NCP had been written using an 8-bit addressing scheme, and 8-bit schemes only allow for the coding of 256 addresses. (See below for why.) TCP/IP uses a 32-bit addressing scheme that allows more than 4 billion addresses. Even that 32-bit scheme will lead to problems soon because there are more than 20 million computers on the Internet today and many more addresses. Again, the early designers of the Internet completely underestimated how popular networked computers would become. For example, the international use of networking was certainly not anticipated, but we now routinely correspond on electronic mail with Internet users all around the world.

Another early issue was what to do with computers once they were networked. The software applications that we take for granted today did not exist. Among the first software packages written were TELNET and FTP. TELNET (see Chapter 4) allows users to access remote computers as if users were physically at the computer site. In other words, the network acts as a long wire from the user to the remote computer. FTP (see Chapter 4) allows users to transfer programs and data from a remote computer to their own. These applications had never been created previously because they had not been needed in the pre-Internet world of non-networked computers. Electronic mail was another early use of the network, as were mailing lists (see Chapter 3). Gopher and WWW browsers (see Chapters 5 and 6, respectively) are much newer, dating from the late 1980s. The network enhancements of the operating system UNIX also did not exist until DARPA commissioned them from UC-Berkeley for use on ARPANET. Today, UNIX is the most common operating system on the Internet.

Implementation and Growth

The first four ARPANET sites or nodes (a computer connected to the Internet) were UCLA, the Stanford Research Institute (SRI), UC-Santa Barbara, and the University of Utah (Aboba, 1993). They were chosen because researchers at those various sites were already conducting research into aspects of computer networking. That research included projects concerning communications network topologies (e.g., designs and structures), bundling of information into "packets," distributed communication, and satellite communication[1]. By 1971, the network had grown to 15 sites, a slow pace to many in the project. But, after a demonstration at a conference in 1972, ARPANET began to grow quickly, to 111 sites by 1977[2].

In the 1980s, the National Science Foundation started to influence the development of networks. NSFnet was originally created to network supercomputers at five American universities, but it quickly became obvious that NSFnet could also be used for other network activity. That other activity, mostly electronic mail, soon swamped the capacity of the network, so the NSFnet was upgraded to faster communication links, and management was given to three private companies. Other networks also sprung up, notably BITNET, CSNET, and Usenet, and their servers and users also fueled Internet growth. By 1989, the number of nodes on the NSFnet exceeded 100,000[3]. At about the same time, ARPANET had split into two networks, ARPANET and MILNET. That split was done mainly to make MILNET secure, but it also reflected how the ARPANET had changed into a more open system. Eventually, ARPANET was shut down and its remaining users migrated to NSFnet. MILNET continues as a secure military network.

Today and Tomorrow

This loosely organized and growing collection of networks is what today comprises the Internet. The number of nodes now easily exceeds 20 million, and no one can really guess at the number of total users because new users and nodes are added daily. The technical issues that were researched in the 1970s, combined with the various types of equipment and communications protocols that emerged from that research, have made the Internet possible. Future growth is a certainty, as are changes in equipment and associated software.

The future of the Internet is nearly boundless. However, technical issues like communications infrastructure and bandwidth and political issues like governmental policies and international cooperation could limit Internet growth. A recent example of the latter has been Congress's concern with the proliferation of violent and pornographic materials on the Internet. As you surely have already seen, the Internet has made its presence known in education. Today, many university faculty and students are routinely given electronic mail accounts and access to the World Wide Web and other Internet software tools. Unfortunately, many other faculty and students are still waiting for Internet access at their schools. Likewise, some secondary schools have already achieved Internet access, but most have yet to do so. The same pattern of wide variations in Internet connectivity exists on the international level. Many countries have minimal Internet connectivity, meaning those countries may be limited to electronic mail only at a few nodes. Some countries have yet to achieve any Internet connectivity. Still other countries have levels of connectivity nearly the equal of that in the United States. For some, the growth of the Internet is but another example of technology being split between the "haves" and the "have–nots." At some point, the issue of Internet access will have to be addressed, both in the United States and worldwide.

Much debate is currently taking place about the future of the Internet. During its early growth, it was subsidized by the American government, and commercial use was prohibited. Today, the ban on commercial use has been lifted, but few people have figured out a way to profit financially from the Internet. One problem is security. Determined individuals with computer skills, known as hackers and crackers, can and do use the Internet illegally, sometimes stealing money and services. Many legal issues are yet to be resolved. For example, is electronic mail like a telephone call or like a letter? Is encryption, or secret coding, of electronic mail legal? Should the government have the right to listen in on the Internet? Another problem concerns the philosophy of Internet use. Will it continue as it now is, a loose and informal place? Or will it become more structured, more formal, and more in the mainstream? Finally, what new tools and uses will emerge? What new resources and infrastructure will those new tools require? Whatever the questions, we all have a stake in the answers. So, keep abreast of the news and contact lawmakers when issues concerning the Internet are to be decided.

TECHNOLOGY

For you tinkerers out there, we provide a brief overview of some of the technology that makes the Internet work. Again, many users will never be concerned with these kinds of issues. We believe, though, that it cannot hurt to have some basic knowledge about the workings of the Internet.

Basic Concepts

Here is probably as good a place as any to review some basic concepts surrounding computers and networking.

Analog vs. Digital.   What is the difference between analog and digital? **Analog** representations use an existing physical system to provide an analogy between that system and the representation. Much of the world around you uses such analogies in a useful way. For instance, your stereo speakers are analog devices. An electromagnet causes the speaker components to vibrate in such a way as to reproduce the original recorded sound. An old-fashioned mechanical watch with a sweep second hand is another example. The second hand sweeps smoothly around the watch face, under the control of clockwork. The key to determining whether a representation is analog is noting whether the representation divides into an infinite or finite number of possible states.

    Digital representations are abstract. They do not depend on an existing physical system, and they are finite. Look at a digital watch with a traditional face and a sweep second hand. What do you notice about the movement of the second hand? Does it sweep smoothly like the second hand on an analog watch? No, the digital second hand jumps from second to second, 60 jumps to a minute. The analog second hand, in contrast, moves smoothly around the face, sweeping past an infinite number of fractions of a second, thus dividing each minute into an infinite number of parts. There is even an infinite number of such fractions between each second.

    More generally, digital representations divide any information into a finite number of discrete elements. Let's look at two examples. Time can be divided into a more and more precise representation by splitting it into smaller but discrete pieces. Imagine a digital watch that does not have a traditional watch face . If it just shows hours and minutes and does not show a.m. or p.m., then it divides time into 720 states (12 hours X 60 minutes). If it does show a.m. or p.m., or if it shows military time, then it divides time into 1440 states (24 hours X 60 minutes). If the watch shows hours, minutes, seconds, and a.m. and p.m., then it divides time into 86,400 states (24 hours X 60 minutes X 60 seconds). Timers that show tenths of a second (think of basketball) divide time into 864,000 states. Can you see why?

Similarly, music CDs divide each second into 44,000 separate elements; each element can be coded to represent a particular sound. Those coded elements are converted back into analog sound emanating from your speakers. Programming can be used to eliminate unwanted and nonmusical sounds like hisses and pops, making for much cleaner sound than possible from completely analog systems.

Coding and the Number of Bits. A **bit** is the smallest piece of information that can be coded. One way to think of bits is as "yes" and "no" answers to questions. Then a "yes" answer can be coded as a 1, and a "no" answer as a 0. By grouping sets of bits into longer pieces, a coding system can be developed. The simple formula: 2^n, where n is the number of bits used as a longer element or "word," gives the maximum number of words or code states for a given number of bits. As mentioned above, the ARPANET used 8-bit words and thus could only code for 256 possible states. The modern Internet uses 32-bit words and thus can code for over 4 billion possible states.

Communications Media. The American road system makes for a good analogy for the Internet's communication infrastructure. The Internet is composed of a wide variety of different kinds of communications media that move the digitized information from place to place. The fastest transmission is accomplished by T3 dedicated lines. These are high speed (45 megabits/sec) communication lines, usually made of fiber optic cables; they are like the most modern and widest interstate highways. T3 lines are used as the backbone, or main part, of the Internet. T1 lines, usually made of insulated copper wire, are slower (1.544 megabits/sec) but are fast enough for most of the uses you will have for the Internet. They are like older and narrower interstate highways. They are still primary roads, but their speed limits are lower, and the amount of traffic they can carry is limited. Typically, T3 and T1 cables belong to a communications company and are then leased to Internet service providers. Slower leased lines are also available. The slower leased lines are like the federal and state highway systems. The analogy can be carried to the secondary road level, too.

The Internet can also be accessed through ordinary telephone lines and modems (see Chapter 3). A **modem** (a contraction for "modulator-demodulator") at the sending end of a connection converts the computer's digital signals into analog form so that they can travel along the telephone wire; then another modem at the receiving end converts the analog signals back into digital form. Information travels much slower on this kind of connection. For example, the most commonly available modems today transmit signals at 0.14 megabits/sec, still fast enough for many client computers, but too slow for an Internet server computers. (See below for an explanation of clients and servers.) Higher–speed modems (0.28 megabits/sec) are available, but they cost more and stretch telephone wiring to its practical limits of functionality. Chapter 3 discusses the issues involved in setting yourself up to use the Internet from your home computer using a modem.

Bandwidth.   "Bandwidth" is a term used often in conjunction with Internet communications. In terms of the road analogy above, you can think of bandwidth as the road's capacity for traffic. Interstates can handle much more traffic than secondary roads. You may experience the differences in bandwidth when you connect to the Internet via modem rather than your school's T1 line. The latter will be much faster. However, you are not likely to ever experience the maximum speed achievable by any communications medium because of other traffic or communications bottlenecks.

Client-Server Computing.   The Internet is probably the leading example of the client-server model of computing. In that model, computers may act as **servers**, or distributors of information; or they may act as **clients**, or consumers of information. A particular computer may be both client or server at different times, as well. For you, the main advantage of the client-server model is that it puts a world of information at your fingertips. Potential problems for you include finding all of that information and running out of storage space on your computer for information you want to keep.

Packet Switching.   If you recall the recent earthquakes in California and Japan or other similar disasters, you might remember that the telephone companies requested that callers not attempt to call loved ones in those areas in order to keep the circuits clear. A less dramatic example occurs every Mother's Day, when you may get a recorded message that all circuits are busy. Such problems are a result of the telephone system's use of circuit–switching technology.

You use circuit–switching technology every time you make a telephone call. When a call goes through, you and the person you called have physically established a connection or circuit between the two of you. That circuit is maintained as long as both phones are off the hook, even if no words are being spoken. The Internet could have been designed around circuit–switching technology, but that technology is not really suited for the kind of information that travels the Internet. Nor is it suited for providing reliable communications in the event of nuclear war and other disasters. Thus, packet switching was developed.

So what is **packet switching**? Krol's (1992) analogy of packets as mail envelopes is informative. A packet contains information about where it is supposed to go, and where it came from, and about the number and order of packets comprising a particular piece of information. Digital information is placed inside one or more packets and sent on the Internet. In Krol's envelope analogy, humans read the address and route the envelope accordingly. In the Internet, the IP part of the TCP/IP protocol handles the routing of packets using IP addresses. (How addresses work on the Internet is described below.) The TCP part disassembles information into smaller chunks and puts those chunks into one or more packets, labelling them in the process. At the destination, TCP reassembles and reorders the packets. If any are missing or damaged, it requests that the sender send them again.

Again, vehicles and roads provide a useful analogy of how the Internet works, if you make a few simple changes. First, imagine that all vehicles on the road are exactly the same size and that all travel the fastest speed that they can without causing collisions. Next, substitute information for people and goods, and assume that if shippers cannot fit all of the goods that customers ordered into one vehicle, they simply add vehicles until the entire order is accommodated. Finally, each vehicle is labelled with the shipper's address, the customer's address, and with the number of vehicles making up the order. The same logic would apply to passenger vehicles, except that they would be labelled with the passengers' origin and destination.

Notice how the highway analogy deals with the issue of bandwidth. Two-lane roads can only accommodate a certain volume of traffic before that traffic has to slow down to avoid collisions. On the other hand, six-lane interstates can handle a much larger volume of traffic before they become as congested. Also, notice that individual vehicles need not travel together or travel the same route. If we can switch metaphors, each packet is like a rail car, but those rail cars are not connected. If you were watching such disconnected, self-powered rail cars, each one that passed in front of you might be bound for a different destination (see Figure 2-1). Regardless of the metaphor, the routing information on the packets allows the customer to put them and their contents back into their original order. If a packet is missing or empty, the customer simply labels another packet and sends it back with a request to resend the missing items. On the Internet, such tasks are handled automatically by the TCP/IP protocol.

Unlike in circuit-switching networks, users in packet-switching networks may share the same physical network connections simultaneously. As more users access the network, it begins to degrade by slowing down. In contrast, circuit-switching networks respond to increased user demand by not allowing new users on the network. You may have already noticed that some servers also deny access to Internet users as well. That

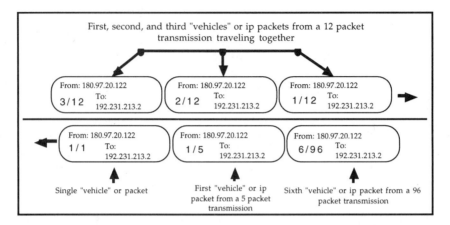

Figure 2-1. IP packets as "vehicles"

denial occurs because servers monitor the number of users accessing them and are programmed to reject new access attempts when they exceed programmed limits in order to protect themselves, not the network, from overloads.

Internet Addressing and the Domain Name System (DNS)

Internet protocol (IP) addresses consist of four sets of numbers ranging from 0 to 255 (notice that is 256 states if you count the zero), each separated by a period (said as "dot" in common use). Such addresses are called "dotted-octet" addresses, and they are not user-friendly. So, for human use, IP addresses are converted into the more user-friendly domain name system They have to be converted back to dotted-octet again for use by the computers on the Internet.

The **domain name system** is a hierarchical arrangement designed to avoid the problems that surfaced on the ARPANET. When the ARPANET was first set up under the NCP protocol, one server was set up to keep track of all of the network's addresses. That server was housed at the Stanford Research Institute. However, when ARPANET switched to the TCP/IP protocol, that system rapidly proved insufficient because of the large and rapidly growing number of new users. The domain name system (DNS) was the solution to that problem.

The structure of the DNS is very similar to the structure of UNIX files, or what computer scientists call a "tree" structure. Seven top–level domains were created: "edu" (educational institutions), "mil" (military), "org" (nonprofit organizations), "net" (network organizations), "com" (for profit commercial organizations), "int" (international organizations), and "gov" (government organizations). However, other countries may use different systems, so do not expect the addresses of all universities in the world to end in "edu". Below the top level are the registered names for the organizations themselves. For example, "nsf.gov" indicates the National Science Foundation, a division of the federal government. Note that "nsf.org", "nsf.com", and "nsf.edu" are all different (and fictional) addresses. Addresses at this level must be registered with NIC, the Network Information Center, to prevent duplication, obviously. Recently, and because of the rapic growth of the Internet, NIC began to impose a $50 per year charge for DNS names.

The domain that you will probably spend the most time in is "edu", educational institutions. Table 2-1 shows the registered domain names of some colleges and universities. Network administrators at this level have the authority to set the names of servers below their registered name. That naming privilege illustrates the distributed nature of DNS and is one of its main advantages. Distributed control makes it possible to avoid maintaining a central listing of a large number of constantly changing server names and user addresses. Unfortunately, it is also one of the reasons that making a directory of the Internet is extremely difficult.

The servers on the Internet, however, do not use the DNS to send and receive packets. Instead, they use the IP address system. How is the conversion made between both systems? That is the job of a system of specialized servers, domain name servers.

The Domain Name Server System

Domain name servers–or, more simply, name servers–keep track of servers and their users in local portions of the Internet. The system is organized in the same hierarchical order as UNIX. So, finding or resolving a particular IP address from a DNS address may involve taking a number of steps down the hierarchy of name servers until one server is found that contains the sought address. Southern Arkansas University's name server is in Little Rock at the University of Arkansas at Little Rock.

By using another such hierarchical search algorithm, it is possible for the reverse process to occur as well, namely, going from an IP address to the DNS address.

The Requests For Comments System

The publication of requests for comments (RFCs) began early in the development of the Internet. They were begun by Steve Crocker, a graduate student at the time, as a democratic method of sharing new developments and promoting communication (Aboba, 1993). RFCs quickly evolved into the main medium of communication about Internet

University	Registered Domain Name
Louisiana State University	lsu.edu
South Dakota State University	sdstate.edu
Southeast Missouri State University	semo.edu
Stanford University	stanford.edu
Sweet Briar College	sbc.edu
The Johns Hopkins University	jhu.edu
UCLA	ucla.edu
United States Naval Academy	nadn.navy.mil
University of Wisconsin-Milwaukee	uwm.edu
University of Nebraska	unl.edu
University of Baltimore	ubalt.edu
University of Illinois	uiuc.edu
University of Maryland	umd.edu
University of Northern Iowa	uni.edu
Washington College	washcoll.edu

Table 2-1. Registered Domain Names of selected colleges and universities

developments. Most RFCs are available on-line[4], and they constitute a kind of primary source about the history of the Internet.developments and promoting communication (Aboba, 1993).

CONCLUSION

You should now understand how the Internet was born and how it developed. No one has any real idea what the future of the Internet will be, but at least you know where the future will begin. This chapter also covered the basic technical issues concerning the Internet. Many other books and articles have been written about such issues. Any library or bookstore will have some of them. Also, you can look in the Internet itself, as we have, to find more information on both the history and the technology of the Internet.

We now turn our attention to actually using the Internet in research and practice. The next five chapters cover the software tools that have been developed to use the Internet to good purpose. We move first to the most common use of the Internet, electronic mail.

NOTES

1.   http://info.isoc.org/guest/zakon/Internet/History
      /Timeline_of_Network_History

2.   http://info.isoc.org/guest/zakon/Internet/History/How_the_Inter-
      net_came_to_Be

3.   http://info.isoc.org/guest/zakon/Internet/History/Brief_History_-
      of_the_Internet

4.   http://www.apocalypse.org/pub/rfcs/ghindex.html

3

E–Mail and Mailing Lists

CHAPTER PREVIEW

Electronic mail was conceived and developed shortly after the Internet was first set up. It quickly became and still is the leading use of the Internet. **Mailing lists**, an automated form of electronic mail that allows you to send mail to fellow subscribers all at once, soon followed. Below we provide you with the basic information you need to start using electronic mail and mailing lists.

WHAT IS ELECTRONIC MAIL?

Electronic mail easily accounts for most of the present usage of the Internet. **Electronic mail** is a tool that allows users to communicate with each other easily from anywhere in the world. All that is required to use electronic mail is a computer, an electronic mail address, and connection to the Internet. Obtaining an electronic mail address and a connection can be accomplished in a variety of ways. In any case, electronic mail allows you to communicate directly with anyone else in the world who also has electronic mail.

HOW DOES ELECTRONIC MAIL WORK?

New users are often mystified by the workings of electronic mail. You, too, may experience a little disorientation when you first begin reading messages from faraway places. What is really going on beyond your screen?

Actually, your electronic mail is waiting for you someplace else. Mail is not on your computer until you ask for it. Before you ask for it, your mail is waiting on a mail server, a networked remote computer that runs 24 hours a day and that sends and receives electronic mail to and from other mail servers. You already may have an electronic mail account

27

on a mail server somewhere, even if you did not set it up yourself. Of course, you may have set up your own electronic mail service. If you do not have electronic mail yet, but would like to, see the section "Getting Connected" below.

Most human face-to-face communication is synchronous, meaning that messages are sent and received nearly simultaneously. Electronic mail is a form of asynchronous communication, meaning that messages are sent but are not retrieved until later. A good analogy for asynchronous communication is a telephone answering machine. On it, like electronic mail, messages wait for you to pick them up. Of course, synchronous communication is impossible if you cannot find the person with whom you wish to communicate. Another example of the failure of synchronous communication is getting a busy signal on the telephone. So, one of the big advantages of electronic mail is that the recipients need not be present when you send them a message. All that is needed for communication is that both sender and recipient check on a regular basis to see if they have received electronic mail and send electronic mail replies to each other as needed.

When you ask for your electronic mail, you are really making a request, via a computer network, to the mail server that stores your electronic mail. As you might imagine, the location of your mail on the server is called a mailbox. It is not a real mailbox like the kind used for postal mail; rather, it is a metaphorical mailbox that serves the same purpose as your postal mailbox does, namely, holding your mail until you retrieve it. Once you retrieve it, you can read it. Then you may dispose of it or save it, just like postal mail. Yes, you may even receive the equivalent of junk mail, especially if you subscribe to listservers (see below). Because so many different kinds of electronic mail systems exist, you will have to check with your individual electronic mail provider to obtain the details of working with your particular electronic mail system.

Unlike with postal mail, with electronic mail you can quickly reply to the sender of your message, or you can forward electronic mail to another electronic mail address. The ease of replying has led to a phenomenon called **flaming**. Flaming is the equivalent of speaking your mind without thinking of the consequences of your reply. Ordinarily, social constraints keep us from telling our boss, spouse, or friends what we really think of them. On electronic mail, though, the interpersonal cues that keep those thoughts inside us are unavailable. Sometimes, flaming develops into a vicious, escalating cycle called flame wars. See the section "Netiquette" in Chapter 1 for a pointer to a WWW source for avoiding flaming. Seabrook (1994) also wrote about a particularly disturbing example of flaming that happened to him.

Electronic mail systems work by converting messages to a standard protocol, TCP/IP protocol (Transmission Control Protocol

/Internet Protocol). As mentioned in Chapter 2, TCP/IP makes all Internet traffic, including electronic mail, possible. Any computer connected to the Internet must convert its native format into TCP/IP. Fortunately, most users will seldom, if ever, have to immerse themselves in the details of TCP/IP.

INTERNET ADDRESSES

All electronic mail users need their own individual and unique addresses. Internet addresses specify a particular user on a particular server. Although your first experiences with addresses may be confusing, realize that there is a logic to those addresses. The system consists of a username, a servername, and a domain. Additionally, a country domain may follow. The Internet is set up so that the United States' country domain, "us ," is the default domain. So, addresses in the United States need not contain the country domain. Those addresses will still work, however, if the "us" is specified. Here are four examples of Internet addresses. The first and third are generic; the second and fourth are ours. Feel free to send us electronic mail.

username@servername.domain.country domain

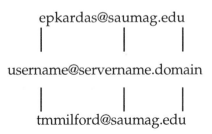

epkardas@saumag.edu

username@servername.domain

tmmilford@saumag.edu

Note that NO spaces are used inside an address. Sometimes, however, you will see the underscore character "_" used as in
<John_Smith@computer.edu>
Do not substitute a space for the underscore character. When I say my address to someone, I say (one letter at a time)
"E-P-K-A-R-D-A-S AT S-A-U-M-A-G DOT E-D-U"
and I take care to spell it out slowly. If I am dealing with new users, I may tell them what symbol the word "AT" stands for, that "DOT" is a period, and not to put in any spaces.

TYPES OF INTERNET ORGANIZATIONS

The domain after the servername designates the type of organization on the Internet. Most of the domains you will probably encounter will have "edu" in their addresses. The "edu" domain is for educational institutions like colleges and universities. If you use a commercial Internet provider, you may notice the domain "com", which is for commercial, for-profit, organizations. The "gov" domain is for government organizations. Other domains include "mil" for military organizations, "org" for not-for-profit organizations, and "net" for Internet-related groups.

GETTING CONNECTED

If you are a student at an institution that already has electronic mail, then getting an account may be as simple as asking the proper administrator at your school for it. Or your instructor may have already set up your account for you. In either of those cases, you will simply have to learn to use the existing system at your institution.

Personal Equipment

If your institution does not yet have electronic mail, or if you simply want your own personal account, you can still get one in a variety of ways. You will first need a computer and a modem. The computer can be nearly any one of the many types available today. However, you should not simply purchase a computer without first checking a few things. For example, what kind of software do you plan to use? Does your school or class require a particular kind of software or computer? If not, what kind of software and computer do you wish to use? Will you want to use your computer for more Internet functions than electronic mail? Probably the best strategy before purchasing a computer is to ask around at your campus, department, or local computer stores. A good bit of advice is to buy the fastest computer, the most RAM (random access memory), and the biggest hard drive you can afford.

Purchasing a modem is much simpler. What is a modem? **Modem** is a contraction for "modulator-demodulator," and it is a device that allows you to connect your computer to a server using existing telephone lines. Modems are the most commonly used devices for connecting to the Internet outside of institutions with direct connections to the Internet. Modems transmit information at various speeds or baud rates. The higher the baud rate, the faster the modem. A popular baud rate now is 14,400 bps (bits per second) because such modems are sufficiently fast for many Internet applications and are priced at around $100. Higher–baud–rate modems are available, that allow faster access, but they are more expensive and will not operate at full speed with Internet providers whose modems are slower. So, before you buy a modem, call the service (e.g., America Online, Compuserve, etc; see below) and check their maximum baud rate. If the provider's baud rate is less than yours, then the connection between the provider's modem and yours will be made at the slower rate. Obviously, the reverse is true—if your modem is slower than the provider's, then the connection will also be made at the slower rate. Also, be sure to purchase a modem that is compatible with the computer you will use to make your connection to the provider, and do not forget to get the proper cables. Finally, decide what Internet services other than electronic mail you will want to use. That decision will affect both the provider and the speed of the modem you choose. For instance, it is possible to access the World Wide Web (see Chapter 6) with a modem whose baud rate is less than 14,400 bps, but that access will be very tedious for you because of the slower modem speeds.

Internet Service Providers

Many companies are now providing several hours' worth of Internet access on a nationwide basis for less than $10 per month. They include companies like CompuServe, America Online, MCI, Prodigy, GEnie, and Delphi. Again, one of the best ways to make a choice among them is to ask others in your local area who are using the services provided by these companies. Internet access can also be made through local companies in some areas. Some colleges and universities also provide free or cheap access to residents of their local communities. You may want to check into that option as well. Regardless of which route you choose, do not forget to factor in the price of making the initial call to the Internet provider. For example, where we live that call must be a long-distance call, so those long-distance charges become part of the cost of access. The provider you choose should help you set up your computer and modem properly. Some providers will even supply the necessary software to make the connection. If your provider does not offer such software, then you will have to use communications software that you either purchase or obtain as freeware (free software) or shareware (software you may try out before paying for it).

USING ELECTRONIC MAIL

Now that you have electronic mail access, what can you do with it? How can you use it for research in the social sciences? Obviously, the simplest use of electronic mail is to communicate with other users. Before you can do that, however, you need to determine whether the user you wish to contact is local or remote. By local users, we mean users who are on the same Internet access system as you: all the student users at a university or all of the members of CompuServe, for example. The addressing rules are slightly simpler when users are local. Think of the following analogy using a telephone system with extension numbers. If I want to call my dean, I just dial her extension, 4201. But I could also get an "outside" line first by dialing a 9 and then dialing her complete number, 235-4201. Either way, her telephone rings. The same analogy applies to the Internet. Using the same example, I could send electronic mail to my dean by using her local address, "ehdavis". Or, I could go outside the campus network by typing in "MX%" (our local mail system's equivalent of dialing a 9) and use her full Internet address, "ehdavis@saumag.edu". Using that address causes my electronic mail to first travel to Little Rock, our Internet access point, and then back to our campus server, and finally to her. So, if you know someone is on your local system, use the simpler addressing scheme. If the person is not local, then you will have to use the longer addressing scheme. You can to get the details of each scheme, local or remote, from your Internet provider.

Sending and Receiving Electronic Mail

Electronic mail programs require that you know the address of the person to whom you intend to send electronic mail. Most will allow you to simultaneously send a copy of that message to yourself or to others. This last function is sometimes called a "carbon copy" function because of its metaphorical resemblance to the process of making carbon copies on a typewriter. It is often useful to send such copies to yourself or to others.

Some electronic mail programs have a graphical user interface and others have a command line interface. If your computer requires you to type in commands like "Read 1" or "Del 1," then you have a command line interface. If your computer has the ability to display layers of windows and icons and requires a mouse or other pointing device, you have a graphical user interface. Computers that cannot display graphical user interfaces may be able to display menu interfaces, and menus are easier to use than command line interfaces. Regardless of the interface, however, the same actions are carried out by all types of electronic mail programs; namely, some text is sent to the desired addressee(s). Figure

3–1 shows an example of a graphical user interface style of electronic mail program.

Parts of an Electronic Mail Message

As you can see from Figure 3-1, an electronic mail message contains a number of parts. Probably the most important is the **recipient's address**. In Figure 3-1, a remote address was used for the recipient for purposes of illustration. Note that the carbon copy was sent to a local address. In this example, the recipient's address could have been simply "ehdavis," because she is a local user. The form illustrated also allows the user to set his or her full name in the space marked "local user name." The software automatically places the sender's local address in the place marked "local user address."

The **subject header** should contain a brief description of the message. Many new users neglect to include a subject header. When you begin to receive a large number of messages, you will come to appreciate the subject header because it will allow you to read important mail first. That is why netiquette calls for subject headers. Some electronic mail programs will insert the words "no header" when mail is sent without a header, but others will just leave the space blank.

The **message** is the main part of any piece of electronic mail. Electronic mail has developed a kind of writing style that emphasizes short paragraphs, abbreviations, and "smileys." These last are sideways-facing faces created by keystroke combinations such as ";-)" (notice wink) or ":-(" that are used to indicate the writer's mood. Angell and Heslop (1994) have written a style manual for electronic mail in the style of Strunk and White's famous writing manual. In a more humorous vein, Greenberg[1] posted a satiric set of rules for writing electronic mail.

Signatures or **sig blocks** are lines at the end of a piece of electronic mail that identify the sender. Most electronic mail programs provide a method for inserting a signature automatically following the message. Sig blocks are controversial[2]. Some people believe they are a waste of bandwidth; others, especially owners of listservers (see below), want users to use sig blocks because some electronic mail software strips the sender's information from the mail, making it impossible for other users to reply directly to the original message. Long (over eight lines) sig blocks, however, are universally regarded as a nuisance and a waste of bandwith.

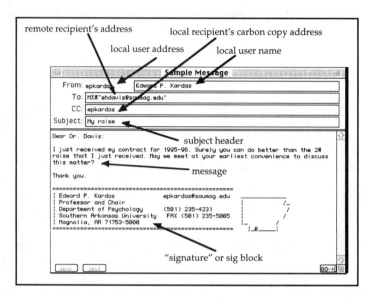

Figure 3-1. A sample message on a graphical user interface electronic mail form (Mail for Macintosh®)

Soon, you will be sending and receiving electronic mail daily. If you are like us, it will become an integral part of your daily routine. When receiving messages from remote users, most of you (those whose mail programs leave the headers on) will see quite a bit of text above the body of the message itself. For the most part you may ignore that material. It simply shows where the message originated and how it got to you.

ADVANCED FEATURES IN ELECTRONIC MAIL

Presently, most electronic mail systems are limited to sending text data in **ASCII** (American Standard Code for Information Interchange). ASCII is a code for the characters of alphabets only, and can only code 256 characters. **MIME** (Multipurpose Internet Mail Extensions)[3], a newer standard, supports text and other forms of data like sound and graphics. But it is not yet a commonly used protocol. Thus, sending pictures, particular fonts, or particular formatting via electronic mail is possible, but not yet on all computers attached to the Internet. However, even with ASCII alone, it is possible to attach documents to electronic mail messages. The sender attaches a document coded in a more generic form, binary, to an electronic mail message, and then the receiver must decode the document. Check with your Internet provider if you wish to learn how to attach documents to your electronic mail.

Distribution Lists

A distribution list is another advanced feature of electronic mail. A distribution list is a named text file of electronic mail addresses. After you create a distribution list, you may send the same piece of electronic mail to everyone on the list by simply using the list's name as an electronic mail address. Then, your mail server will automatically send electronic mail to every address on the distribution list. Naturally, you may have any number of distribution lists. For example, you could have one called "family" for each of your family members, one called "methods" for everyone in your research methods course, or one called "studyg" for a study group you set up. Again, your Internet provider can show you how to set up distribution lists on your system.

Mailing Lists

A more complex form of a distribution list is the **mailing list**. Unlike the distribution list described above, mailing lists are remote to the user. A specialized server called a "listserver" manages the mailing list(s); listservers are managed by a human being, the list owner. Users who subscribe to lists of interest (see below for instructions on subscribing) receive all of the mail sent to the listserver by other subscribers. Subscribers may choose only to read the mail from the mailing list, or they may choose to post (send) messages as well. Those posted messages are then sent to all subscribed members (including the poster of the message). So, listservers act as automated deliverers of mail to and from all of the subscribers to a mailing list.

Mailing lists exist for a wide variety of topics. Some are particularly appropriate for social science research. The names and addresses of many of those lists are given in the appropriate discipline-related chapters. Mailing lists may be either open or closed and moderated or unmoderated. Open lists allow any Internet user with electronic mail access to subscribe. Closed lists restrict their membership in some way. For example, the list "SUBSTANCE-RELATED-DISORDERS*" is closed and accepts membership only from professionals working in the field of substance abuse. In moderated lists, the list owner reads and edits posted messages before sending them to the mailing list's subscribers. The owner may also choose not to post the message. In unmoderated lists, posted messages are distributed without any reading or editing. As you might suspect, flaming is more likely on open, unmoderated mailing lists.

Before you subscribe to a mailing list, be aware that such action may increase your volume of electronic mail substantially. Some mailing lists generate over 100 messages per day. In such an event, you will have to keep up with your electronic mail daily, or you will soon have more mail than you can comfortably read. Also, check with your instructor or your computer center director before subscribing to a mailing list. You may find that your mailbox size is limited. If so, your full mailbox may cause problems for the mailing lists to which you subscribed. Turn off any automatic acknowledging functions if your electronic mail provides them. Those automatically inform the sender that you read the message. However, when used on mailing lists, they cause large volumes of useless mail—a waste of bandwidth and bad netiquette. Again, a good strategy would be to ask others at your institution for information about mailing lists to which they subscribe.

Subscribing to Mailing Lists

Fortunately, subscribing to mailing lists is a fairly simple process. The most common mistake that new users make is to subscribe to the wrong address. Mailing lists have two addresses. One address is to the server that handles the chores involved in the listserver. That is the address users should use to subscribe, unsubscribe, stop mail temporarily (e.g., for vacations or other time away from electronic mail), and restart mail after such periods. Upon subscribing, users will receive a list of instructions from the server. Those instructions should be kept for future reference.

The other address is the one used to post mail or to reply to mail. Some mailing lists are set up so that replies are automatically sent to the list. Others are set up so that replies go to the person who posted the mail. In either system, all subscribed users who have their mail option turned on will receive all of the mail generated by the list.

Some mailing lists will allow users to receive mail in a digest form. When in digest form, the mailing list sends all recent mail to the user at some regular interval. In the normal form, the mailing list sends mail to users as it comes into the server. Check with the instructions you receive when you first subscribe to see whether the digest form is supported, and, if so, how to set the mailing list to digest form.

FINDING ELECTRONIC MAIL ADDRESSES

Unfortunately there is no easy way to find an electronic mail address. No equivalent yet exists to telephone white or yellow pages. Many universities maintain address lists that are accessible via TELNET (see Chapter 4), gopher (see Chapter 5), or World Wide Web (see Chapter 6).Addresses may also be found if you know where the person works and that work location maintains an Internet phone book. See the example

---

Subscribing to an Internet Mailing List

If you have permission from your local computer administrator, find a mailing list from one of the discipline-related chapters (Chapters 9-15). Then subscribe by sending a message to its server computer address as listed in those chapters. Remember that you will now be getting electronic mail automatically, so be sure to check your mailbox often. If you decide you no longer want to subscribe use the same syntax as below but substitute "UNSUBSCRIBE" or "LEAVE" (for Mailbase). The syntax for most lists (Listproc, LISTSERV, Mailserv, Majordomo) is:

SUBSCRIBE <LISTNAME> <Firstname> <Lastname>

Some lists (Mailbase) use

JOIN <LISTNAME> <Firstname> <Lastname>

Do NOT put in the "<" or ">". Do leave a space between the command "SUB-SCRIBE" and the LISTNAME. Also, leave a space between Firstname and Lastname. Obviously, you should substitute your real first name and last name in their places. See the example below:

SUBSCRIBE ACUMUG-L Edward Kardas

When sent to the proper address, the above line would subscribe me to the list ACUMUG-L or the Arkansas College and University Macintosh Users Group list.

Addresses may also be found if you know where the person works and that work location maintains an Internet phone book. See the example below for the phone book information for my colleague Douglas Chute of Drexel University:

-200:1:Drexel Directory Assistance, version 2.0, (c) 1992-93, Drexel University.
-200:1:Data copied on May 14, 1995 from OCS, OSIR and Personnel databases.
-200:1:Send comments about the DDA service to: dda-comm ents@noc.drexel.edu
-200:1:
-200:1:Detailed information...
-200:1:Douglas Chute Dr   I 314 Exeter Road
-200:1: Professor   I Devon, PA 19333
-200:1: Psychology-Sociology-Anthropol I
-200:1: Tel: 895-6105 NeuroPsy 110   I Phone: (610) 688-3114
-200:1: Fax: 895-1333 Email: CHUTE@duvm.ocs.drexel.edu

RESEARCH USES OF ELECTRONIC MAIL

The obvious uses of electronic mail in research involve gathering information from people who have it and requesting materials from people who created them. Look at the example below. I needed a reference citation for an instructor's manual I was writing; but I had misplaced my copy of the book. I found the address of Dr. Johnson-Laird, editor of the book I was looking for, by telnetting to Princeton University's telephone book. Then, I sent him a short electronic mail message. As you can see, he very graciously sent me the information I needed. By the way, I had never communicated with him before.

> Hi,
> Here's the reference:
> Keith G. Oatley (1977) Inference, navigation, and cognitive maps. In Johnson-Laird, P.N., and Wason, P.C. (Eds) Thinking: Readings in Cognitive Science. Cambridge: Cambridge University Press. pp. 537-547.
> It was a chapter specially written for the book.
> Cheers,
> Phil J-L

Another research use of electronic mail is to tap the expertise of members of particular lists. You could simply read the mail in a list of interest, or more directly, you could post a question. Look at the following example concerning the placement of demographic information from the METHODS-L list. Here is the original post:

> Dear Colleagues
> In teaching questionnaire construction to undergraduate Social Science students it has been my practice to recommend that profile data be left to the end of the questionnaire which should begin at an early stage to move directly into substantive questions in pursuit of the research question (- an exception to this rule being when dealing with children). However, I have colleagues who give the opposite advice to students - ie. profile questions first (- on the logic that this gives an easy start to the questionnaire?)
> I wonder if anyone would care to clarify for me what the conventional wisdom and or methodological research findings happen to be on this subject?

Here are the replies(edited for typos and punctuation):

> I teach my undergraduate planning students to arrange the order of the questions as though they were planning a conversation. If rapport needs to be established before any questions can be asked, place the profile data first. If the "conversation" can begin with substantive questions, then leave the profile data to the end.
>
> I'm eager to hear the opinions of others on the placement of the profile questions. I explain the tradeoffs to students. That it is more interesting (for the respondent) to get to the substantive questions and leave the demographic stuff to the end (and also when the respondent may be experiencing fatigue or boredom or impatience, etc. On the other hand, by putting the profile first, the respondents know what identifying information you will have about them, an aspect that seems ethically desirable -- before they answer your queries.

I had always been told to put sensitive demographic questions, such as age, income, etc., at the end of the questionnaire in order to keep response rates up. Many individuals, when seeing that the first question involves personal info, may just not complete the questionnaire. We psychologists like to take advantage of the prior commitment hypothesis by having Rs fill out most of the Q, and *then* asking the personal stuff.

Unless certain demographics are required for screening (e.g., certain age groups, household composition, and the like) we put demographic questions at the end of the survey, emphasizing that they are for statistical purposes only and reemphasizing that any and all responses to such questions are strictly confidential. We find this seems to work best for our purposes and appears to be generally less off-putting to the respondents, encouraging them to complete the survey.

My understanding of the research on question order is that profile data should be placed at the end (it's better to get immediately into the substantive research questions) UNLESS the substantive questions are sensitive (sex, drugs, etc.) in which case profile questions can acclimate the respondent.

I have been the director of a survey firm for a few years and I've never seen profile questions at the beginning of a questionnaire, at least in telephone surveys. I have seen it in 'paper' surveys but very rarely. I teach my students to put profile questions at the end of the survey though I think that in some rare situations, perhaps when you do a personnel interview (face to face), it could be appropriate. It would be a way to initiate contact before going into delicate questions.

In my experience, it's better to put demographic questions up front in a face-to-face interview survey and at the end in a self-administered questionnaire.

The conventional wisdom has usually been to ask demographic questions (age, sex, income, ethnicity, party ID, etc...) at the end of questionnaires. I think the reason being that some of these rather personal questions are ones respondents are most likely not to want to answer. Also if you start with questions like income or age and you have them at the beginning and people refuse to answer them they may simply decide to not complete the questionnaire and therefore you'll have no useful data from the respondent. Whereas if they refuse to answer these questions at the end of the questionnaire you at least have the substantive part of the questionnaire answered and therefore a lot of usable data.
The above is especially the case in telephone surveys and mail questionnaires. I've never seen a large scale national survey like the GSS or NES ever ask demographic questions anyplace other than at the end.

In our industrial surveys we follow Don Dillman's Total Design Method as
closely as possible. Dillman's approach is designed to maximize
response rates. Compared to published reports of other surveys
(sometimes of the same industry), we do get a response rate about twice
as high. So the method seems to work.
Dillman suggests putting identifying questions at the end for many of
the reasons people have spelled out here. High response rates depend on
arousing the respondent's interest and not boring the respondent. So,
putting routine questions at the end seems appropriate. Of course, I
can't say our high response rates are due to this one feature, since
Dillman's method is a "total" method as the name suggests.

The focus of this thread concerns whether profile data should be placed
at the beginning or at the end of the questionnaire. I note that some
respondents explicitly offer the opinion and others imply that,
especially for "sensitive" questions, placing the profile questions at
the end may help improve the response rate.
My question is whether anyone knows of any empirical evidence (as opposed
to experience or intuition), either published or unpublished, on this
issue: does the location of the profile section in a questionnaire
influence the response rate? This would be useful information, and
likely not very difficult to obtain.

It all depends on your subjects, I did a self-administered survey among first time
arrested offenders. I have to ask a lot of sensitive questions. I tried both ways:
demographic questions at the beginning and the end.
I found in my sample profile questions first can generate higher
response rates than at the end. Even though the conventional wisdom
tells us to ask profile data later, it may not apply to everywhere.
It all depends on your subjects and survey situation.

Notice that there was a consensus among the respondents. By far, most
agreed that the demographic items should be held back until the end of
the questionnaire. This give–and–take on electronic mail points out one of
the big advantages of the Internet, namely, the ability to form and to tap
into virtual communities–in this case a community of scholars interested
in methodological issues in social science. How else could such an
exchange of ideas take place so easily and so quickly? After our students
read these exchanges, they had to write a questionnaire. Where do you
think they put the demographic items?

    Conducting surveys and polls, either formal or informal, is another
good research use of mailing lists. Before doing so, however, be sure that
the mailing list you are surveying allows such activity. How can you tell?
After you have subscribed to a mailing list for a while, you should be able
to tell. For instance, if others are already surveying the list and they do
not get flamed, then that is an obvious sign of tacit approval. When we
were planning this book, we surveyed the membership of TIPS (Teaching

in Psychological Science; see Chapter 9), a mailing list devoted to issues in the teaching of psychology. The mostly favorable responses were instrumental in our being able to write this text. A word of caution: remember that ANY Internet sample will be highly selected. (Can you see why?) So, the external validity of any data you collect will be tenuous, at best.

CONCLUSION

After reading this chapter and after securing access to a computer with an Internet connection, you should be able to communicate with other users all around the world. Also, you should be able to subscribe and unsubscribe to mailing lists. There you can read or post messages that will be seen by others with similar interests as you. Imagine the power you now have at your fingertips, and as you will see in subsequent chapters, electronic mail is only the beginning. We turn next to TELNET and file transfer protocol (FTP).

NOTES

1.   gopher://ftp.std.com:70/00/obi/book/Nerd.Humor/Mail.Style

2.   http://beast.cc.emory.edu/Jargon30/JARGON_S/SIGBLOCK.HTML

3.   http://home.netscape.com/assist/helper_apps/what-is-mime.html

4

TELNET and FTP

CHAPTER PREVIEW

TELNET and file transfer protocol (FTP) are two closely related software applications that were developed at around the same time as ARPANET and its networking protocols. Recall that the main thrust behind the creation of ARPANET was the notion of connecting computers together (see Chapter 2). TELNET allows authorized remote users access to any networked computer, and FTP enables users to move files from one networked computer to another. Despite their age, both applications are still heavily used today. In this chapter we show you how to use these old but still useful programs. We also introduce OCLC's FirstSearch™ databases and show you how to use them.

WHAT IS TELNET?

TELNET is a very useful software application that makes it possible for users to interact with a remote computer. Unlike FTP, no easier-to-use Internet applications have been created to replace it. The reason for TELNET's long life has mainly to do with the original ARPANET problem, namely, linking a wide variety of computers together. When you use a TELNET application, you essentially convert your computer into a simpler kind of machine, an Internet–wide standard terminal or "network virtual terminal," or NVT. The NVT is simply a conceptual framework specifying the standard terminal. Each host's TELNET software implements the NVT for its particular hardware. However, do not let TELNET's simplicity fool you. Some of the most useful research and practice applications in social science are accomplished via TELNET—access to off-site libraries and databases, for example.

HOW DOES TELNET WORK?

RFC 854[1] describes the TELNET protocol (RFC is short for Requests for Comments)[a]. Specifically, according to RFC 854 (p.1):

> The purpose of the TELNET Protocol is to provide a fairly general, bi-directional, eight-bit byte oriented communications facility. Its primary goal is to allow a standard method of interfacing terminal devices and terminal-oriented processes to each other. It is envisioned that the protocol may also be used for terminal-terminal communication ("linking") and process-process communication (distributed computation).

Stated simply, TELNET allows you to connect to other computers on the Internet and to use them as if you were on-site.

USING TELNET

Logging In

TELNET sessions may be public or private. Public sessions allow any Internet user to log in, whereas private sessions require users to demonstrate authorization, usually via a password system. Below we will demonstrate a private TELNET session to the FirstSearch™ on-line information system included with this text. Public TELNET sessions are conducted similarly, but without the necessity of a password.

Before you can conduct a TELNET session, you will need TELNET software. Usually, such software is already installed on computers that are directly connected to the Internet. If you have such a connection or if you have Internet service from a commercial provider, check with your local system administrator or with your provider to see if TELNET software is already installed and to learn how to use it. Otherwise, you may have to secure the software in some other fashion. For example, you might have to find someone with Internet access, locate TELNET software, download it, and then copy it to disk. Then you could load that disk on your computer. Be sure not to violate existing copyright laws concerning the use of freeware, shareware, and commercial software. Assuming that you now have a TELNET program that runs on your computer, you are ready to begin. First, you will need an address of a TELNET site. In the following example, we will TELNET to the FirstSearch™ on-line information system using the address:

FSCAT.OCLC.ORG

and the account and password included with your book.

---

a   Requests for Comments (RFCs): the information dissemination system developed
        during the early days of the ARPANET

Sample TELNET Session

```
TELNET> connect
_To: fscat.oclc.org
Trying...132.174.100.5
Connected to FSCAT.OCLC.ORG.
Escape character is '^]'.
```

The lines above demonstrate how to establish your connection.

```
You are connected to OCLC Reference Services.
Enter your authorization.
=> XXXXXXXXX
Enter your password.
=> XXXXXXXXX
```

After connection is established, you are prompted for your account number and password.

```
* * * * * * *      WELCOME TO FIRSTSEARCH !     * * * * * * * * *
Use The FirstSearch service to find books, articles, theses,
films, computer software, and other types of material on the
subject you need.

The actions you can take are listed on each screen.  Just type
the ACTION name or first letter.
OCLC MAKES NO EXPRESS WARRANTIES OR REPRESENTATIONS
AND DISCLAIMS ALL IMPLIED WARRANTIES WITH RESPECT
TO THE DATABASES VIA THE FIRSTSEARCH SERVICE,
INCLUDING ABOUT ITS ACCURACY, MERCHANTABILITY OR
 FITNESS FOR A PARTICULAR PURPOSE.
```

This is the first screen you will see.

```
NEWS: *Now you can email the results of your search!  On the next
screen, type H NEWS for information on FirstSearch 3.1.
```

This is an announcement of a new feature.

```
PRESS ENTER TO CONTINUE
* * * * * * * * * * * * Topic Area Selection * * * * * * * * * * * * * * *
__NO.__TOPIC AREA_____     NO.__TOPIC AREA_____
|
|  1  Arts and Humanities             8   General Science
|  2  Business and Economics          9   Life Sciences
|  3  Conferences and Proceedings     10  Medicine and Health Sciences
|  4  Consumer Affairs and People     11  News and Current Events
|  5  Education                       12  Public Affairs and Law
|  6  Engineering and Technology      13  Social Sciences
|  7  General and Reference           14  List of All Databases
|_____
```

HINTS: Select a topic area . . . . type topic area number.
Get help . . . . type H.
Get News . . . . type H NEWS.
See hours of operation . . . . type H HOURS.
ACTIONS: Help Database BYE Reset

Above are the topic areas available to you. There are a total of 50 databases available.

TOPIC AREA NUMBER (or Action): 13

Here we selected Social Sciences (naturally enough) by entering its code: 13.

* * * * * * * * * * * * Database Selection * * * * * * * * * * * * * * *
TOPIC AREA: Social Sciences
__NO.__DATABASE_____DESCRIPTION_____

| 1 WorldCat   Books and other materials in libraries worldwide.
| 2 Article1st   Index of articles from nearly 12,500 journals.
| 3 Contents1st   Table of contents of nearly 12,500 journals.
| 4 FastDoc   Index of articles with text online or by email.
| 5 EconLit   An index of economic literature.
| 6 LibraryLit   Materials on libraries and librarianship.
| 7 PsycFIRST   Psychology abstracts from over 1300 journals.
| 8 SocioAbs   Abstracts to articles on all aspects of sociology.
| 9 SocSciInd   Guide to the literature of the social sciences.

HINTS: Select a database . . . . type database number or name.
              Help on a database . . . . type H and database name.
              Return to Topic Area screen . . . . just press Enter.
ACTIONS: Help BYE Reset
              DATABASE NUMBER (or Action): 7

Here we selected code number 7 to access the database PsycFIRST.

* * * * * * *   PSYCFIRST   * * * * * * * * *
COVERAGE: More than 1,300 journals on psychology and related fields.
Coverage is current year plus the most recent three years.
 Updated monthly.

Copyright American Psychological Association, 1995.

The American Psychological Association takes care to provide
accurate representation of the behavioral literature, but assumes
no liability for errors or omissions and makes no warranties, express
or implied, including, but not limited to, any implied warranty of
merchantability or fitness for a particular purpose and assumes
no responsibility for Customer's use of the information.

Above is PsychFIRST's opening screen.

PRESS ENTER TO CONTINUE

```
* * * * * * * * * * * * * * * Search * * * * * * * * * * * * * * * * * *
DATABASE: PsycFIRST
__SEARCH_____DESCRIPTION_____EXAMPLES_____
|
| Subject    Type the label SU: and a word(s).          su:mania
|            (Descriptors, titles, abstracts, notes)     su:man machine
|
| Author     Type the label AU: and the author          au:geri
|            name or any part of the name.               au:george a geri
|
| Title      Type the label TI: and the title            ti:parents
|            or any word(s) in the title.                 ti:child's knowledge
|_____
HINTS:  Other ways to search . . . . . . . type H <database name> LABELS.
Include plural (s and es) or possessive . . . type + at end of word.
Return to Database Selection screen . . . . . . . just press Enter.
ACTIONS: Help Limit Database Wordlist BYE Reset
```

Note that on-line help is available by pressing H.

```
SEARCH WORD(S) (or Action): su:Internet
Searching for su:Internet
```

Above we searched for articles on the subject "Internet" abstracted in PsychFIRST.

```
        + * * * * * * * * * * * * List of Records * * * * * * * * * * * * * * * +
        DATABASE: PsycFIRST             LIMITED TO:
        SEARCH: su:Internet FOUND 2 Records
____NO.__ARTICLETITLE_____YEAR
|
|   1  Teaching via the internet.                      1994
|   2  The Whitaker database of dysarthric (cerebral palsy) speech.  1993
|_____
HINTS :
View a record . . . . . . . . . . . . . . . . type record number.
Decrease number of records . . . . type L (to limit) or A (to 'and').
 Do a new search . . . . . . . . . . . . . . . . type S or SEARCH.
ACTIONS: Help Search And Limit Print Email Database BYE
RECORD NUMBER (or Action): 1
```

Entering a "1" brings up the first record.

```
* * * * * * * * * * * * Full Record Display * * * * * * * * * * * * * * *
DATABASE: PsycFIRST              LIMITED TO:
SEARCH: su:Internet
Record 1 of  2_____( Page 1 of 4)
|
|        RECORD NO: 82-07510
|        AUTHOR: Bailey, Elaine K.; Cotlar, Morton
|        CORP. SOURCE: U Hawaii, Coll of Business Administration, US
|        TITLE: Teaching via the internet.
|        SOURCE: Communication Education
```

| DATE: 1994 Apr Vol 43(2) 184-193
| YEAR: 1994
| ISSN/ISBN: 0363-4523
| LANGUAGE: English
| DOC. TYPE: Journal Article
|_____

HINTS: Forward one page . . type F.   Another record . type record number.
See which libraries may own this item . . . . .type LIB.
Return to Record List . . . . just press Enter.
ACTIONS: Help Search Print Email Order LIBraries Forward
RECORD NUMBER (or Action): F

Entering an "F"" takes us to the next page of the first record.

* * * * * * * * * * * * Full Record Display * * * * * * * * * * * * * *
DATABASE: PsycFIRST   LIMITED TO:
SEARCH: su:internet
Record 1 of 2_____(Page 2 of 4)
|
| DOC. TYPE: Journal Article
| ABSTRACT: Explores the techniques and methodologies used in efforts to
| integrate computers and telecommunications technology into
| existing educational curricula. As the content of teaching
| moves toward helping students develop thinking skills,
| emphasis needs to be placed on deeper learning through
| extended student-teacher interactions. Through the use of the
| Internet, students and professors located remotely from each
| other can engage in cooperative learning experiences,
| potentially maximizing the learning benefit for both students
|_____

HINTS: Another page . type F or B.   Another record . type record number.
 Return to Record List . . . . just press Enter.
ACTIONS: Help Search Print Email Order LIBraries Forward Back
RECORD NUMBER (or Action): F

Entering an "F"" takes us to the next page of the first record.

* * * * * * * * * * * * Full Record Display * * * * * * * * * * * * * *
DATABASE: PsycFIRST   LIMITED TO:
SEARCH: su:Internet
Record 1 of 2_____(Page 3 of 4)
| and faculty and providing a high level of interaction for all
| participants. Use of tools such as electronic mail and
| bulletin boards can allow students to interact with other
| students from diverse cultures and in remote locations. In
| addition to curricula, behavioral patterns, values, and
| beliefs can be explored. The use of electronic mail for
| electronic guest lecturers and forums is also discussed.
| (PsycINFO Database Copyright 1995 American Psychological Assn,
| all rights reserved)
|_____

HINTS: Another page . type F or B.   Another record . type record number.
See which libraries may own this item . . . . .type LIB.
 Return to Record List . . . . just press Enter.

ACTIONS: Help Search Print Email Order LIBraries Forward Back
RECORD NUMBER (or Action): BYE
Entering "BYE" ends the session.

BYE disconnects FirstSearch.
Are you sure you want to disconnect? (Y/N): Y
You are prompted for confirmation of your "BYE" command.

You are disconnected from FirstSearch.
Remote connection closed
Your session is over.

Research Uses of TELNET

TELNET allows you to find information from many places on the
Internet. Libraries, databases, and directories of names and addresses are
examples of the kinds of information you can access. See chapters 9-15
for TELNET addresses of interest to particular social science disciplines.

WHAT IS FILE TRANSFER PROTOCOL (FTP)?

FTP originally provided a method for moving files from one computer to
another. Later, to accommodate users who did not have accounts on FTP
servers, "anonymous FTP"servers were set up. Anonymous servers
enabled users who did not have assigned accounts to download files to
their own computers, too. Anonymous clients are usually allowed access
to a restricted portion of an anonymous server's files, but they are not
usually allowed to upload their own files to the server. (See below for a
more detailed discussion of anonymous FTP.)

Despite its ancient age (in computer terms), FTP is still widely
used today. Recent software developments have made FTP easier to use,
either by creating a user-friendly interface or by incorporating FTP
functions into software like gopher or World Wide Web (WWW)
browsers. Regardless, you should still know how to use FTP in its original
form because you may find yourself in a situation where FTP is the only
software available. Also, if you have electronic mail capability only, you
can still send FTP commands via electronic mail. Using FTP in that
manner is slower, but at least you can download files from FTP sites.
Ironically, one of the main uses of FTP is downloading newer Internet
software like gopher or WWW browsers. Those newer kinds of Internet

software allow you to perform FTP searches as well as many other tasks easily. In fact, we hardly ever use FTP anymore ourselves.

HOW DOES FTP WORK?

RFC 959[2] discusses FTP's history and implementation.. FTP's objectives, according to RFC 959 (p. 1) are:

   1) to promote sharing of files (computer programs and/or data)
   2) to encourage indirect or implicit (via programs) use of remote computers
   3) to shield a user from variations in file storage systems among hosts
   4) to transfer data reliably and efficiently.

Most of you will probably never use FTP to its full extent or capabilities because you will be unlikely to have user accounts on two separate servers. If you did have two or more accounts, however, you could use FTP to move files back and forth between those servers. On the other hand, most of you will likely to use anonymous FTP at some point.

Anonymous FTP

One of FTP's main uses is in accessing files placed in "public" files on Internet servers. Such public files are made available to anyone with an Internet connection. Those files may be accessed without having a designated account on that server. Instead, users typically log in using the account name "anonymous" and use their Internet address as a password. The tradition of providing public files demonstrates the communal nature of the Internet. Local system administrators do not have to provide such access; that they do so is commendable. The practice of using one's Internet address for a password allows system administrators to see easily where their traffic is coming from.

Most files that you will download have been compressed to make them smaller and thus require less time for downloading. You will have to decompress those files yourself before you can use them. How do you decompress them? You use decompressing software. Where do you get decompressing software? You download it via anonymous FTP. By now you should be getting an idea about how useful FTP can be. Each different kind of computer will have its own decompressing software, so you will have to find the proper kind for your particular software. IBM PC software is usually compressed with PKZIP software, Mac software with BINHEX software, and UNIX software with TAR.Z software. See the two locations indicated by the notes in this sentence to find PC[3] and Mac[4] anonymous FTP sites.

FTP Made Easier

Since FTP's creation, a number of other applications have been created to make the process of file transfer easier for nearly every kind of computer. Find those new, easier–to–use applications at various sites like the one[5] indicated by the note in this sentence. FTP functions have also been built into more recent Internet software like gopher (see Chapter 5) and WWW browsers (see Chapter 6). So, you will very likely be using FTP in some way even if you never actually use FTP by itself.

USING FILE TRANSFER PROTOCOL (FTP)

Logging in

Before you can conduct an FTP session, you will need FTP software. Usually, such software is already installed on computers that are directly connected to the Internet. If you have such a connection or if you have Internet service from a commercial provider, check with your local system administrator or with your provider to see if FTP software is already installed and to learn how to use it. Otherwise, you may have to secure the software in some other fashion. For example, you might have to find someone with Internet access, locate FTP software, download it, and then copy it to disk. Then you could load that disk on your Internet-connected computer. Be sure not to violate existing copyright laws concerning the use of freeware, shareware, and commercial software.

Assuming that you now have an FTP program that runs on your computer, you are ready to begin. First, you will need an address of an FTP site. In the following example, we will download a compressed image from the Smithsonian Institution's Office of Printing and Photographic Services[6] indicated by the note in this sentence.

Sample FTP Session

user
The "user" command starts the session.
Username: anonymous
This is the anonymous *account open to all.*
331 Guest login ok, send your complete e-mail address as password.
Password: epkardas@saumag.edu
The password will not show up on the screen. You would use your electronic mail account for a password.

230-   WELCOME TO THE "PHOTO1.SI.EDU" ANONYMOUS FTP SERVER
230-   --
230-
230-Welcome to "photo1.si.edu" located in the Smithsonian Institution's
230-Office of Printing & Photographic Services in Washington, D.C.
230-"Photo1" is designed to make a variety of Smithsonian photographs
230-available as electronic image files.
230-
230-Photo1 is available through the Internet as a result of Project Chapman,
230-a joint effort between this office and the Apple Library of Tomorrow
230-program.
230-
230-We request that you always provide a working E-mail address when
230-answering our FTP server's password prompt. All accesses to and file
230-transfers from this FTP server are logged with your host name and
230-E-mail address. Guests abusing the few rules that we have will be
230-denied access. See the "smithsonian.photo.info.txt" file which is
230-located in the "/images" directory for a complete list of rules.
230-Anonymous users *MAY NOT* upload (PUT) files on to this FTP server.
230-
230-If you have any unusual problems, please report them via E-mail to
230-the address below. If you do have problems, please try using a dash (-)
230-as the first character of your password -- this will turn off the
230-continuation messages that may be confusing your ftp client.
230-
230-We hope you enjoy these images and we invite comments via E-mail to
230-PSDMX@SIVM.SI.EDU.
230-
230-
230 Guest login ok, access restrictions apply.

Above is the first screen of this FTP server.

cd

The "cd" command changes directories.

To: images

"Images" is the directory we selected.

250 CWD command successful.
Dir

The "dir" command lists the contents of the current directory.

200 PORT command successful.
150 Opening ASCII mode data connection for /bin/ls.
total 19
drwxrwxr-- 8 root   bin   1024 May 22 14:31 .
dr-xr-xr-x 11 root   wheel   1024 Jun 14 14:24 ..
drwxrwxr-x 5 root   bin   1024 May 23 19:50 catalogs
drwxrwxr-x 5 root   bin   1024 May 22 12:59 electronic.times
drwxrwxr-x 8 root   bin   1024 Jun 14 01:05 gif89a

```
drwxrwxr-x  7 root    bin              1024 May 22 14:08 jfif.uuencode
drwxrwxr-x  7 root    bin              1024 May 22 14:14 jpeg
drwxrwxr-x  4 root    bin              1024 May 22 14:25 preview-text
-rw-rw-r--  1 root    bin             10405 May 22 14:31 smithsonian.photo.info.txt
```

Above are the contents of the directory "Images."

cd

The "cd" command changes directories again.

To: catalogs

"Catalogs" is the directory selected.

250 CWD command successful.

dir

The "dir" command lists the contents of the current directory.

```
200 PORT command successful.
150 Opening ASCII mode data connection for /bin/ls.
226 Transfer complete.
total 23
drwxrwxr-x  5 root    bin      1024 May 23 19:50 .
drwxrwxr--  8 root    bin      1024 May 22 14:31 ..
-rw-rw-r--  1 root    bin     16910 May 22 12:51 P1TREE.GIF
drwxr-xr-x  2 root    root     1024 May 24 23:17 dos
drwxrwxr-x  2 root    bin      1024 May 22 12:51 hypercard
drwxrwxr-x  2 root    bin      1024 May 22 12:51 others
```

Above are the contents of the directory "Catalogs."

cd

The "cd" command changes directories still another time.

To: hypercard

"hypercard" is the directory selected.

250 CWD command successful.

Dir

The "dir" command lists the contents of the current directory.

```
200 PORT command successful.
150 Opening ASCII mode data connection for /bin/ls.
226 Transfer complete.
total 255
drwxrwxr-x  2 root    bin        1024 May 22 12:51 .
drwxrwxr-x  5 root    bin        1024 May 23 19:50 ..
-rw-rw-r--  1 root    bin      257195 May 22 12:51 Photo1.sit.hqx
```

Above are the contents of the directory "hypercard."

get Photo1.sit.hqx

The "get" command starts the file transfer.

```
200 PORT command successful.
150 Opening ASCII mode data connection for Photo1.sit.hqx (257195 bytes).
```

Above, the file transfer has begun.

49198 bytes received.
126224 bytes received.
202256 bytes received.

The prompts above appeared as the file was being downloaded.

226 Transfer complete.

The above message lets the user know that the file transfer is complete.

257195 bytes received.

Note that the number of bytes immediately above is exactly the same as the number of bytes listed after the get command for the directory "hypercard."

Bye

The "Bye" command ends the FTP session.

At this point, you will have to find the downloaded file on your computer and decompress it. In this example, we downloaded a HyperCard stack. HyperCard stacks are Macintosh software, so we need to use decompressing software that uses the BINHEX compression algorithm. Recall that we discussed the various compression schemes for PCs, Macs, and UNIX computers above. Prior to downloading the file above, we had downloaded the program Stuffit Expander™, a freeware program, also by using FTP. When we decompressed the file above, we found it to be a HyperCard-based catalog of the Smithsonian's photo file. Figure 4-1 shows the first page of the decompressed file.

Help

Most FTP servers will have a "help" command. Figure 4-2 shows the result of invoking that command, a list of all FTP commands. Additionally, typing "help" followed by a particular command from the list will provide more detailed information about using that command.

ARCHIE

Archie, which is short for "archive," is a popular use of anonymous FTP. **Archie** servers contain the names of other anonymous FTP sites, thus acting as a kind of index. Archie makes it possible for users to look to one server when trying to find a particular file instead of having to look at many servers for that same file. Archie is like a card catalog of Internet FTP sites. There are many duplicate or "mirror" servers for Archie. Those mirror sites diminish the load on any particular server. They also serve to reduce bandwidth problems by making it possible for users to access

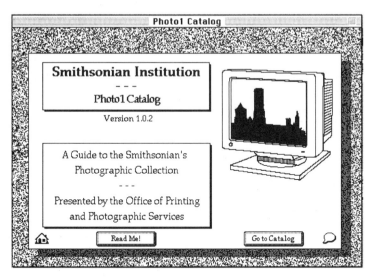

Figure 4-1. First page or card of decompressed HyperCard stack "Photo1 Catalog" downloaded from the Smithsonian's anonymous FTP server

FTP Commands

acct	ascii	bell	bget	binary
bput	bye	cd	close	delete
debug	dir	get	glob	hash
help	interactive	lcd	ldir	lls
ls	macb	mdelete	mdir	mget
mkdir	mls	mode	mput	noninteractive
open	prompt	put	pwd	quit
quote	recv	remotehelp	rename	rm
rmdir	send	sendport	slashflip	status
struct	type	user	verbose	

Figure 4-2 Standard FTP commands. Most FTP servers use these commands. Notice that "help" is a command, too. Typing in "help" followed by a command will usually open a screen giving information about that command.

Archie servers near them. Table 4-1 shows a worldwide list of Archie servers. You should use one near you for maximum efficiency. However, recall the advice given in Chapter 1 about using time zones to help you get around traffic bottlenecks caused by local daily usage patterns. So, there may be occasions when you will want to use a more distant Archie server located in a time zone where usage is less due to daily patterns (e.g., early morning, local time). Further information about Archie can be found on Internet sites like the one[7] referenced by the note in this sentence.

Server	IP Address	Country
archie.au	139.130.4.6	Australia
archie.edvz.uni-linz.ac.at	140.78.3.8	Austria
archie.univie.ac.at	131.130.1.23	Austria
archie.uqam.ca	132.208.250.10	Canada
archie.funet.fi	128.214.6.102	Finland
archie.univ-rennesl.fr	129.20.128.38	France
archie.th-darmstadt.de	130.83.128.118	Germany
archie.ac.il	132.65.16.18	Israel
archie.unipi.it	131.114.21.10	Italy
archie.wide.ad.jp	133.4.3.6	Japan
archie.hana.nm.kr	128.134.1.1	Korea
archie.sogang.ac.kr	163.239.1.11	Korea
archie.uninett.no	128.39.2.20	Norway
archie.rediris.es	130.206.1.2	Spain
archie.luth.se	130.240.12.30	Sweden
archie.switch.ch	130.59.1.40	Switzerland
archie.ncu.edu.tw	192.83.166.12	Taiwan
archie.doc.ic.ac.uk	146.169.11.3	United Kingdom
archie.hensa.ac.uk	129.12.21.25	United Kingdom
archie.unl.edu	129.93.1.14	USA (NE)
archie.internic.net	198.49.45.10	USA (NJ)
archie.rutgers.edu	128.6.18.15	USA (NJ)
archie.ans.net	147.225.1.10	USA (NY)
archie.sura.net	128.167.254.179	USA (MD)

Table 4-1. Addresses of Archie servers worldwide

CONCLUSION

If you are like us, then you will probably agree that using FTP is a lot like working a standard transmission on a car. You have to know when and how to shift gears. Still, FTP is an efficient and fast method for downloading files, especially if you know exactly where the file you want is. In the next two chapters, we will look at two Internet applications, gopher and the WWW browsers; they are more like automatic transmissions in that they make the process of file transfers much easier. They make browsing through servers easier, too. Still, you will need to learn both TELNET and FTP before you become an accomplished Internet user. Both applications will pay you dividends as a social science researcher or practitioner. You may be able to bypass FTP by using the newer Internet software like gopher and WWW browsers, but you likely will need to use TELNET sometime as well.

NOTES

1.   http://www.apocalypse.org/pub/rfcs/rfc854.txt

2.   http://www.w3.org/hypertext/WWW/Protocols/rfc959/Overview.html

3.   http://proper.com:70/0/pc/files/long-ftp

4.   http://ici.proper.com/mac/files/

5.   http://wwwhost.ots.utexas.edu/mac/internet-ftp.html

6.   ftp://photo1.si.edu/

7.   http://www2.hawaii.edu/itsdocs/archie.html

5

Gopher

CHAPTER PREVIEW

Gopher, one of the earliest interactive Internet software applications developed, is another implementation of client-server computing and is based on a hierarchical model of folders and files. That model makes it intuitively easy for you to navigate the Internet because of its familiarity. Further, gopher is designed so that you can easily set up gopher servers as well as use gopher clients. Shortly after gopher's introduction in 1989, gopher's design led to a veritable explosion of new gopher servers that is continuing today. In this chapter, we show how gopher's design and ease of use led to the first surge of Internet server growth.

TUNNELING THE INTERNET

The name "gopher" was chosen for several reasons. One was that gopher was developed at the University of Minnesota, the mascot of which is the "Golden Gopher." Another was the term's similarity to the slang expression "go fer" to describe entry-level employees who are sent on errands. Still another was real gophers' habit of digging tunnels. This last reason serves as an apt metaphor because gopher software seemingly links you to an Internet site as if you had "tunneled" directly to it.

WHAT IS GOPHER?

Originally designed as a campus wide information distribution system, the **gopher** model has been extended to the entire Internet. The file folder model chosen is familiar to most users already, and it maps readily to the file structure of most microcomputers. Unlike TELNET and FTP, gopher's design is explicitly linked to microcomputers, not to UNIX computers (although it does work on UNIX, too). Gopher servers and clients have been written for nearly any type of computer. Because of the design of the gopher protocol, it does not matter what kind of computer is running the gopher server or the gopher client. Gopher clients and servers communicate regardless of the computers they are running on. One way to look at gopher, then, is as a method for achieving compatibility across computer platforms and as another step toward solving the problem of making different types of computers work together on the Internet.

Because the gopher design puts most of the "intelligence" of the gopher protocol on the side of the server, gopher clients, the software you use to access a gopher server, may be written to match the interface features and other capabilities of the computer running the gopher client. Thus, graphical user interface (GUI) features may be implemented in gopher clients running on computers that support GUI and not implemented on computers that do not. Similarly, gopher clients running on computers with modest hardware features may implement only features of the gopher protocol that the computer can handle. Typically, the users of such computers need not or will not know that their gopher client is so limited. On the other hand, computers with powerful hardware will be able to support all or most of the current or future features of the gopher protocol. Such design flexibility for clients is one of the conceptual advances created by the gopher model and is in large part responsible for the rapid creation of both gopher client software and gopher servers. A recent Veronica harvest (a method for finding gopher servers; see below) revealed that there are probably over 11,000 gopher servers, counting both registered and unregistered servers, currently operating on the Internet, with more being started daily (Steven Foster, personal communication).

HOW DOES GOPHER WORK?

RFC 1436[1] describes the gopher protocol as follows (p. 1):

> The Internet Gopher protocol is designed primarily to act as a distributed document delivery system. While documents (and services) reside on many servers, Gopher client software presents users with a hierarchy of items and directories much like a file system. In fact, the Gopher interface is designed to resemble a file system since a file system is a good model for locating documents and services.

Gopher presents you with a familiar system of organization, folders and files, and then allows you to browse through them easily without your having to worry about the address or location of the remote servers you access.

USING GOPHER

Obtaining Gopher Software

Gopher software is easily obtained by anonymous FTP (see Chapter 4) to the Home Gopher site at the University of Minnesota[2] referenced by the note in this sentence. Follow the instructions to install the gopher client software appropriate to your particular computer. After you install the appropriate gopher client, you will also need to install a set or suite of "helper applications" (see the section "Helper Applications" below). Together, the gopher and the helper applications suite complete your installation.

Using Helper Applications

Helper applications are applications that perform useful functions like handling audio, graphic, and compression tasks. Gopher and the World Wide Web browsers (see Chapter 6) also invoke these helper applications automatically. Helper applications can be obtained from a variety of sites including the one[3] referenced by the endnote in this sentence. Helper applications further extend gopher's ease of use. Recall that when using FTP, users must perform such tasks manually by finding and running the appropriate software.

   If you do not install helper applications, you will not be able to view graphic files, hear sound files, or decompress compressed files. So, be sure to install the helper applications as well as the appropriate gopher client for your computer. Helper applications are a part of the basic design of the gopher protocol. Using them keeps the gopher client design simple and makes it possible to update the client's functionality by adding new helper applications as they are developed. The alternative would be to rewrite the gopher client each time an improvement was desired, a much more difficult task.

Sample Gopher Session

Figure 5–1 shows a sample gopher session using a GUI client, TurboGopher. As indicated in the figure, each mouse click opens a new screen window in a hierarchical fashion, starting with the "Home Gopher" at the University of Minnesota and ending at the gopher server at Louisiana Tech University.

Research and Practice Uses of Gopher

Gopher allows you to find information from many places on the Internetinteractively using a familiar metaphor. In addition, gopher automates the process of TELNET, decompressing and viewing graphic files, and listening to sound files, by invoking helper applications. These applications are called into action by gopher as needed. See Chapters 9 - 15 for gopher server addresses of interest to particular social science disciplines.

VERONICA

Veronica is gopher's near-analog to FTP's Archie (see Chapter 4). Veronica (short for Very Easy Rodent-Oriented Net-Wide Index To Computerized Archives) searches and displays gopher titles on your gopher client. You may then select any title found, and your gopher client will take you to the gopher server that holds that title. Veronica searches are conducted simply by finding a Veronica menu item within gopher— as, for instance, within the Home Gopher Hierarchy at the University of Minnesota site or at many other sites. So, Veronica is not a separate piece of Internet software that you load on your computer, but rather another gopher file that you find and select. The managers of each Veronica server count or "harvest" the number of gopher servers on a routine basis. You use the results of those harvests each time you conduct a Veronica search.

GOPHER IN 3-D

A new and exciting prospect is a protocol called VRML (Virtual Reality Markup Language). **VRML** enables gopher and other types of Internet clients to display resources in a seemingly three–dimensional format. The first, experimental gopher clients that use VRML have already been released. However, those clients are still a long way from everyday use because of their slowness, their propensity to crash, and their need for fast processors and large amounts of RAM. However, VRML may be one of the standards of future Internet browsing software.

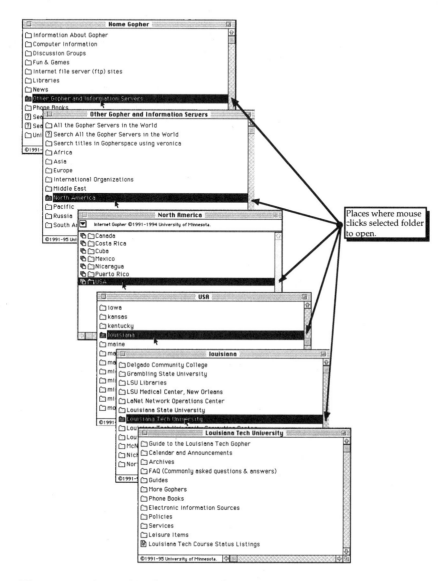

Figure 5-1. A graphical user interface gopher (TurboGopher) file hierarchy

CONCLUSION

Gopher is a user-friendly, file folder-based Internet software tool that provides access to gopher servers and to other Internet resources without your having to know much about computers or networking. Its design allows you to easily browse through the Internet, something not easily done via FTP. Helper applications are part of gopher's design, and they open automatically as needed to handle audio and graphic files as well as decompression of files. Gopher clients' ease of use combined with the ready availability of gopher servers has led to heavy use of the gopher protocol. Finally, the gopher protocol may be seen as one of the first steps toward a world where all networked computers can easily communicate with each other. In the next chapter, we will cover another set of Internet software tools, the World Wide Web browsers, which are also easy to use but that use a different model for their implementation, hypertext.

NOTES

1.   http://www.apocalypse.org/pub/rfcs/rfc854.txt

2.   boombox.micro.umn.edu

3.   http://www.netscape.com/MCOM/tricks_docs/helper_docs/

6

World Wide Web

CHAPTER PREVIEW

The World Wide Web is a hypertext-based distributed information system originally created at CERN, the European Center for Nuclear Research, to provide a channel for communication and collaboration between CERN scientists. Today, however, the World Wide Web has completely outstripped its original bounds and has become a new publishing paradigm, a method for tapping into the vast repository of different types of information created in all previous Internet formats, a means for corporate and personal expression, and much more. The WWW has surpassed even gopher's phenomenal growth (see Chapter 5) in an even shorter time. A recent survey by SRI[1] found that users of the WWW break into two groups: "upstream" and "other half." The former represents mostly those with subsidized direct connections (e.g., professionals in universities and businesses); the latter consists primarily of students or recent graduates. Both groups share high levels of education but differ in terms of gender breakdown: females, in general, use the WWW less than males, but more females are found in the "other half" group than in the "upstream" group. Also, the "upstream" group, while fully half of the SRI sample, represents only 10% of the U.S. population. On the other hand, the "other half" group represents 90% of the population, and SRI predicts that it is in that group where the bulk of future Internet growth will have to occur because of market saturation in the "upstream" group. Which group are you in? Incidentally, SRI conducts such surveys periodially, and you may participate by using theURL[2] referenced in this sentence.

In this chapter, you will learn how the World Wide Web started, how it is designed, how to get connected to it, and how to use it in social science research and practice.

WHAT IS THE WORLD WIDE WEB?

Recall our discussion of hypertext and hypermedia from Chapter 1. Both hypertext and hypermedia are the models upon which the World Wide Web is based. The **World Wide Web** can be viewed as a huge hypermedia network where Web servers form the nodes of that network. Web browsers (see below for more detail) are the software tools that allow you to navigate easily from node to node. Both Web browsers and servers are written in a language called HTML (Hypertext Markup Language, see below for more detail). The browsers interpret HTML documents as you "surf" or explore the Web. Browsers have been written for nearly every type of computer and for both graphical and text-based interfaces (below we tell you where to obtain a browser appropriate for your computer). Like gopher clients, Web browsers can access information from a variety of servers and protocols. Naturally, Web browsers can access Web servers, but they can also access gopher servers, FTP servers, WAIS servers (see Chapter 7), and Usenet news groups (see Chapter 8), and perform TELNET. Some browsers will even allow you to send electronic mail directly from them. Thus, the Web protocol is very inclusive, and the ability of its browsers to access older protocols is a major reason for the Web's popularity and rapid growth. To paraphrase from Tolkein's *The Lord of the Rings*, the Web is "one tool to rule them all."

HOW DOES THE WORLD WIDE WEB WORK?

Authoring vs. Writing

World Wide Web pages, the basic units of the Web, are said to be "authored," not written. That distinction is made because the process of creating Web pages involves more than writing in the traditional sense. A page may contain original text, to be sure, but it may also take the reader to pages created by others. The creator of a Web page may not write a single word, but may find text, still pictures, sound files, and movie files all created by others and placed on different Web pages, and then make it possible for you to access those resources from one Web page. So, the word "authoring" attempts to include that kind of activity. In traditional text, writers are the source of the text and provide references to indicate where they have drawn from the work of others. In hypertext, however, that model no longer applies. Many hypertext authors may explicitly still use the old model governing the creation of text, but many more are taking advantage of the properties of hypertext and making it possible for you to go to other sites on the Web that they have found. In writing this text, we find ourselves in between the two paradigms. On the one hand, we are "writing" a traditional text, and at the same time, we are "authoring" a Web page where you can explore many of the topics we discuss in this text.

Web Browsers

The Web browser is the key to your easy use of the web. A **browser** is a fairly complex piece of software whose job is to interpret HTML (the language used on the Web; see below) statements on Web pages and then carry out the appropriate action. Browsers are most impressive when they are graphically based, but text-based browsers also exist. Usually, text-based browsers are used by those whose computers do not support a graphical user interface. But some use them because they can be faster. That time savings results because text-based browsers cannot display downloaded graphic items but must substitute a text message instead. Graphic items are larger than text items, so that accounts for text-based browsers' greater speed (all other factors being equal, that is). See below for instructions on how to obtain a Web browser appropriate for your computer.

At its simplest, you can think of a browser as a navigational tool for the Web. Nearly all browsers will allow you to type in the URL (Uniform Resource Locator) of a node you wish to visit, move up and down the path you have taken through the Web during a particular session, and perform typical tasks like saving and printing files. More powerful browsers may allow you to send electronic mail, access Usenet (see Chapter 8), jump to a particular location you have already visited during a current session, or save a "bookmark"—a URL of a website you find interesting—into a bookmark file. A bookmark file, then, consists of all the URLs you might want to revisit sometime. The discipline-specific chapters (9-15) are bookmark files. They are websites we have found that may be interesting to you. By using the disk that came with this text, you can download all or some of the bookmarks we found into your own browser and save yourself a lot of typing.

A good browser should make it easy for you to navigate the Web, allow you to find sites, retrace your steps, and save URLs, as well as show you websites you have already visited during a session. In an almost literal sense, browsers are hyperspace vehicles: they allow you to drive through the Web, and, like real vehicles, some have more speed, options, and horsepower than others.

Hypertext Markup Language

Hypertext Markup Language, or HTML., is a language created from
another language, SGML, or Standard Generalized Markup Language. The
current version of HTML is 3.0. But, not all Web browsers support the
newest version yet. Older versions of HTML do not support features of
version 3.0 like tables, right-justified text, or single-spaced line breaks.
The main difference between versions 1.0 and 2.0 of HTML is that 2.0
supports the use of "forms." Forms allow you to enter text into a box on
a Web page and have the Web server interpret that text. For example, a
Web "search engine" (see below) may use forms to help you search for a
string of text you specify. Version 3.0 does support the use of forms.
        HTML statements consist of ordinary text surrounded by
tags—the commands of HTML. Some of those tags dictate what you will
see on your screen and how it will be displayed, while other tags may
take you to another location on the page or elsewhere on the Web. Buttons
and/or underlining are the main ways that browsers tell you that a
particular section of a Web page will take you elsewhere or perform some
other action such as downloading a file. Fortunately, you need not learn
HTML in order to use the Web. Most browsers are sufficiently user-
friendly that even the most computer-illiterate can use them with very
little effort or training.
        Here is a Web site[3] for those of you who may wish to learn HTML.

Web Pages

Web pages are the main units, or nodes, of the Web. You, too, could
author a Web page by simply writing the proper HTML statements.
Surprisingly, a simple text editor or a word processor is all that you need
in order to write HTML (other than knowledge of HTML, that is).
However, if you want to create your own Web page, you should probably
look into a text editor that has been designed specifically to create
HTML. Also, many of the popular word processing programs now have
added HTML creation capabilities. You may want to look into them as
well. You will need Web server software and an Internet connection to
display your Web page. Many colleges and universities allow their
students to display their personal Web pages through their institution's
Internet connection. Also, it is now possible to rent space on the Web
from an Internet provider. Some providers will even create those pages for
you, for a fee. These endnotes [4,5,6,7,8] reference some of those page
designers found by a quick search using a "search engine" (see the section
"Web Search Engines" below for information). There are many more such
providers. (Note: we neither know, use, nor endorse any of these
providers. We simply list them for your possible benefit.)

Anchors and Hyperlinks

In addition to HTML statements, Web pages consist of anchors and hyperlinks. An **anchor** is the starting point of a hyperlink. A **hyperlink** consists of the instructions to the browser from activating an anchor. Can you see the hyperspace implications of those definitions? Anchors are nodes, too. Hyperlinks are the mechanisms that enable you to jump from node to node. HTML statements govern both the creation of anchors and hyperlinks. Can you see how each Web page author creates a small portion of the Web? Now, can you see how, when you hyperlink to other pages or when other pages hyperlink to your page, the Web grows a little more? Finally, imagine how literally thousands of people all over the world are adding to the Web daily. When you put all that activity together, it becomes easier to explain the Web's growth.

As the Web grows, it also becomes more difficult to navigate and easier to get lost. That is why a good browser is an essential tool for you. But a good browser is not enough. You will need to organize your bookmark file so that you can find your way back to those sites you find useful. If you begin to write Web pages, you will soon discover how good design principles will help those who land on your page find their way through it easily. Such principles are not obvious, so you may need to look at a site[9] like the one referenced in this sentence for help.

USING THE WORLD WIDE WEB

Obtaining World Wide Web Browsers

World Wide Web browsers, both graphical or text-based, are easily obtained by anonymous FTP (see Chapter 4) to the University of Illinois[10] referenced in this sentence. Other sources include national commercial Internet providers such as America Online and CompuServe, among others. Recently, the Well, a longtime on-line service provider, announced "the Whole Works," a package furnishing a complete suite of Internet software tools for home use, including Netscape, one of the more popular browsers. Additionally, the Well announced a network of local–access telephone numbers in 50 U.S. cities. Local Internet service providers are another place you may wish to look to obtain a browser.

Using Helper Applications (again)

Helper applications are applications that handle audio, graphic, compression, or other tasks. Recall that the gopher design was the first to use helper applications (see Chapter 5). Web browsers use helper applications to perform tasks that would otherwise have to be performed by the browser. If the helper applications model were not used, then browser software would be much more complicated because then the browser itself would have to handle all of the tasks now handled by the helper applications as well as the browsing task. The helper applications model also makes it easier to incorporate new features and protocols as they emerge. Browsers can be updated much more simply in the helper applications model. You can obtain helper applications[11] from a variety of sites including the one referenced in this sentence. Both gopher clients and Web browsers invoke helper applications automatically. Recall that when using FTP, tasks like decompressing files require you to perform the task with appropriate software. So, a complete browser installation will also include a suite of helper applications.

A Sample World Wide Web Session

Figure 6-1 shows the Buena Vista Corporation's home page as seen using the Netscape browser. Notice that the hyperlinks on this page are both buttons and underlined items. Also notice that provision is made for users with nongraphical browsers via another hyperlink.

Research and Practice Uses of the World Wide Web

In the discipline-specific chapters (9-15), we provide you with URLs for many websites that may be useful to your research or practice interests. Your Web browser will allow you access not only to Web pages but also to gopher sites, FTP sites, WAIS sites (see Chapter 7), and Usenet groups (see Chapter 8). Some browsers, when properly configured, may allow you to send electronic mail directly from them.

WEB SEARCH ENGINES

Like archie and Veronica in FTP and gopher, respectively, you may search the Web using "search engines" found at specific websites. A **search engine** is software that will search the Web for you using keywords that you give it. The notes in this sentence give you the URLs for InfoSeek Search[12], Lycos[13], WebCrawler™[14], and other search engines[15]. Note that we used all of those search engines in compiling the URLs listed in this book.

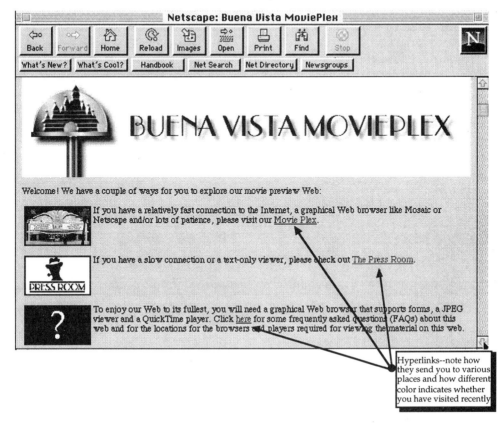

Figure 6-1. A Web browser (Netscape) and the Buena Vista Corporation's home page.

CONCLUSION

The World Wide Web is a fast-growing collection of Web pages created by individuals and institutions. You navigate the Web using browser software and an Internet connection. The model guiding the development of the Web is hypermedia in all of its forms. That model has created a hyperspace where users can leap from section to section within a Web page, or from continent to continent between Web pages. The Web has become the most popular Internet software tool for several reasons: the browser's ease of use, the browser's ability to use all previous Internet protocols, and a relatively easy way for users to provide new home pages. Next, we turn to yet another valuable tool, the Wide Area Information Server (WAIS).

NOTES

1. http://future.sri.com/vals/vals-survey.results.html

2. http://future.sri.com/

3. http://info.med.yale.edu/caim/M_Resources.HTML

4. http://www.usa.net/~data/

5. http://hamp.hampshire.edu/~jtsF93/Jamie/Flea.html

6. http://www.garlic.com/rfwilson/writserv.htm

7. http://www.halcyon.com/ah/HDC.html

8. http://www.teleport.com/~wpdp/

9. http://info.med.yale.edu/caim/StyleManual_Top.HTML

10. http://union.ncsa.uiuc.edu:80/HyperNews/get/www/browsers.html

11. http://www.netscape.com/MCOM/tricks_docs/helper_docs/

12. http://home.netscape.com/home/internetñsearch.html

13. http://lycos.cs.cmu.edu/

14. http://webcrawler.com/

15. http://cuiwww.unige.ch/metañindex.html

7

WAIS (Wide Area Information Server)

CHAPTER PREVIEW

WAIS is an early example of a rapidly developing area of computer science, intelligent agents. **Intelligent agents** are a type of software designed to cope with the rapidly expanding knowledge base of the Internet. In the future, intelligent agents like WAIS will learn what kind of items you will want to look at and then provide them for you, automatically. That level of intelligent agent has yet to materialize, but right now you could subscribe to news services that provide you with news of personal interest. So, for example, you could specify that you wanted college lacrosse scores, a digest of soap opera plots, or the latest job openings in your field delivered to you electronically. Eventually, electronic agents will learn your preferences as you read your daily electronic newspaper and tailor the precedence of items you see accordingly. In this chapter, we explain WAIS and illustrate its use.

WHAT IS WAIS?

WAIS is still another example of Internet client-server computing. WAIS is based on a database model that supports natural–language queries (e.g., questions in plain English) and a form of feedback called **relevance matching**. Relevance matching allows WAIS users to see how closely their information requests correspond to the returned database information. Unlike the client-server software tools discussed thus far, WAIS is a commercial product from a consortium of companies: Thinking Machines Corp., Apple Computer Inc., and the *Wall Street Journal*. Each company has a compelling interest in developing WAIS. Thinking Machines Corp. is a producer of supercomputer hardware. Apple Computer Inc. has long used a conceptual model, "The Knowledge Navigator," as a blueprint for its vision of the future of computing. In that model, intelligent client-server interfaces will make retrieving any kind of on-line information extremely easy. Finally, the *Wall Street Journal* is the owner of the Dow-Jones News Retrieval Service.

HOW DOES WAIS WORK?

WAIS's design is discussed in RFC 1625[1], which. which describes it as follows (p. 1):

> The network publishing system, Wide Area Information Servers (WAIS), is designed to help users find information over a computer network. The principles guiding WAIS development are:
>
> 1.   A wide-area networked-based information system for searching, browsing, and publishing
> 2.   Based on standards
> 3.   Easy to use
> 4.   Flexible and growth oriented.
>
> From this basis, a large group of developers, publishers, standards bodies, libraries, government agencies, schools, and users have been helping further the WAIS system. The WAIS software architecture has four main components: the client, the server, the database, and the protocol. The WAIS client is a user-interface program that sends requests for information to local or remote servers. Clients are available for most popular desktop environments. The WAIS server is a program that services client requests, and is available on a variety of UNIX platforms. The server generally runs on a machine containing one or more information sources, or WAIS databases. The protocol, Z39.50-1988, is used to connect WAIS clients and servers and is based on the 1988 Version of the NISO Z39.50 Information Retrieval Service and Protocol Standard. The goal of the WAIS network publishing system is to create an open architecture of information clients and servers by using a standard computer-to-computer protocol that enables clients to communicate with servers.

Thus, WAIS relies on a great deal of cooperation between database providers, adherence to a protocol (Z39.50-1988), and appropriate client-server software.

The WAIS protocol (Z39.50-1988) was designed to work on the Internet using the TCP protocol (see Chapter 2 for a discussion of TCP). When you use WAIS client software, you send a request to a database. Databases of all kinds exist, and they are registered with the Directory-of-servers maintained by Thinking Machines Corp. Currently, there are over 500 WAIS databases. If your request to the database generates some "hits" or matches, the database returns the titles of those hits to you along with a score indicating the closeness of the match; the higher the score, the closer the match with 1000 being a perfect match. See Figure 7-1 for an example of the first few hits from a database of the speeches made by Bill Clinton using the request "Information highway." Those speeches could be downloaded and looked at in their entirety. WAIS servers store text items primarily, but they can also store graphic or binary items.

WAIS searches can also be made through gopher and the World Wide Web. Each of those Internet software tools has "gateways" (methods of access) to WAIS. Gopher gateways are folders and files, and Web gateways are hyperlinks. So, you need not actually possess WAIS client software in order to perform WAIS searches.

The Directory-of-Servers

The Directory-of-Servers maintained by Thinking Machines Corp. serves as a kind of white pages for WAIS databases. As new databases are created, they are listed with the Directory-of-Servers. A partial list of social science WAIS databases is provided for you in Table 7-1. Notice that WAIS databases always end with the extension "src," which stands for "source."

USING WAIS

Obtaining WAIS Software

WAIS client software is easily obtained by anonymous FTP (see Chapter 4) to the FTP site maintained by the Thinking Machines Corp[2] as referenced in this sentence. Follow the instructions to install the WAIS client software appropriate to your particular computer.

Research and Practice Uses of WAIS

WAIS can be a very useful tool in social science research and practice, provided you can find an appropriate database. You may want to obtain a WAIS client and then search through some of the databases listed in Table 7-1 to see the kind of information available to you.

WAIS searches can also be made on the archives of many Internet listservers (see Chapter 3) or news groups (see Chapter 8), provided those resources have been converted into WAIS databases (and many are). Those kinds of archives let you find information about topics that were discussed in the past, but in which you may still have an interest. Using WAIS in that way saves bandwidth for listservers and news groups and may prevent you from being flamed (see Chapter 3).

Sample WAIS Session

Figure 7-1 shows a sample WAIS session using the client MacWAIS. The example shown is a search through the database "clinton-speechess.src," or the speeches made by Bill Clinton, for the search terms "information highway."

Score	Size	Headline
1000	1.5K	UNESCO-DARE-Social-Science-Institutes.src
720	3.6K	ANU-Vietnam-SocSci.src
694	3.2K	ANU-Coomspapers-Index.src
631	2.8K	ANU-Demography-Publications.src
606	4.3K	ANU-SSDA-Australian-Census.src
600	4.6K	ANU-SSDA-Australian-Opinion.src
591	1.4K	STAR-Data.src
589	5.1K	ANU-SSDA-Australian-Studies.src
585	2.5K	ANU-Internet-Voyager-Guide.src
570	1.7K	ASK-SISY-Software-Information.src
560	2.4K	Academic_email_conf.src
556	1.6K	MacPsych.src
552	2.9K	ANU-Hist-Aust-Sci-Tech-L.src
528	1.9K	STAR-NIPO-Data.src
526	2.1K	ANU-Vietnam-NatSci.src
518	1.8K	Ersa.src
489	2.9K	ANU-Theses-Abstracts.src
485	2.4K	ANU-Vietnam-SciTech-L.src
456	2.0K	Hst-status.src
456	2.7K	ANU-SocSci-WWW-Gopher-News-L.src
451	3.3K	ANU-Australian-Economics.src
447	2.1K	ANU-Coombswais-Index.src
441	2.2K	ANU-Philippine-Studies-L.src
403	3.0K	ANU-SocSci-Internet-Rscrces.src
396	1.7K	Arctic_Environmental_Data_Directory.src
386	720	Unimelb-research.src

Table 7-1 Social science WAIS databases (servers)
Note: ANU stands for Australian National University

Score	Size	Headline
365	5.5K	Stsci-ulas-db.src
348	1.3K	Science-Fiction-Series-Guide.src
348	2.5K	ANU-CAUT-Academics.src
347	2.5K	ANU-CAUT-Projects.src
340	7.5K	OnePgrs.src
336	11.9K	Health-Security-Act.src
333	2.0K	ANU-Austral-SocPol-Theor-L.src
320	1.8K	ANU-Complex-Systems.src
320	2.6K	ANU-AustPhilosophyForum-L.src
318	492	Scholastic-ms-lib.src
318	3.2K	ANU-Gesture-L.src
317	1.9K	ANU-Sociology-ANU-RSSS-L.src
311	2.0K	ANU-Coombseminars-L.src
1	699	Query Report for this Search

Table 7-1 (Cont.)

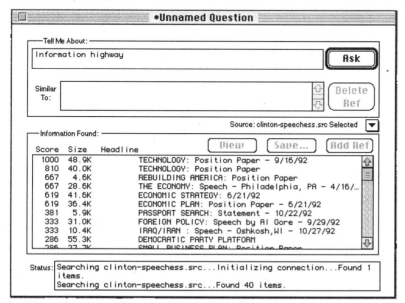

Figure 7-1. High relevance WAIS results for "information highway" in the database "clinton-speeches.src" (MacWAIS)

CONCLUSION

WAIS lets you quickly search through published databases without your having to learn a syntax for making search queries. Instead, you simply type in your queries in natural language. The hits you get from that query are then listed in the order of closeness of match. In the next chapter, we will look at one of the biggest uses of the Internet, Usenet News.

NOTES

1.   http://www.apocalypse.org/pub/rfcs/rfc1625.txt

2.   Think.com:/public/wais

8

Usenet

CHAPTER PREVIEW

Usenet is different from the other Internet software tools previously discussed. For one, Usenet is not an Internet software tool. Instead, **Usenet** is a vast collection of people who communicate with each other in thousands of news groups, or groups that share a special interest. Usenet is so big that you cannot possibly sample it all. Instead, you will want to look for the parts of Usenet you might find useful. In this chapter, we provide you with some of the knowledge necessary to find and read news groups of interest to social science research and practice. But realize that Usenet is much, much more than that.

BULLETIN BOARDS

Although the term "bulletin board" does not strictly apply to Usenet in the context of networked computers, the term does apply in a broader sense. Strictly speaking, bulletin board systems (BBSs) refer to computers running bulletin board software and accessed primarily via modems. We will not cover BBSs in this text.

More generally, Usenet can be seen as a system of bulletin boards. In this context, we describe Usenet via the metaphor of the common, ordinary bulletin board--a place where people post notices and others read them. Indeed, the term "post" is used to describe the same process (albeit in electronic fashion) on Usenet **news groups**.

In order to differentiate Usenet from other electronic bulletin board systems, a different terminology is used on Usenet to describe similar people, roles, and behaviors. For example, the person running a news group is called a "news administrator" (not a "sysop" for system operator), and news groups are not called "areas," "boards," groups, or "rooms."[1] Such terms are used, but they are not properly applied to news groups.

WHAT IS USENET?

Usenet's origins date back to the early days of the ARPANET (see Chapter 2). One of the creators of Usenet, Stephen Daniel, described Usenet as "the poor man's ARPANET." In 1979, he and Tom Truscott, Duke University graduate students, made a connection between a computer at Duke with another at the University of North Carolina used by Steve Bellovin. The connection was via two 300–bps modems and used UUCP (UNIX–to–UNIX Copy Program), a new feature of the then-current UNIX release. Since that first connection, Usenet has grown into a huge worldwide network running on many types of connection media including, but not limited to, the Internet. Much of the impetus for creating Usenet was as a response to the structure, formality, and restricted access of ARPANET. From its very origin, Usenet was designed to embody the opposite of those ARPANET characteristics. You will see the reflection of those origins still in today's Usenet, for it is a place with few rules, many flames, and an "anything goes" kind of atmosphere.

HOW DOES USENET WORK?

RFC 977[2] describes NNTP, the Network News Transfer Protocol. RFC 1036[3] describes the format for Network News articles. RFC 977 describes the workings of **NNTP** as follows (p. 3):

> Using NNTP, hosts exchanging news articles have an interactive mechanism for deciding which articles are to be transmitted. A host desiring new news, or which has new news to send, will typically contact one or more of its neighbors using NNTP. First it will inquire if any new news groups have been created on the serving host by means of the NEWGROUPS command. If so, and those are appropriate or desired (as established by local site-dependent rules), those new newsgroups can be created. The client host will then inquire as to which new articles have arrived in all or some of the newsgroups that it desires to receive, using the NEWNEWS command. It will receive a list of new articles from the server, and can request transmission of those articles that it desires and does not already have.
>
> Finally, the client can advise the server of those new articles which the client has recently received. The server will indicate those articles that it has already obtained copies of, and which articles should be sent to add to its collection. In this manner, only those articles which are not duplicates and which are desired are transferred.

NNTP, then, works via communication from server to server. Thus, servers are sometimes referred to as being "upstream" or "downstream" from each other in terms of news flow. In practice, however, those terms are somewhat misleading. Instead, you can think of Usenet news flowing to and from local and more remote servers. The Usenet news you can read will depend primarily upon the settings made on your local server by that server's system administrator and the news groups sent from upstream.

Because there are so many news groups (over 10,000), you will not be able to read them all. Your local server can only carry a small portion of those news groups. Each individual post has a short lifetime, chiefly determined by the system administrator of the server from which you get your Usenet news. Although individual posts have a limited lifespan, many news groups archive or collect their postings, making them available to you for much longer periods.

USING USENET

Obtaining Usenet Software and Getting on Usenet

Usenet news software is easily obtained by anonymous FTP (see Chapter 4) to the Indiana University site[4] referenced by the note in this sentence. Follow the instructions to install the Usenet news client software appropriate to your particular computer. After you install the appropriate Usenet news client, you will also need to configure the application properly with the domain name or IP address of the server from which you will get your Usenet news. If you do not know that address, see your local system administrator. The commercial Internet providers also provide access to Usenet news. You can also read Usenet news and post messages to news groups from some World Wide Web browsers (e.g., Netscape or Mosaic.) You will have to configure those Web browsers with the address of your local news server before you can read Usenet news, however.

Posting and Lurking

Usenet news is generated by people "posting," or writing and sending, articles to a news group. The length of those articles ranges from one line on up. Other people read the posted articles, and more people read than post articles. Those who only read articles and never post are called "lurkers." They are the silent audience of the news group. "Delurking" occurs when those readers switch from being only readers to being readers and posters. Some news groups have semi-formal traditions regarding the process of delurking; others do not. For new users, a safe strategy is to lurk a while before posting to any news group. That will lower the likelihood of being flamed or making "newbie" (new Internet user) errors.

News Servers

You will get your Usenet news from a news server. That news server will most likely be located on your campus or somewhere else nearby. Ask your local system administrator or fellow users in your area for information about your local news server. If you do not have a local news server, you may have to resort to using the services of a commercial Internet provider. Even if you cannot access Usenet, you can still get Usenet news postings via electronic mail or the World Wide Web. For example, Stanford University sponsors a free "NetNews Filtering Service" in which you can specify the subjects that you would like to read. Those are then sent to you via electronic mail or via a Web home page created for you by the service. To get the electronic mail version instructions, send an electronic mail message to

NETNEWS@HOTPAGE.STANFORD.EDU

In the body of the message type the word "help".

The URL[5] referenced by the note in this sentence will take you to the World Wide Web version of this service. Table 8-1 shows the news groups searched by this service.

NEWS GROUPS

As mentioned above, there are thousands of news groups, and you cannot hope to read them all. However, a hierarchical naming system has been devised to make the selection of news groups that you might wish to read easier.

The Usenet Hierarchy

Usenet news groups have been divided, taxonomically (classified), into subject categories. The "Big 8" categories are (in alphabetical order):

comp	topics related to computers, in general
humanities	topics related to arts and literature, in general
misc	topics that do not easily fit into the others (e.g., employment)
news	topics related to news
rec	topics related to recreation, in general
sci	topics related the sciences, both pure and applied
soc	topics related to social behaviors and to cultures
talk	discussions of problems and issues.

Another popular (and controversial) category is "alt," which includes subjects of all kinds including sexual behaviors in all possible forms, weddings, education, binaries (graphic items), radio, games, and feminism, just to name a few. Figure 8-1 shows the results of a recent survey of Usenet usage by selected subject categories.

News Group Naming Conventions

News groups are named in a structured, arbitrary, and hierarchical fashion. Additionally, loose taxonomic relationships can be implied between news groups by analyzing their respective names. These taxonomies exist because name parts become more specific as you read to the right. For example, the group "sci.psychology" covers more general subject matter than "sci.psychology.consciousness." Look at Table 8-1 and study the names of the news groups. Can you see some possible taxonomic relationships?

Insofar as possible, abbreviations are discouraged in naming news groups. Because news group names are not definitive, the only way to really know what a particular news group is interested in is to read that group's posts.

Starting Your Own News Group

Starting a new news group is not a task for new users. News group creation is the only really organized process that exists on Usenet. In fact, a vote is taken on each new news group. You should not consider starting your own news group until you have had a significant amount of experience (at least one year) on Usenet.

Research and Practice Uses of Usenet

Usenet is extremely useful for keeping track of current issues of interest in the various social sciences. You will have to develop your own mental filters, however, to weed out articles with little or no relevance to research or practice. That is just another way of saying, "Don't believe everything you read." Each of the discipline-specific chapters (9–15) contains a list of news groups covering topics of interest to that discipline.

FINDING NEWS GROUPS

Most news reader software packages have a feature that will allow you to search the news server you use for particular topics. If you cannot find a news group that you know exists on your news server, contact your system administrator.

alt.3d
alt.abortion.inequity
alt.abuse.recovery
alt.activism
alt.activism.death-penalty
alt.adoption
alt.aldus.freehand
alt.aldus.pagemaker
alt.alien.visitors
alt.amateur-comp
alt.angst
alt.anybody
alt.appalachian
alt.aquaria
alt.archery
alt.architecture
alt.artcom
alt.ascii-art
alt.asian-movies
alt.astrology
alt.atheism
alt.atheism.satire
alt.autos.antique
alt.banjo
alt.bbs
alt.bbs.ads
alt.bbs.allsysop
alt.bbs.doors
alt.bbs.internet
alt.beer
alt.best.of.internet
alt.binaries.multimedia
alt.binaries.pictures.anime
alt.binaries.pictures.celebrities
alt.binaries.pictures.erotica
alt.binaries.pictures.
erotica.anime
alt.binaries.pictures.erotica.d
alt.binaries.pictures.
erotica.female
alt.binaries.pictures.
erotica.male
alt.binaries.pictures.misc
alt.binaries.pictu
res.supermodels
alt.binaries.sounds.cartoons
alt.binaries.sounds.mods
alt.binaries.sounds.music
alt.bitterness
alt.books.anne-rice
alt.books.isaac-asimov
alt.books.kurt-vonnegut
alt.books.m-lackey
alt.books.reviews
alt.books.stephen-king
alt.books.tom-clancy
alt.buddha.short.fat.guy
alt.business.misc
alt.business.multi-level

alt.cad
alt.cad.autocad
alt.california
alt.callahans
alt.cd-rom
alt.censorship
alt.chess.ics
alt.child-support
alt.chinchilla
alt.chinese.computing
alt.chinese.text
alt.chinese.text.big5
alt.coffee
alt.collecting.autographs
alt.college.college-bowl
alt.college.fraternities
alt.college.sororities
alt.comedy.british
alt.comics.alternative
alt.comp.acad-freedom.talk
alt.comp.shareware
alt.computer.consultants
alt.config
alt.consciousness
alt.conspiracy
alt.conspiracy.jfk
alt.consumers.free-stuff
alt.cuddle
alt.cult-movies
alt.cult-movies.rocky-horror
alt.culture.hawaii
alt.culture.indonesia
alt.culture.internet
alt.culture.karnataka
alt.culture.kerala
alt.culture.ny-upstate
alt.culture.oregon
alt.culture.tuva
alt.culture.us.asian-indian
alt.culture.us.southwest
alt.culture.usenet
alt.current-events.bosnia
alt.current-events.korean-
crisis
alt.cyberpunk
alt.cyberpunk.chatsubo
alt.cyberpunk.movement
alt.cyberspace
alt.dads-rights
alt.dcom.telecom
alt.desert-storm
alt.devilbunnies
alt.discordia
alt.discrimination
alt.dragons-inn
alt.dreams
alt.drugs
alt.drwho.creative
alt.education.disabled

alt.emusic
alt.exotic-music
alt.fan.bill-gates
alt.fan.cecil-adams
alt.fan.conan-obrien
alt.fan.dan-quayle
alt.fan.david-bowie
alt.fan.douglas-adams
alt.fan.dragons
alt.fan.eddings
alt.fan.frank-zappa
alt.fan.furry
alt.fan.gene-scott
alt.fan.goons
alt.fan.howard-stern
alt.fan.james-bond
alt.fan.jimmy-buffett
alt.fan.letterman
alt.fan.madonna
alt.fan.monty-python
alt.fan.oj-simpson
alt.fan.piers-anthony
alt.fan.pooh
alt.fan.pratchett
alt.fan.rush-limbaugh
alt.fan.tolkien
alt.fan.u2
alt.fan.warlord
alt.fan.wodehouse
alt.fan.woody-allen
alt.fandom.cons
alt.fashion
alt.feminism
alt.fishing
alt.flame
alt.flame.roommate
alt.flame.spelling
alt.folklore.college
alt.folklore.computers
alt.folklore.ghost-stories
alt.folklore.herbs
alt.folklore.science
alt.folklore.urban
alt.food.chocolate
alt.food.fat-free
alt.food.taco-bell
alt.games.doom
alt.games.lynx
alt.games.marathon
alt.games.mk
alt.games.sf2
alt.games.torg
alt.games.vga-planets
alt.good.morning
alt.gopher
alt.gothic
alt.graffiti
alt.great-lakes
alt.guitar

Table 8–1 (cont.)   85

alt.guitar.bass
alt.guitar.tab
alt.hackers.malicious
alt.hemp
alt.history.what-if
alt.homosexual
alt.horror
alt.horror.cthulhu
alt.hypertext
alt.hypnosis
alt.individualism
alt.internet.access.wanted
alt.internet.services
alt.irc
alt.irc.ircii
alt.irc.questions
alt.journalism
alt.journalism.music
alt.kids-talk
alt.law-enforcement
alt.locksmithing
alt.lycra
alt.magic
alt.magick
alt.mcdonalds
alt.med.cfs
alt.meditation
alt.meditation.transcendental
alt.messianic
alt.military.cadet
alt.misc
alt.missing-kids
alt.models
alt.mud
alt.mud.lp
alt.music.a-cappella
alt.music.alternative
alt.music.alternative.female
alt.music.amy-grant
alt.music.beastie-boys
alt.music.bela-fleck
alt.music.billy-joel
alt.music.blues-traveler
alt.music.bootlegs
alt.music.brian-eno
alt.music.byrds
alt.music.chapel-hill
alt.music.complex-arrang
alt.music.danzig
alt.music.deep-purple
alt.music.enya
alt.music.filk
alt.music.fleetwood-mac
alt.music.genesis
alt.music.independent
alt.music.james-taylor
alt.music.journalism
alt.music.kylie-minogue
alt.music.led-zeppelin

alt.music.lyrics
alt.music.misc
alt.music.monkees
alt.music.nin
alt.music.nirvana
alt.music.paul-simon
alt.music.pearl-jam
alt.music.peter-gabriel
alt.music.pink-floyd
alt.music.prince
alt.music.producer
alt.music.queen
alt.music.roger-waters
alt.music.rush
alt.music.ska
alt.music.smash-pumpkins
alt.music.sonic-youth
alt.music.soul
alt.music.synthpop
alt.music.techno
alt.music.the-doors
alt.music.tmbg
alt.music.u2
alt.music.weird-al
alt.music.who
alt.music.world
alt.music.yes
alt.mythology
alt.mythology.mythic-animals
alt.native
alt.news.macedonia
alt.news-media
alt.non.sequitur
alt.online-service
alt.online-service.america-
online
alt.online-service.compuserve
alt.online-service.prodigy
alt.os.multics
alt.out-of-body
alt.pagan
alt.paranet.abduct
alt.paranet.paranormal
alt.paranet.skeptic
alt.paranet.ufo
alt.paranormal
alt.peace-corps
alt.peeves
alt.periphs.pcmcia
alt.personals
alt.personals.ads
alt.personals.bondage
alt.personals.misc
alt.personals.poly
alt.personals.spanking
alt.philosophy.objectivism
alt.politics.british
alt.politics.clinton
alt.politics.correct

alt.politics.economics
alt.politics.elections
alt.politics.equality
alt.politics.homosexuality
alt.politics.libertarian
alt.politics.media
alt.politics.radical-left
alt.politics.reform
alt.politics.usa.constitution
alt.politics.usa.misc
alt.politics.usa.republican
alt.polyamory
alt.president.clinton
alt.prisons
alt.privacy.anon-server
alt.prophecies.nostradamus
alt.pub.coffeehouse.amethyst
alt.punk
alt.punk.straight-edge
alt.quotations
alt.radio.networks.npr
alt.radio.pirate
alt.radio.scanner
alt.rap
alt.rave
alt.recovery
alt.recovery.aa
alt.recovery.codependency
alt.recovery.na
alt.religion.islam
alt.religion.kibology
alt.religion.mormon
alt.religion.scientology
alt.revenge
alt.revisionism
alt.rhode_island
alt.rock-n-roll
alt.rock-n-roll.classic
alt.rock-n-roll.metal
alt.rock-n-roll.metal.heavy
alt.rock-n-roll.metal.metallica
alt.rock-n-roll.stones
alt.romance
alt.romance.chat
alt.rush-limbaugh
alt.satanism
alt.sb.programmer
alt.sci.physics.new-theories
alt.sci.planetary
alt.scooter
alt.security
alt.security.pgp
alt.sega.genesis
alt.sewing
alt.sex
alt.sex.bestiality
alt.sex.bondage
alt.sex.fetish.feet
alt.sex.fetish.startrek

alt.sex.magazines
alt.sex.motss
alt.sex.movies
alt.sex.spanking
alt.sex.stories
alt.sex.strip-clubs
alt.sex.wanted
alt.sex.wizards
alt.sexual.abuse.recovery
alt.shenanigans
alt.showbiz.gossip
alt.skate-board
alt.skinheads
alt.slack
alt.smokers
alt.snowmobiles
alt.society.anarchy
alt.society.generation-x
alt.sources
alt.sources.mac
alt.sport.bowling
alt.sport.jet-ski
alt.sport.paintball
alt.sport.pool
alt.sports.baseball.atlanta-braves
alt.sports.baseball.balt-orioles
alt.sports.baseball.bos-redsox
alt.sports.baseball.chicago-cubs
alt.sports.baseball.cinci-reds
alt.sports.baseball.cleve-indians
alt.sports.baseball.col-rockies
alt.sports.baseball.fla-marlins
alt.sports.baseball.la-dodgers
alt.sports.baseball.ny-mets
alt.sports.baseball.ny-yankees
alt.sports.baseball.oakland-as
alt.sports.baseball.sea-mariners
alt.sports.baseball.sf-giants
alt.sports.baseball.texas-rangers
alt.sports.baseball.tor-bluejays
alt.sports.basketball.ivy.penn
alt.sports.basketball.nba.char-hornets
alt.sports.basketball.nba.hou-rockets
alt.sports.basketball.nba.la-lakers
alt.sports.basketball.nba.miami-heat
alt.sports.basketball.nba.orlando-magic
alt.sports.basketball.nba.sa-spurs
alt.sports.basketball.pro.ny-knicks

alt.sports.football.mn-vikings
alt.sports.football.pro.buffalo-bills
alt.sports.football.pro.cleve-browns
alt.sports.football.pro.dallas-cowboys
alt.sports.football.pro.denver-broncos
alt.sports.football.pro.gb-packers
alt.sports.football.pro.jville-jaguars
alt.sports.football.pro.la-raiders
alt.sports.football.pro.miami-dolphins
alt.sports.football.pro.ne-patriots
alt.sports.football.pro.no-saints
alt.sports.football.pro.ny-giants
alt.sports.football.pro.pitt-steelers
alt.sports.football.pro.sea-seahawks
alt.sports.football.pro.sf-49ers
alt.sports.football.pro.wash-redskins
alt.sports.hockey.nhl.boston-bruins
alt.sports.hockey.nhl.mtl-canadiens
alt.sports.hockey.nhl.ny-islanders
alt.sports.hockey.nhl.ny-rangers
alt.sports.hockey.nhl.phila-flyers
alt.sports.hockey.nhl.tor-mapleleafs
alt.sports.hockey.nhl.vanc-canucks
alt.startrek.klingon
alt.stupidity
alt.suicide.holiday
alt.supermodels
alt.support.arthritis
alt.support.cancer
alt.support.depression
alt.support.diet
alt.support.divorce
alt.support.mult-sclerosis
alt.support.stop-smoking
alt.surfing
alt.sustainable.agriculture
alt.sys.intergraph
alt.sys.pc-clone.dell
alt.sys.pc-clone.gateway2000

alt.sys.pc-clone.micron
alt.sys.pdp11
alt.sys.sun
alt.tasteless
alt.test
alt.toys.hi-tech
alt.toys.transformers
alt.transgendered
alt.tv.animaniacs
alt.tv.babylon-5
alt.tv.beakmans-world
alt.tv.bh90210
alt.tv.comedy-central
alt.tv.forever-knight
alt.tv.friends
alt.tv.game-shows
alt.tv.highlander
alt.tv.kids-in-hall
alt.tv.mad-about-you
alt.tv.melrose-place
alt.tv.muppets
alt.tv.mwc
alt.tv.nickelodeon
alt.tv.northern-exp
alt.tv.nypd-blue
alt.tv.picket-fences
alt.tv.prisoner
alt.tv.real-world
alt.tv.red-dwarf
alt.tv.ren-n-stimpy
alt.tv.saved-bell
alt.tv.seinfeld
alt.tv.simpsons
alt.tv.simpsons.itchy-scratchy
alt.tv.talkshows.late
alt.tv.twin-peaks
alt.tv.wiseguy
alt.tv.x-files
alt.tv.x-files.creative
alt.usage.english
alt.usenet.kooks
alt.usenet.offline-reader
alt.uu.comp.os.linux.questions
alt.vampyres
alt.video.laserdisc
alt.visa.us
alt.war
alt.war.civil.usa
alt.war.vietnam
alt.wedding
alt.windows.cde
alt.windows.text
alt.winsock
alt.wolves
ba.announce
ba.bicycles
ba.broadcast
ba.food
ba.general

Table 8–1 (cont.) 87

ba.internet
ba.jobs.contract
ba.jobs.misc
ba.jobs.offered
ba.market.computers
ba.market.housing
ba.market.misc
ba.market.vehicles
ba.motorcycles
ba.motss
ba.mountain-folk
ba.music
ba.news.group
ba.politics
ba.singles
ba.transportation
comp.ai
comp.ai.alife
comp.ai.fuzzy
comp.ai.games
comp.ai.genetic
comp.ai.philosophy
comp.apps.spreadsheets
comp.arch
comp.arch.bus.vmebus
comp.arch.embedded
comp.bbs.majorbbs
comp.bbs.misc
comp.bbs.waffle
comp.benchmarks
comp.cad.cadence
comp.cad.microstation
comp.cad.pro-engineer
comp.client-server
comp.compression
comp.databases
comp.databases.gupta
comp.databases.ibm-db2
comp.databases.informix
comp.databases.ingres
comp.databases.ms-access
comp.databases.object
comp.databases.olap
comp.databases.oracle
comp.databases.paradox
comp.databases.progress
comp.databases.sybase
comp.databases.theory
comp.databases.xbase.fox
comp.dcom.cabling
comp.dcom.cell-relay
comp.dcom.fax
comp.dcom.isdn
comp.dcom.lans.ethernet
comp.dcom.lans.token-ring
comp.dcom.modems
comp.dcom.sys.cisco
comp.dcom.telecom.tech
comp.dsp

comp.edu
comp.emacs.xemacs
comp.emulators.apple2
comp.emulators.cbm
comp.emulators.misc
comp.emulators.ms-
windows.wine
comp.fonts
comp.graphics.animation
comp.graphics.apps.gnuplot
comp.graphics.a
pps.lightwave
comp.graphic
s.packages.3dstudio
comp.graphics.rendering.misc
comp.groupware.lotus-
notes.misc
comp.home.automation
comp.infosystems
comp.infosystems.gis
comp.infosystems.gopher
comp.infosystems.
www.announce
comp.infosystems.
www.authoring.cgi
comp.infosystems.
www.authoring.html
comp.infosystems.
www.authoring.images
comp.infosystems.
www.browsers.misc
comp.infosystems.
www.browsers.ms-windows
comp.infosystems.
www.browsers.x
comp.infosystems.www.misc
comp.infosystems.
www.servers.mac
comp.infosystems.
www.servers.unix
comp.internet.net-
happenings
comp.lang.ada
comp.lang.basi
c.visual.3rdparty
comp.lang.basic.
visual.database
comp.lang.basic.visual.misc
comp.lang.c
comp.lang.c++
comp.lang.clipper
comp.lang.cobol
comp.lang.forth
comp.lang.forth.mac
comp.lang.lisp
comp.lang.modula2
comp.lang.oberon
comp.lang.pascal
comp.lang.pascal.borland

comp.lang.pascal.
delphi.components
comp.lang.pascal.
delphi.databases
comp.lang.pascal.delphi.misc
comp.lang.pascal.mac
comp.lang.pascal.misc
comp.lang.perl
comp.lang.perl.misc
comp.lang.prograph
comp.lang.python
comp.lang.rexx
comp.lang.smalltalk
comp.lang.tcl
comp.lang.verilog
comp.lang.vhdl
comp.mail.elm
comp.mail.list-admin.policy
comp.mail.misc
comp.mail.multi-media
comp.mail.pine
comp.mail.zmail
comp.misc
comp.multimedia
comp.music
comp.networks.n
octools.wanted
comp.object
comp.org.cpsr.talk
comp.org.eff.talk
comp.os.cpm
comp.os.geos
comp.os.linux.de
velopment.apps
comp.os.linux.de
velopment.system
comp.os.linux.hardware
comp.os.linux.misc
comp.os.linux.networking
comp.os.linux.setup
comp.os.linux.x
comp.os.magic-cap
comp.os.minix
comp.os.ms-
windows.advocacy
comp.os.ms-
windows.apps.financial
comp.os.ms-
windows.apps.misc
comp.os.ms-
windows.apps.utilities
comp.os.ms-
windows.apps.word-proc
comp.os.ms-windows.misc
comp.os.ms-
windows.networking.misc
comp.os.ms-
windows.networking.tcp-ip
comp.os.ms-

windows.networ
king.windows
comp.os.ms-windows.nt.misc
comp.os.ms-
windows.nt.setup
comp.os.ms-
windows.program
mer.controls
comp.os.ms-
windows.programmer.drivers
comp.os.ms-
windows.program
mer.graphics
comp.os.ms-
windows.program
mer.memory
comp.os.ms-
windows.programmer.misc
comp.os.ms-
windows.program
mer.multimedia
comp.os.ms-
windows.program
mer.networks
comp.os.ms-
windows.programmer.ole
comp.os.ms-
windows.programmer.tools
comp.os.ms-
windows.programmer.win32
comp.os.ms-windows.setup
comp.os.ms-windows.video
comp.os.msdos.djgpp
comp.os.msdos.misc
comp.os.msdos.programmer
comp.os.netware.connectivity
comp.os.netware.misc
comp.os.netware.security
comp.os.os2.advocacy
comp.os.os2.apps
comp.os.os2.bugs
comp.os.os2.comm
comp.os.os2.games
comp.os.os2.mail-news
comp.os.os2.misc
comp.os.os2.multimedia
comp.os.os2.networking.misc
comp.os.os2.networking.tcp-ip
comp.os.os2.networking.www
comp.os.os2.programmer.misc
comp.os.os2.prog
rammer.porting
comp.os.os2.setup
comp.os.os2.setup.storage
comp.os.os2.utilities
comp.os.qnx
comp.os.vms
comp.periphs

comp.periphs.printers
comp.periphs.scsi
comp.programming
comp.programming.contests
comp.protocols.dicom
comp.protocols.iso
comp.protocols.kerberos
comp.protocols.ppp
comp.protocols.smb
comp.protocols.snmp
comp.protocols.tcp-ip
comp.protocols.tcp-ip.domains
comp.protocols.tcp-ip.ibmpc
comp.protocols.time.ntp
comp.publish.cd
rom.hardware
comp.publish.cdrom.software
comp.publish.prepress
comp.realtime
comp.robotics
comp.security.misc
comp.security.unix
comp.soft-sys.app-builder.uniface
comp.soft-sys.dce
comp.soft-sys.khoros
comp.soft-sys.matlab
comp.soft-sys.nextstep
comp.soft-sys.powerbuilder
comp.soft-sys.sas
comp.soft-sys.spss
comp.software.international
comp.software.testing
comp.software-eng
comp.sources.wanted
comp.speech
comp.std.c
comp.std.c++
comp.std.lisp
comp.std.wireless
comp.sw.components
comp.sys.acorn.apps
comp.sys.acorn.hardware
comp.sys.acorn.misc
comp.sys.acorn.networking
comp.sys.acorn.programmer
comp.sys.amiga.advocacy
comp.sys.amiga.applications
comp.sys.amiga.audio
comp.sys.amiga.datacomm
comp.sys.amiga.emulations
comp.sys.amiga.games
comp.sys.amiga.graphics
comp.sys.amiga.hardware
comp.sys.amiga.marketplace
comp.sys.amiga.misc
comp.sys.amiga.networking
comp.sys.amiga.programmer

comp.sys.amstrad.8bit
comp.sys.apple2
comp.sys.atari.8bit
comp.sys.atari.st
comp.sys.att
comp.sys.cbm
comp.sys.dec
comp.sys.hp.hardware
comp.sys.hp.hpux
comp.sys.hp.misc
comp.sys.hp.mpe
comp.sys.hp48
comp.sys.ibm.pc.demos
comp.sys.ibm.pc.games.action
comp.sys.ibm.pc.games.adventure
comp.sys.ibm.pc.games.flight-sim
comp.sys.ibm.pc.games.marketplace
comp.sys.ibm.pc.games.misc
comp.sys.ibm.pc.games.rpg
comp.sys.ibm.pc.games.strategic
comp.sys.ibm.pc.hardware.cd-rom
comp.sys.ibm.pc.hardware.chips
comp.sys.ibm.pc.hardware.comm
comp.sys.ibm.pc.hardware.misc
comp.sys.ibm.pc.hardware.storage
comp.sys.ibm.pc.hardware.systems
comp.sys.ibm.pc.hardware.video
comp.sys.ibm.pc.misc
comp.sys.ibm.pc.soundcard.advocacy
comp.sys.ibm.pc.soundcard.music
comp.sys.ibm.pc.soundcard.tech
comp.sys.ibm.ps2.hardware
comp.sys.intel
comp.sys.laptops
comp.sys.mac.advocacy
comp.sys.mac.apps
comp.sys.mac.comm
comp.sys.mac.databases
comp.sys.mac.games
comp.sys.mac.games.action
comp.sys.mac.ga
mes.adventure
comp.sys.mac.games.flight-sim
comp.sys.mac.games.misc

Table 8–1 (cont.) 89

comp.sys.mac.games.strategic
comp.sys.mac.graphics
comp.sys.mac.hardware.misc
comp.sys.mac.ha
rdware.storage
comp.sys.mac.hardware.video
comp.sys.mac.hypercard
comp.sys.mac.misc
comp.sys.mac.portables
comp.sys.mac.pr
ogrammer.codewarrior
comp.sys.mac.pr
ogrammer.help
comp.sys.mac.pr
ogrammer.misc
comp.sys.mac.pr
ogrammer.tools
comp.sys.mac.scitech
comp.sys.mac.system
comp.sys.mac.wanted
comp.sys.misc
comp.sys.newton.misc
comp.sys.newton.programmer
comp.sys.next.advocacy
comp.sys.next.hardware
comp.sys.next.misc
comp.sys.next.programmer
comp.sys.next.software
comp.sys.next.sysadmin
comp.sys.palmtops
comp.sys.pen
comp.sys.powerpc
comp.sys.psion
comp.sys.sgi.bugs
comp.sys.sgi.hardware
comp.sys.sun.admin
comp.sys.sun.hardware
comp.sys.tandy
comp.sys.unisys
comp.text.desktop
comp.text.frame
comp.text.tex
comp.theory
comp.unix.admin
comp.unix.aix
comp.unix.amiga
comp.unix.aux
comp.unix.bsd.freebsd.misc
comp.unix.bsd.netbsd.misc
comp.unix.internals
comp.unix.misc
comp.unix.osf.osf1
comp.unix.programmer
comp.unix.questions
comp.unix.sco.misc
comp.unix.shell
comp.unix.solaris
comp.unix.sys5.r3
comp.unix.sys5.r4

comp.unix.unixware.misc
comp.windows.misc
comp.windows.x
comp.windows.x.apps
comp.windows.x.i386unix
dc.jobs
de.admin.news.groups
de.admin.news.misc
de.alt.drogen
de.alt.flame
de.alt.fotografie
de.alt.test
de.alt.tv.misc
de.comm.gateways
de.comm.internet
de.comp.graphik
de.comp.infosystems
de.comp.lang.pascal
de.comp.misc
de.comp.os.linux
de.comp.os.misc
de.comp.os.unix
de.comp.sys.amiga.advocacy
de.comp.sys.amiga.misc
de.comp.sys.amiga.tech
de.comp.sys.apple
de.comp.sys.ibm
de.comp.sys.next
de.etc.finanz
de.etc.sprache.deutsch
de.markt.comp.misc
de.markt.misc
de.markt.wohnen
de.newusers.questions
de.org.ccc
de.rec.fahrrad
de.rec.games.rpg
de.rec.modelle
de.rec.motorrad
de.rec.reisen
de.rec.sf.misc
de.rec.sf.perry-rhodan
de.rec.sf.startrek
de.sci.electronics
de.sci.medizin
de.sci.misc
de.soc.kontakte
de.soc.kultur
de.soc.netzwesen
de.soc.politik
de.soc.recht
de.soc.verkehr
de.soc.weltanschauung
de.talk.bizarre
de.talk.chat
de.talk.jokes
de.talk.jokes.d
de.talk.romance
de.talk.sex

de.test
es.uniovi
fr.comp.os.linux
fr.comp.sys.amiga
fr.petites-annonces.divers
fr.petites-
annonces.informatique
fr.rec.cuisine
fr.rec.divers
fr.soc.divers
fr.test
gnu.chess
gnu.emacs.bug
gnu.emacs.help
gnu.g++.bug
gnu.gcc.bug
gnu.gdb.bug
gnu.misc.discuss
info.bind
info.grass.user
info.ietf
info.snmp
info.wisenet
misc.books.technical
misc.consumers
misc.consumers.house
misc.education
misc.education.home-
school.christian
misc.education.l
anguage.english
misc.education.science
misc.emerg-services
misc.entrepreneurs
misc.fitness
misc.fitness.aerobic
misc.fitness.misc
misc.fitness.weights
misc.forsale.com
puters.discussion
misc.forsale.computers.mac-
specific.cards.video
misc.forsale.computers.mac-
specific.misc
misc.forsale.computers.mac-
specific.portables
misc.forsale.computers.mac-
specific.software
misc.forsale.computers.mac-
specific.systems
misc.forsale.com
puters.memory
misc.forsale.com
puters.modems
misc.forsale.computers.net-
hardware
misc.forsale.computers.
other.misc
misc.forsale.computers.

other.software
misc.forsale.computers.
other.systems
misc.forsale.computers.pc-
specific.misc
misc.forsale.computers.pc-
specific.motherboards
misc.forsale.computers.pc-
specific.portables
misc.forsale.computers.pc-
specific.software
misc.forsale.computers.pc-
specific.systems
misc.forsale.comp
uters.printers
misc.forsale.computers.storage
misc.forsale.comp
uters.workstation
misc.forsale.non-computer
misc.health.aids
misc.health.alternative
misc.health.diabetes
misc.immigration.canada
misc.immigration.usa
misc.industry.utilities.electric
misc.invest
misc.invest.canada
misc.invest.funds
misc.invest.futures
misc.invest.real-estate
misc.invest.stocks
misc.invest.technical
misc.jobs.contract
misc.jobs.misc
misc.jobs.offered
misc.jobs.offered.entry
misc.jobs.resumes
misc.kids
misc.kids.computer
misc.kids.consumers
misc.kids.health
misc.kids.pregnancy
misc.kids.vacation
misc.legal
misc.legal.computing
misc.misc
misc.rural
misc.survivalism
misc.taxes
misc.test
misc.transport.air-industry
misc.transport.rail.americas
misc.transport.rail.australia-nz
misc.transport.rail.europe
misc.transport.rail.misc
misc.transport.urban-transit
misc.wanted
misc.writing
misc.writing.screenplays

news.admin.net-
abuse.announce
news.admin.net-abuse.misc
news.answers
news.groups
news.groups.questions
news.newusers.questions
news.software.anu-news
news.software.nntp
news.software.readers
rec.animals.wildlife
rec.antiques
rec.antiques.marketplace
rec.antiques.radio+phono
rec.aquaria
rec.arts.animation
rec.arts.anime
rec.arts.anime.marketplace
rec.arts.bodyart
rec.arts.bonsai
rec.arts.books
rec.arts.books.childrens
rec.arts.books.marketplace
rec.arts.books.tolkien
rec.arts.comics.alternative
rec.arts.comics.dc.lsh
rec.arts.comics.dc.universe
rec.arts.comics.dc.vertigo
rec.arts.comics.marketplace
rec.arts.comics.m
arvel.universe
rec.arts.comics.marvel.xbooks
rec.arts.comics.misc
rec.arts.comics.other-media
rec.arts.comics.strips
rec.arts.comics.xbooks
rec.arts.dance
rec.arts.disney
rec.arts.disney.animation
rec.arts.disney.parks
rec.arts.drwho
rec.arts.fine
rec.arts.int-fiction
rec.arts.manga
rec.arts.marching.colorguard
rec.arts.marching.drumcorps
rec.arts.marching.misc
rec.arts.misc
rec.arts.movies.current-films
rec.arts.movies.lists+surveys
rec.arts.movies.past-films
rec.arts.movies.people
rec.arts.movies.production
rec.arts.mystery
rec.arts.poems
rec.arts.puppetry
rec.arts.sf.fandom
rec.arts.sf.marketplace
rec.arts.sf.movies

rec.arts.sf.starwars.collecting
rec.arts.sf.starwars.games
rec.arts.sf.starwars.misc
rec.arts.sf.tv
rec.arts.sf.tv.babylon5
rec.arts.sf.tv.quantum-leap
rec.arts.sf.written
rec.arts.sf.written.robert-
jordan
rec.arts.startrek.current
rec.arts.startrek.fandom
rec.arts.startrek.misc
rec.arts.startrek.tech
rec.arts.theatre.misc
rec.arts.theatre.musicals
rec.arts.theatre.plays
rec.arts.theatre.stagecraft
rec.arts.tv
rec.arts.tv.mst3k.misc
rec.arts.tv.soaps.abc
rec.arts.tv.soaps.cbs
rec.arts.tv.soaps.misc
rec.arts.tv.uk.comedy
rec.arts.tv.uk.eastenders
rec.audio.car
rec.audio.high-end
rec.audio.marketplace
rec.audio.misc
rec.audio.opinion
rec.audio.pro
rec.audio.tech
rec.autos.4x4
rec.autos.antique
rec.autos.driving
rec.autos.makers.chrysler
rec.autos.makers.
ford.mustang
rec.autos.makers.saturn
rec.autos.marketplace
rec.autos.misc
rec.autos.rod-n-custom
rec.autos.simulators
rec.autos.sport.f1
rec.autos.sport.indy
rec.autos.sport.misc
rec.autos.sport.nascar
rec.autos.sport.tech
rec.autos.tech
rec.autos.vw
rec.aviation.hang-gliding
rec.aviation.homebuilt
rec.aviation.ifr
rec.aviation.marketplace
rec.aviation.military
rec.aviation.misc
rec.aviation.owning
rec.aviation.piloting
rec.aviation.products
rec.aviation.rotorcraft

Table 8–1 (cont.)   91

rec.aviation.simulators
rec.aviation.soaring
rec.aviation.student
rec.backcountry
rec.bicycles.marketplace
rec.bicycles.misc
rec.bicycles.off-road
rec.bicycles.racing
rec.bicycles.rides
rec.bicycles.soc
rec.bicycles.tech
rec.birds
rec.boats
rec.boats.building
rec.boats.cruising
rec.boats.paddle
rec.boats.racing
rec.climbing
rec.collecting
rec.collecting.cards.discuss
rec.collecting.cards.non-sports
rec.collecting.coins
rec.collecting.dolls
rec.collecting.phonecards
rec.collecting.sport.baseball
rec.collecting.sport.basketball
rec.collecting.sport.football
rec.collecting.sport.hockey
rec.collecting.stamps
rec.crafts.beads
rec.crafts.brewing
rec.crafts.jewelry
rec.crafts.marketplace
rec.crafts.metalworking
rec.crafts.misc
rec.crafts.polymer-clay
rec.crafts.textiles.misc
rec.crafts.textiles.needlework
rec.crafts.textiles.quilting
rec.crafts.textiles.sewing
rec.crafts.textiles.yarn
rec.crafts.winemaking
rec.drugs.cannabis
rec.drugs.psychedelic
rec.equestrian
rec.food.cooking
rec.food.drink
rec.food.drink.beer
rec.food.historic
rec.food.preserving
rec.food.recipes
rec.food.restaurants
rec.food.veg
rec.gambling
rec.gambling.blackjack
rec.gambling.lottery
rec.gambling.other-games
rec.gambling.poker
rec.gambling.racing

rec.gambling.sports
rec.games.backgammon
rec.games.board
rec.games.board.marketplace
rec.games.bolo
rec.games.bridge
rec.games.chess
rec.games.chess.analysis
rec.games.chess.misc
rec.games.chess.play-by-email
rec.games.computer.
doom.editing
rec.games.computer.
doom.help
rec.games.computer.
doom.misc
rec.games.computer.
doom.playing
rec.games.diplomacy
rec.games.empire
rec.games.frp.advocacy
rec.games.frp.cyber
rec.games.frp.dnd
rec.games.frp.gurps
rec.games.frp.live-action
rec.games.frp.marketplace
rec.games.frp.misc
rec.games.go
rec.games.int-fiction
rec.games.mecha
rec.games.miniat
ures.historical
rec.games.miniat
ures.warhammer
rec.games.mud.diku
rec.games.netrek
rec.games.pbm
rec.games.pinball
rec.games.programmer
rec.games.roguelike.angband
rec.games.roguelike.nethack
rec.games.trading-cards.jyhad
rec.games.trading-
cards.magic.misc
rec.games.trading-
cards.magic.rules
rec.games.trading-
cards.magic.strategy
rec.games.trading-
cards.marketplace
rec.games.trading-cards.misc
rec.games.video.3do
rec.games.video.advocacy
rec.games.video.arcade
rec.games.video.
arcade.collecting
rec.games.video.atari
rec.games.video.cd-i
rec.games.video.classic

rec.games.video.marketplace
rec.games.video.nintendo
rec.games.video.sega
rec.games.video.sony
rec.gardens
rec.gardens.orchids
rec.gardens.roses
rec.humor
rec.hunting
rec.juggling
rec.kites
rec.martial-arts
rec.models.railroad
rec.models.rc
rec.models.rockets
rec.models.scale
rec.motorcycles
rec.motorcycles.dirt
rec.motorcycles.harley
rec.motorcycles.racing
rec.music.a-cappella
rec.music.afro-latin
rec.music.ambient
rec.music.artists.beach-boys
rec.music.artists.bruce-
hornsby
rec.music.beatles
rec.music.bluenote
rec.music.bluenote.blues
rec.music.cd
rec.music.celtic
rec.music.christian
rec.music.classical
rec.music.classical.recordings
rec.music.compose
rec.music.country.old-time
rec.music.country.western
rec.music.dylan
rec.music.early
rec.music.filipino
rec.music.folk
rec.music.funky
rec.music.gdead
rec.music.hip-hop
rec.music.indian.classical
rec.music.indian.misc
rec.music.industrial
rec.music.makers.bagpipe
rec.music.makers.bands
rec.music.makers.bass
rec.music.makers.builders
rec.music.makers.french-horn
rec.music.makers.guitar
rec.music.makers.
guitar.tablature
rec.music.makers.marketplace
rec.music.makers.percussion
rec.music.makers.piano
rec.music.makers.songwriting

rec.music.makers.synth
rec.music.makers.trumpet
rec.music.marketplace
rec.music.misc
rec.music.newage
rec.music.opera
rec.music.phish
rec.music.progressive
rec.music.reggae
rec.music.rem
rec.music.reviews
rec.nude
rec.org.mensa
rec.org.sca
rec.outdoors.fishing
rec.outdoors.fishing.fly
rec.outdoors.fishing.saltwater
rec.outdoors.national-parks
rec.outdoors.rv-travel
rec.parks.theme
rec.pets
rec.pets.birds
rec.pets.cats
rec.pets.dogs.activities
rec.pets.dogs.behavior
rec.pets.dogs.breeds
rec.pets.dogs.health
rec.pets.dogs.misc
rec.pets.dogs.rescue
rec.pets.herp
rec.photo.advanced
rec.photo.darkroom
rec.photo.help
rec.photo.marketplace
rec.photo.misc
rec.puzzles
rec.puzzles.crosswords
rec.pyrotechnics
rec.radio.amateur.antenna
rec.radio.amateur.digital.misc
rec.radio.amateur.equipment
rec.radio.amateur.homebrew
rec.radio.amateur.misc
rec.radio.cb
rec.radio.scanner
rec.radio.shortwave
rec.radio.swap
rec.roller-coaster
rec.running
rec.scouting
rec.scuba
rec.skiing.alpine
rec.skiing.nordic
rec.skiing.resorts.misc
rec.skiing.resorts.north-
america
rec.skiing.snowboard
rec.skydiving
rec.sport.archery

rec.sport.baseball
rec.sport.baseball.fantasy
rec.sport.basketball.college
rec.sport.basketball.pro
rec.sport.billiard
rec.sport.boxing
rec.sport.cricket
rec.sport.disc
rec.sport.fencing
rec.sport.football.australian
rec.sport.football.canadian
rec.sport.football.college
rec.sport.football.fantasy
rec.sport.football.pro
rec.sport.golf
rec.sport.hockey
rec.sport.misc
rec.sport.olympics
rec.sport.orienteering
rec.sport.paintball
rec.sport.pro-wrestling
rec.sport.rugby
rec.sport.skating.ice.figure
rec.sport.skating.inline
rec.sport.soccer
rec.sport.swimming
rec.sport.table-soccer
rec.sport.tennis
rec.sport.triathlon
rec.sport.volleyball
rec.sport.waterski
rec.toys.cars
rec.toys.lego
rec.toys.misc
rec.travel.asia
rec.travel.cruises
rec.travel.europe
rec.travel.latin-america
rec.travel.marketplace
rec.travel.misc
rec.travel.usa-canada
rec.video
rec.video.cable-tv
rec.video.desktop
rec.video.production
rec.video.releases
rec.video.satellite.dbs
rec.video.satellite.europe
rec.video.satellite.tvro
rec.windsurfing
rec.woodworking
relcom.commerce.chemical
relcom.humor
sci.agriculture
sci.agriculture.beekeeping
sci.aquaria
sci.archaeology
sci.astro
sci.astro.amateur

sci.astro.planetarium
sci.astro.research
sci.bio
sci.bio.ecology
sci.bio.entomology.lepidoptera
sci.bio.entomology.misc
sci.bio.evolution
sci.bio.fisheries
sci.bio.food-science
sci.bio.microbiology
sci.bio.misc
sci.bio.paleontology
sci.bio.technology
sci.chem
sci.chem.analytical
sci.chem.labware
sci.cryonics
sci.crypt
sci.econ
sci.edu
sci.electronics
sci.energy
sci.energy.hydrogen
sci.engr
sci.engr.biomed
sci.engr.chem
sci.engr.civil
sci.engr.control
sci.engr.heat-vent-ac
sci.engr.lighting
sci.engr.manufacturing
sci.engr.mech
sci.engr.surveying
sci.engr.television.advanced
sci.engr.television.broadcast
sci.environment
sci.fractals
sci.geo.earthquakes
sci.geo.geology
sci.geo.hydrology
sci.geo.meteorology
sci.geo.oceanography
sci.geo.satellite-nav
sci.image.processing
sci.lang
sci.lang.japan
sci.lang.translation
sci.life-extension
sci.logic
sci.materials
sci.math
sci.math.num-analysis
sci.med
sci.med.dentistry
sci.med.diseases.cancer
sci.med.immunology
sci.med.informatics
sci.med.nursing
sci.med.nutrition

Table 8–1 (cont.)   93

sci.med.pharmacy
sci.med.physics
sci.med.psychobiology
sci.med.telemedicine
sci.med.vision
sci.military.naval
sci.misc
sci.op-research
sci.physics
sci.physics.comp
utational.fluid-dynamics
sci.physics.cond-matter
sci.physics.electromag
sci.physics.fusion
sci.physics.particle
sci.polymers
sci.psychology
sci.psychology.consciousness
sci.research.careers
sci.skeptic
sci.space.news
sci.space.policy
sci.space.shuttle
sci.stat.consult
sci.stat.edu
sci.stat.math
sci.techniques.xtallography
soc.bi
soc.college.admissions
soc.college.financial-aid
soc.college.grad
soc.couples
soc.couples.intercultural
soc.couples.wedding
soc.culture.african
soc.culture.african.american
soc.culture.arabic
soc.culture.argentina
soc.culture.asian.american
soc.culture.austria
soc.culture.baltics
soc.culture.bangladesh
soc.culture.belgium
soc.culture.bengali
soc.culture.bosna-herzgvna
soc.culture.brazil
soc.culture.british
soc.culture.bulgaria
soc.culture.canada
soc.culture.caribbean
soc.culture.celtic
soc.culture.chile
soc.culture.china
soc.culture.croatia
soc.culture.cuba
soc.culture.czecho-slovak
soc.culture.ecuador
soc.culture.egyptian
soc.culture.europe

soc.culture.filipino
soc.culture.french
soc.culture.german
soc.culture.greek
soc.culture.hongkong
soc.culture.hong
kong.entertainment
soc.culture.indian
soc.culture.indian.delhi
soc.culture.indian.kerala
soc.culture.indian.marathi
soc.culture.indian.telugu
soc.culture.indonesia
soc.culture.iranian
soc.culture.iraq
soc.culture.irish
soc.culture.israel
soc.culture.italian
soc.culture.japan
soc.culture.jewish
soc.culture.korean
soc.culture.kurdish
soc.culture.kuwait
soc.culture.latin-america
soc.culture.lebanon
soc.culture.malagasy
soc.culture.malaysia
soc.culture.mexican
soc.culture.native
soc.culture.nepal
soc.culture.netherlands
soc.culture.new-zealand
soc.culture.nigeria
soc.culture.nordic
soc.culture.pakistan
soc.culture.portuguese
soc.culture.puerto-rico
soc.culture.romanian
soc.culture.russian
soc.culture.scientists
soc.culture.scottish
soc.culture.singapore
soc.culture.somalia
soc.culture.soviet
soc.culture.spain
soc.culture.sri-lanka
soc.culture.swiss
soc.culture.syria
soc.culture.taiwan
soc.culture.tamil
soc.culture.thai
soc.culture.turkish
soc.culture.ukrainian
soc.culture.usa
soc.culture.venezuela
soc.culture.vietnamese
soc.culture.welsh
soc.culture.yugoslavia
soc.genealogy.computing

soc.genealogy.french
soc.genealogy.german
soc.genealogy.jewish
soc.genealogy.medieval
soc.genealogy.methods
soc.genealogy.misc
soc.genealogy.nordic
soc.genealogy.surnames
soc.genealogy.uk+ireland
soc.history
soc.history.science
soc.history.war.misc
soc.history.war.us-civil-war
soc.history.war.vietnam
soc.history.war.world-war-ii
soc.history.what-if
soc.libraries.talk
soc.men
soc.motss
soc.org.nonprofit
soc.penpals
soc.religion.bahai
soc.religion.quaker
soc.religion.shamanism
soc.singles
soc.support.fat-acceptance
soc.support.transgendered
soc.veterans
soc.women
talk.abortion
talk.bizarre
talk.environment
talk.euthanasia
talk.origins
talk.philosophy.misc
talk.politics.animals
talk.politics.china
talk.politics.drugs
talk.politics.guns
talk.politics.libertarian
talk.politics.mideast
talk.politics.misc
talk.politics.theory
talk.politics.tibet
talk.rape
talk.religion.buddhism
talk.religion.misc
talk.religion.newage
talk.rumors
vmsnet.misc

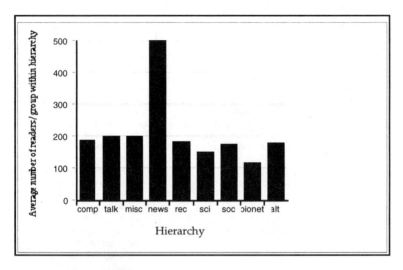

Figure 8-1 Recent Usenet usage levels (Based on Allbery and Reid, 1995. Data used with permission)

NETIQUETTE (AGAIN)

Netiquette is probably more important on Usenet than anywhere else on the Internet. The news group "news.announce.newusers" maintains an article that is periodically reposted called "A Primer on How to Work With the Usenet Community." It is reproduced in this text as Appendix B. You should read it carefully so that you will not be as easily flamed or perceived as a newbie.

CONCLUSION

Usenet is the world's largest bulletin board in the broadest sense of the word. Once you learn how to read and post on it, you will find a wealth of information available to you. Remember, though, that much of that information is raw and unedited. So be a wise Usenet user. Take the time necessary to find news groups of interest to you, and then read them for a period before posting. Follow the rules of netiquette, and you will avoid being the target of flaming.

NOTES

1. http://www.lib.ox.ac.uk/internet/news/faq/archive/usenet.what-is.part1.html

2. http://www.apocalypse.org/pub/rfcs/rfc977.txt

3. http://www.apocalypse.org/pub/rfcs/rfc1036.txt

4. http://scwww.ucs.indiana.edu/NetRsc/#reader

5. http://hotpage.stanford.edu

9

Psychology

CHAPTER PREVIEW

Psychology, the study of human and animal behavior, has a large Internet presence, reminiscent of the breadth and depth of psychology itself. In this chapter, we survey topics from neuroscience to psychopathology. A good place to begin our look at psychology is with Human-Computer Interaction at the University of Maryland[1], which studies a topic of interest to readers of this text.

GENERAL PSYCHOLOGY HYPERLINKS

Many psychologists have put together index pages that make it easy to find Internet resources in psychology. Among these are Psych Web by Russ Dewey[2], Addresses of Note[3], and Psychology Resources[4]. Psychological organizations have also created similar lists of Internet sites. For example, the American Psychological Association (APA) has a Web page, American Psychological Association PsychNET (SM)[5], and a gopher[6], both with extensive hyperlinks to a variety of psychology-related sites. A newer and more research-oriented organization, the American Psychological Society, also maintains a Web page, American Psychological Society (APS)[7]. It, too, has a long list of hyperlinks to Internet resources in psychology. APA– and APS–specific information can also be found on the appropriate server. A few of the APA's many divisions have established Internet sites, notably, Division 28, APA Division of Psychopharmacology and Substance Abuse[8], Division 12, Clinical Psychology[9], and Division 2, Teaching[10]. Students in psychology may want to look at the PSYCGRAD Project[11], a Web server that contains mailing lists in psychology, including it own list, "psychtalk," that is specifically designed for students.

Some commercial servers also have lists of psychology sites. For instance, Galaxy's Psychology (Social Sciences)[12] Web page contains hyperlinks to many topics in psychology. Yahoo, another commercial site, has its own psychology section, <u>Yahoo - Science: Psychology</u>[13]. The <u>Self-Help Psychology Magazine</u>[14] is an on-line magazine dedicated to the self-help concept.

Other servers of general interest to psychologists are maintained by other specialized groups. For example, the <u>Society for Computers in Psychology</u> (SciP)[15] maintains a Web page with information about its programs and how to become a member. Another such page is <u>Behavior Analysis</u>[16], which serves as an index to resources in that area of psychology. The Society for Quantitative Analyses of Behavior (SQAB) maintains the <u>1995 SQAB Welcome Page</u>[17], which contains information specific to that group and includes a mailing list of its members. Another such page is <u>European Society for Developmental Psychology WWW server</u>[18]. A relatively new group devoted to the study of evolutionary psychology maintains a page, too—<u>Center for Evolutionary Psychology at UCSB</u>[19]. Another group with similar interests also has its own page, <u>Human Behavior and Evolution Society Title Page</u>[20]. <u>The Behavior Genetics Association</u>[21] has an informational page. <u>The Jean Piaget Society</u>[22] maintains a Web page for those interested in his theories and applications of them.

Another useful set of URLs are those that find or list new sites. The University of Albany's <u>All-in-One Search Page</u>[23] is a collection of search engines, and <u>What's New Too!</u>[24] is a collection of new Internet announcements. When used together they make it possible for you to stay current (as if that were possible) with the recent changes on the Internet. A very useful service from Division 28's page is a search form for finding psychologists' electronic mail addresses, <u>Send email to an APA member (or other psychologist)</u>[25]. It works; we tried it successfully several times.

PSYCHOLOGY HISTORY HYPERLINKS

Psychologists have always been conscious of their own history. So, we were not surprised to find Internet resources related to historical figures in the field. Both Freud and Jung have pages devoted to them. They are <u>Freud OV</u>[26] and <u>Carl Gustav Jung</u>[27], respectively. Two of Abraham Maslow's articles, "Eupsychian Management" and "Politics 3," can be found on a <u>Web page</u>[28]. We did not find any historical references to William James, B. F. Skinner, John B. Watson, or other scientifically oriented psychologists. A relatively new mailing list of potential interest to historically minded psychologists is DESCARTES-L, which is for unmoderated discussion of the philosophy of René Descartes, plus announcements of conferences, books, bibliographies, etc. Send a "SUB DESCARTES-L your name" message to <listserv@bucknell.edu>.

PSYCHOLOGY DEPARTMENT HYPERLINKS

A large number of departments have already set up Web or gopher servers. The APS's page has collected those departments in the Links to Other Psychology Departments[29] portion of its Web page. Large departments like UC-San Diego's UCSD Psychology[30], the University of Texas's U of Texas[31], and Carnegie Mellon's Carnegie Mellon University Psychology[32] are included on that page. But smaller ones like Indiana University East's Indiana University East[33], Ithaca College's Ithaca College-Department of Psychology[34], and John Brown University's JBU Psychology Department Homepage[35] are not.   Another such listing of school home pages is Colleges and University Home Pages[36], which did list Ithaca College and John Brown University, but did not list Indiana University East. Because the Internet, and the World Wide Web especially, are growing so fast, you should not treat lists collected by others as all-inclusive.

PSYCHOLOGY SUBFIELD HYPERLINKS

Clinical Psychology, Counseling and Psychopathology

The National Institute of Mental Health's gopher[37] contains information about that mental health agency of the federal government. Mental Health Resources[38] lists the addresses of professional groups involved in mental health worldwide. Psychiatric and psychological Internet resources are listed in the home page of the University of Michigan's PsychStar Homepage[39]. The Web page The GROHOL Mental Health Page - Main Menu[40] is a large listing of resources in the area of mental health. The psychoanalytic perspective is the focus of Web pages FreudNet: The A.A. Brill Library[41], Dreams[42], and Dreamlink[43]. The Web page Introduction to the Psychoanalytic Connection[44] provides information on how to join restricted, fee-based electronic conferences on psychoanalysis.

Some specific topics include Men's Issues Page[45] and David Baldwin's Trauma Info Pages[46]. We also found a Web page for Martin Seligman's on-line course in abnormal psychology at the University of Pennsylvania, Psychology 162 at Penn[47].

Educational, School, and Teaching Psychology

The journal *Education Theory*[48] now has a Web page where archives from past issues can be found. Those archives can also be searched. Learning disabilities and other information are the focus of the UC-Berkeley School

Psychology's page <u>UC Berkeley School Psychology</u>[49]. ERIC's <u>gopher</u>[50] contains articles relating to schools and school psychology. The Teaching Educational Psychology Special Interest Group of the American Educational Research Association maintains a Web page, <u>Teaching Educational Psychology SIG</u>[51], that covers many issues in teaching and also contains hyperlinks to relevant resources. *Engines for Educators*[52] is an on-line textbook in educational psychology. Suzy Shapiro's page <u>General Psychology Course Introduction</u>[53], featuring a full on-line course, is also worth the trip.

We found resources for help in creating Web pages and other types of instructional media. For example, Yale's page <u>Center for Advanced Instructional Media</u>[54], although primarily medical in orientation, has instructions on how to make effective computer-based instructional media. The Kansas University Medical Center has a series of tutorials including one on preparing effective poster presentations, <u>Introduction.Poster Presentations</u>[55]. Ron Blue's article telling undergraduates how to study, <u>How to Study</u>[56], is useful for students and teachers. Students who wish to publish their research should see the home page of *Der Zeitgeist*, <u>Der Zeitgeist-World-Web Home Page</u>[57], a journal devoted specifically to undergraduate research in psychology.

Linda Walsh of Northern Iowa University has just announced three Web pages that she uses in her course "Pursuing Psychology." The pages are designed to give psychology students information about careers, <u>Some Career Sites to Explore</u>[58]; graduate school, <u>Some Graduate School Information Sites to Explore</u>[59]; and <u>Internet Resources</u>[60]. The three pages will soon be combined into one.

Behavior Analysis

Behavior analysis has staked out a large area of psychology's Internet territory. Marshall Dermer, for instance, has provided a <u>glossary of behavior analytic terms</u>[61] for beginners and others. For a listserver in behavior analysis, see <u>Behavior Analysis ListServ How-To</u>[62]. The University of South Florida maintains the <u>Behavior Analysis</u>[63] home page, which includes an electronic mail directory and hyperlinks to other resources in the subfield. Another useful site is the Web page at Jacksonville State University's <u>SEBAC Psychology Center</u>[64], which features software and a downloadable slide set. *The Journal of Applied Behavior Analysis* and *The Journal of Applied Behavior Analysis* are both available on the Web page <u>Welcome to JEAB & JABA</u>[65] and offer abstract searching, contents lists, and other information.

Developmental Psychology

Internet resources on children and families include Baby Web: The Internet Parenting Resource[66], Infants and Babies[67], and Facts for Families[68]. Neurological issues in childhood are covered by the University of Oulu's (Finland) Laboratory of Developmental Neuropsychology[69]. Another source of research information on children is the University of Texas's Children's Research Laboratory[70]. Dyslexia resources are indexed on the page Dyslexia 2000 Network[71].

Internet resources on adolescence can be found at Indiana University's Center for Adolescent Studies CAS Home Page[72]. A useful hyperlink from this server is Mental Health Risk Factors for Adolescents[73]. Ritual abuse of children and adults, a form of sadism, is the subject of the Ritual Abuse, Ritual Crime, and Healing Home Page[74]. Mental retardation issues hyperlinks can be found on The Arc[75].

Aging and geriatric topics can also be found on the Internet. For instance, TheWorld(TM) Guide to Geriatrics[76] is an index page to geriatric resources. Aging and dementia are the subject of the UC-Irvine's Institute for Brain Aging and Dementia[77]. The National Institute of Aging is constructing a Web page Laboratory of Personality & Cognition[78]. (It uses an IP number as a URL, so you may have to search its upcoming domain name.)

Industrial and Organizational Psychology

The Society for Industrial-Organizational Psychology maintains a Web page for its newsletter The Industrial/Organizational Psychologist[79]. That server has a hyperlink to a page of I/O–related Pages on the WWW[80]. The IAAP Index[81] and Contemporary Applied Psychology[82] are two I/O hyperlinks from Spain.

Cognitive Psychology and Cognitive Science

A large index page to psychology resources in cognitive science and psychology is Cognitive & Psychological Sciences[83]. Cognitive Science[84] is a page featuring information about researchers in artificial intelligence and cognitive science. The page also includes some landmark papers and the home pages of researchers. The GlobalPsych Institute[85] is another large Web site devoted to cognitive psychology and other areas.

Neuropsychology and Biopsychology

Psychology's link to biology is another place where a large number of Internet resources exist. This is also an area with "big science" projects like the Human Brain Project[86] and the human genome project GDB Proposal–Abstract, specific aims, and introduction[87]. You may be interested to know that one of the goals of the human genome project is a hundredfold increase in the quality and speed of computer-based tools for research and dissemination of results.

A good overview to neuroscience is provided by Neurosciences on the Internet[88]. Another introductory server is the Society for Neuroscience's gopher[89]. The Galaxy index page Neurobiology (Human Biology)[90] is another general introduction to this area.

Servers dedicated to the brain and the nervous system include The Harvard BRAIN[91], a Web page maintained by the Harvard Undergraduate Society for Neuroscience. The page consists of an on-line version of several issues of the journal *The Harvard Brain*. Another Harvard server on the brain is The Whole Brain Atlas[92], which contains a large number of brain images. The University of Minnesota's Virtual Brain[93] and Virtual Neuron[94] are another set of servers in neuropsychology. UCLA's Laboratory of Neuro Imaging has a similar Web page, Rat Atlas Image Database[95], but for the rat brain. The brain's connections are the focus of Connections of the Brain[96]. Note that this server is still incomplete. The Cure Paralysis Now Home Page[97] is a large Web page dedicated to the practical issue of curing neurological problems.

The human genome project is very large, and its laboratories are spread around the world. A useful introductory Web page to this vast project is Human Genome Most Used Links[98]. From that page you may navigate to most of the project's many sites. Another useful site in this project is Online Mendelian Inheritance in Man (OMIM)[99], which hyperlinks to pages on specific instances of genetically-based syndromes, diseases, and the like. Chromosome maps are available from another server in this project, CPROP Maps of Human Chromosomes[100].

Evolutionary psychology has begun to establish a presence on the Internet, too. An FAQ archive[101] contains a series of on-line articles on issues in behavioral evolution.

Perception

Perception is one of psychology's oldest areas of research, but it is still a very active area. Visual perception servers are indexed in the Web page Vision Science: The World Wide Web Virtual Library[102]. Newer topics like virtual perception are covered by SRI's Web server SRI Virtual Perception Program[103]. A page on robot perception is Robotics and Perception Lab

Index[104]. Another such page is <u>The Intelligent Perception and Action Lab</u>[105]. <u>Tutorials in Sensation and Perception</u>[106] is a page from the APS's pages and is still under development.

Several servers for auditory perception have been set up. <u>Auditory Perception</u>[107] has a downloadable auditory perception multimedia presentation. A page from the Franklin Institute's "What Makes Music?" home page, <u>Sound Perception Activities</u>[108], explains musical sounds. A similar page is <u>Music Cognition Activities</u>[109].

Olfaction is the subject of the Web page <u>Smell Perception Extravaganza</u>[110]. Unlike for vision and sound, software for the on-line delivery of odor stimuli still lies in the future.

Social Psychology

There are not as many Internet servers for social psychology as there are for other subfields. <u>Social Cognition–Social Psychology Paper Archive</u>[111] is a searchable archive of on-line papers and research. The <u>Society for the Psychological Study of Social Issues</u>[112] is the home page of The Society for the Psychological Study of Social Issues. The Berkeley Psychophysiology Lab conducts research in emotion that is described on the Web server <u>BPL Research</u>[113].

SPECIFIC CLINICAL CONDITIONS HYPERLINKS

A number of servers have been set up for specific clinical conditions. They include <u>Mood Disorders</u>[114], the <u>Sleep Medicine Home Page</u>[115], the <u>Traumatic Stress Home Page</u>[116], <u>Drug-Related Network Resources</u>[117], <u>OCD–Obsessive-Compulsive Disorder</u>[118], <u>STAR (Stress and Anxiety Research) Society</u>[119], and <u>Attention Deficit Disorder</u>[120].

PSYCHOMETRIC HYPERLINKS

<u>The Buros Institute</u>[121] has a Web page that will be of use to most psychologists interested in psychometrics. A general index site, but one that leans toward education, is <u>Assessment and Evaluation on the Internet</u>[122]. The <u>ERIC Clearinghouse on Assessment and Evaluation</u>[123] is a searchable page maintained by the Catholic University. The APA maintains a page, <u>Frequently Asked Questions (FAQ) on Psychological Tests</u>[124] that is especially good for students. A similar page from Great Britain is <u>Mind Tools–Psychometric Testing</u>[125]. Another such file is the

Meyers Briggs FAQ–A Summary of Personality Typing[126].
        Specific tests were also found. They include The Goldberg Mood Scales (11-Aug-1994)[127], the Rorschach Inkblot Test[128] (under construction), and The Keirsey Temperament Sorter[129]. The page Cumulative Data for WWW Jungian Personality Test[130] presents distribution data collected on the Internet on the Keirsey Temperament Sorter from over 124,000 subjects. A PC-based questionnaire based on the DSM-IV can be found at Personality Diagnostic Questionnaire–4 by Alphalogic Ltd.[131], and you can download a computer demo of the program.

RESEARCH HYPERLINKS

A number of sites are useful for conducting and teaching psychological research. For example, a page from Russ Dewey's Psych Web page, the APA Publication Manual Crib Sheet[132], is very handy for all who must write according to APA style. The APA's American Psychological Association Science Programs[133] is part of their PsychNet Web server. It contains information useful to researchers, including the names and URLs of APA scientific journals in APA Science Journals[134].
Psycoloquy Journal, Behavioral and Brain Sciences[135] is Stevan Harnad's page and includes hyperlinks to the electronic journal *Psycoloquy*, the current target articles of the journal *Behavioral and Brain Sciences*, and online versions of his own published papers. The Journey North[136] is a Web page specializing in animal migration, and it features migrations of monarch butterflies, caribou, sea turtles, and other species. The Survey Research Center[137] is an index page for survey research by Herb Abelson and Jonathan Sills of Princeton University. Finally, for a humorous look at research and researchers, see Hot Air[138], the Web server of *The Annals of Improbable Research*.

SOFTWARE

Downloadable software for psychology is available from several sources. The ProGAMMA Home Page[139] offers information about its services and access to the software data bank SIByl HomePage[140]. An FTP site[141] lists Apple Macintosh psychology software and the archive of the mailing list MACPSYCH. Compsych[142] is a gopher that serves as a repository for psychology software of all types.

LISTSERVERS AND MAILING LISTS

There are many listservers and mailing lists in psychology including the gophers[143,144]. Indiana University's searchable Web page Search for Mailing Lists[145] is another such list.

CONCLUSION

Psychologists have started to provide a large number of Internet resources for themselves and their colleagues. However, the distribution of such resources across psychology's subfields is spotty. In time, that distribution should become more even as psychologists see the utility of using the Internet in research, teaching, and service.

NOTES

1.   http://www.lap.umd.edu/LAPFolder/about/propaganda.html

2.   http://www.gasou.edu/psychweb/psychweb.htm

3.   ftp://premier.tulsa.cc.ok.us/pub/psych/aon.txt

4.   http://rs1.cc.und.nodak.edu/misc/jBAT/psychres.html

5.   http://www.apa.org/

6.   gopher://gopher.apa.org/

7.   http://psych.hanover.edu/APS/

8.   http://charlotte.med.nyu.edu/woodr/div28.html

9.   http://rs1.cc.und.nodak.edu/misc/jBAT/div12.html

10.   http://mulerider.saumag.edu/psych/aaproj/d2homepage

11.   gopher://www.cc.utexas.edu:80/hGET%20/psycgrad/psycgrad.html

12.   http://andromeda.einet.net/galaxy/Social-Sciences/Psychology.html

13.   http://www.yahoo.com/science/psychology/

14.   http://www.well.com/user/selfhelp/

15.   http://www.lafayette.edu/allanr/scip.html

16.   http://www.coedu.usf.edu/behavior/behavior.html

17.   http://www.jsu.edu/psychology/sqab.html

18.   http://fnord.dur.ac.uk/eurodev/index.html

19.   http://www.mcl.ucsb.edu/cep/

20.   http://www.mcl.ucsb.edu/cep/hbestie.html

21.   http://www.bga.org/bga/

22.   http://www.wimsey.com/~chrisl/JPS/JPS.html

23.   http://www.albany.net/~wcross/all1srch.html

24.   http://newtoo.manifest.com/WhatsNewToo/index.html

25.   http://charlotte.med.nyu.edu/woodr/apasearch.html

26.   http://www.iris.brown.edu/iris/freud/Freud_OV_274.html

27.   http://miso.wwa.com/~nebcargo/Jung/

28.   http://www.scarletfire.com/maslow/

29.   http://www.hanover.edu/psych/Krantz/other.html

30.   http://psy.ucsd.edu/

31.   http://www.psy.utexas.edu/

32.   http://www.psy.cmu.edu/

33.   http://www.indiana.edu:80/~iuepsyc/

34.   http://www.ithaca.edu/HS/Psych/psych1/

35.   http://www.jbu.arknet.edu/sbs/psych/

36.   http://www.mit.edu:8001/people/cdemello/univ.html

37.   gopher://gopher.nimh.nih.gov/

38.   http://www.cityscape.co.uk/users/ad88/resuk.htm

39.   http://www.psych.med.umich.edu/

40.   http://www1.mhv.net/~grohol/

41.   http://plaza.interport.net/nypsan/

42.   http://lucien.berkeley.edu/dreams.html

43.   http://www.iag.net/~hutchib/.dream/

44.   http://plaza.interport.net/nypsan/psycon.html

45.   http://www.vix.com/pub/men/index.html

46.   http://gladstone.uoregon.edu/~dvb/trauma.htm

47.   http://homepage.seas.upenn.edu/~mengwong/psych162.html

48. http://www.ed.uiuc.edu/coe/eps/Educational-Theory/ET-welcome.html

49. http://www-gse.berkeley.edu/program/SP/sp.html

50. gopher://ericps.ed.uiuc.edu:70/11/npin/res.pared/gen.resources

51. http://seamonkey.ed.asu.edu/~gene/TEPSIG/TEP_SIG.html

52. http://www.ils.nwu.edu/~e_for_e/nodes/I-M-NODE-4121-pg.html

53. http://www.indiana.edu/~iuepsyc/P103Psyc.html

54. http://info.med.yale.edu/caim/

55. http://kumchttp.mc.ukans.edu/instruction/alliedHealth/Occ_Therapy_Ed/jradel/Poster_Presentations/PstrStart.html

56. http://www.indiana.edu/~iuepsyc/Study.html

57. http://www.wwu.edu/~n9140024/index.html

58. http://pages.prodigy.com/IA/linda/linda.html

59. http://pages.prodigy.com/IA/linda/linda2.html

60. http://pages.prodigy.com/IA/linda/linda2.html

61. gopher://alpha1.csd.uwm.edu:70/0ftp%3Aalpha1.csd.uwm.edu@/pub/Psychology/BehaviorAnalysis/educational/course/eab-tech-terms-dermer

62. http://www.coedu.usf.edu/behavior/listserv.html

63. http://www.coedu.usf.edu/behavior/behavior.html

64. http://jsucc.jsu.edu/psychology/sebac.html

65. http://www.envmed.rochester.edu/wwwrap/behavior/jeabjaba.htm

66. http://www.netaxs.com:80/~iris/infoweb/baby.html

67. http://www.efn.org/~djz/birth/babylist.html

68. http://www.psych.med.umich.edu/web/aacap/factsFam/

69. http://grafi.oulu.fi/lab/

70. http://www.psy.utexas.edu/psy/crl.html

71. http://www.futurenet.co.uk/charity/ado/index.html

72. http://education.indiana.edu/cas/cashmpg.html

73. http://education.indiana.edu/cas/adol/mental.html

74. http://www.xroads.com/rainbow/rahome.html

75. http://fohnix.metronet.com/~thearc/welcome.html

76. http://www.theworld.com/HEALTH/GERIATRI/SUBJECT.HTM

77. http://www.alz.uci.edu/

78. http://156.40.66.249/

79. http://cmit.unomaha.edu/TIP/TIP.html

80. http://cmit.unomaha.edu/TIP/iorelatedpages.html

81. http://www.ucm.es/OTROS/Psyap/iaap/index.html

82. http://www.ucm.es/OTROS/Psyap/hispania/index.html

83. http://matia.stanford.edu/cogsci/onepage.html

84. http://www.cudenver.edu/~mryder/itc_data/cogsci.html

85. http://www.shef.ac.uk/uni/projects/gpp/index.html

86. http://www_hbp.scripps.edu/HBP_html/ProgramAnnouncement.html

87. http://gdbwww.gdb.org/gdb/plan/docs/introabs.html#i.

88. http://ivory.lm.com:80/~nab/

89. gopher://gopher.sfn.org/

90. http://galaxy.einet.net/galaxy/Medicine/Human-Biology/Neurobiology.html

91. http://hcs.harvard.edu:80/~husn/BRAIN/index.html

92. http://www.med.harvard.edu:80/AANLIB/home.html

93. http://lenti.med.umn.edu/NEURON_BRAIN/BRAIN.html

94. http://lenti.med.umn.edu/NEURON_BRAIN/NEURON.html

95. http://www.loni.ucla.edu/ratdata/Rat.html

96. http://biogfx.bgsm.wfu.edu/brain/map.html

97. http://www.infowest.com:80/cpn/index.html

98. http://www-ls.lanl.gov/HGhotlist.html

99. http://gdbwww.gdb.org/omim/docs/omimtop.html

100. http://gdbdoc.gdb.org/letovsky/cprop/human/maps.html

101. http://rumba.ics.uci.edu:8080/origins/faqs.html

102. http://vision.arc.nasa.gov/VisionScience/VisionScience.html

103. http://os.sri.com/program.shtml

104. http://www.qucis.queensu.ca/RPL/info.html

105.   http://tinkertoy.ils.nwu.edu/

106.   http://psych.hanover.edu/Krantz/sen_tut.html

107.   http://lecaine.music.mcgill.ca/~welch/auditory/Auditory.html

108.   http://sln.fi.edu/~helfrich/music/psychaco.html

109.   http://www.cs.colorado.edu/~andreas/Teaching/Music/Experiments.html

110.   http://www.mcs.net/~mrutan/rutanpgs/smell.html

111.   http://www.psych.purdue.edu/~esmith/scarch.html

112.   http://www.coled.umn.edu/CAREIwww/SPSSI/SPSSIhome.html

113.   http://violet.berkeley.edu/~lorenmc/research.html

114.   http://avocado.pc.helsinki.fi/~janne/mood/mood.html

115.   http://www.cloud9.net/~thorpy/

116.   http://www.long-beach.va.gov/ptsd/stress.html

117.   http://hyperreal.com/drugs/faqs/resources.html

118.   http://mtech.csd.uwm.edu/~fairlite/ocd.html

119.   http://www.uib.no/STAR/

120.   http://www-leland.stanford.edu:80/group/dss/Info.by.disability/Attention.Deficit.Disorder/

121.   http://www.unl.edu/buros/home.html

122.   http://www.cua.edu/www/eric_ae/intass.html

123.   http://www.cua.edu/www/eric_ae/

124.   http://www.apa.org/science/test.html

125.   http://www.demon.co.uk/mindtool/page12.html

126.   http://sunsite.unc.edu/personality/faq-mbti.html

127.   http://avocado.pc.helsinki.fi/~janne/mood/scales.html

128.   http://www.ac.biola.edu/~markm/rorsch.html

129.   http://sunsite.unc.edu/personality/keirsey.html

130.   http://sunsite.unc.edu/jembin/mb-data.pl

131.   http://travel1.travel-net.com/~alphalog/alpha1.html

132.   http://www.gasou.edu/psychweb/tipsheet/apacrib.htm

133.   http://www.apa.org/science/science.html

134. http://www.apa.org/journals/scjnlind.html

135. http://www.princeton.edu/~harnad/

136. http://www.ties.k12.mn.us/~jnorth/

137. http://www.princeton.edu/~abelson/index.html

138. http://www.improb.com/

139. http://www.gamma.rug.nl/

140. http://www.gamma.rug.nl/sibhome.html

141. ftp://ftp.stolaf.edu/pub/macpsych/

142. gopher://baryon.hawk.plattsburgh.edu/11/.ftp/pub/compsych

143. gopher://gopher.mid.net:7002/11/07menu/09menu

144. http://www.clark.net/pub/listserv/lspsy1.html

145. http://scwww.ucs.indiana.edu/mlarchive/

10

Sociology

CHAPTER PREVIEW

Sociology is the study of social interactions among people. Sociologists attempt to explain and understand social environments and social life. Sociology's scope is broad, ranging from the nature of relationships to the development of societies and their cultures. Sociologists may, for instance, explain the development of social institutions or the problems within social institutions. The Internet is becoming a very valuable tool for studying sociology, as the various Internet resources listed in this chapter show.

THE SOCIOLOGY OF THE INTERNET

The sociological aspects of the Internet itself have come under sociological scrutiny. Previous technological advances like the telephone and television provide the historical basis for predicting that the Internet will have similarly profound sociological effects on society. However, the interactive aspects of the Internet may lead to even greater effects on society than those older technologies. Indeed, the Internet could result in the creation of a worldwide electronic culture. These are interesting times in which to be a sociologist!

The Internet connects sociologists and students of sociology in new ways and also provides new opportunities for research. For example, cultural developments fostered by the Internet provide a new source for study. Discussion of such topics can be found on the Internet already. For instance, the The Sociology of Culture in Computer-Mediated Communication: An Initial Exploration[1] discusses and proposes a science of Internet behavior. The Institute for Advanced Technology in the Humanities home page[2] provides hyperlinks to research in this area and to archives, reports, software, and course materials by Institute fellows and staff. For further exploration into this topic of the Internet and society,

of resources for the study of the relationship between humans and machines, especially computers.

We now turn to more traditional information on sociology that is available on the Internet. We have grouped that information by relevant subject categories.

GENERAL SOCIOLOGY HYPERLINKS

A good place to start sociology Internet "surfing" is with Robert O. Keel's definition of the sociological perspective, found as a hyperlink from the University of Missouri-St. Louis Department of Sociology's Web page[3]. Another good starting point is the EJS Home Page[4]. This hyperlink is the home page for the *Electronic Journal of Sociology*, an on-line, peer–reviewed sociology journal. The electronic journal's front page describes the review process; tables of contents and subscription and submission information are also provided. Another general page of hyperlinks in sociology is the WWW Virtual Library: Sociology[5]. It contains hyperlinks to university sociology departments and to related sociology resources.

Home pages for the various sociological associations can also be found on the Internet. The European Sociological Association home page[6] reviews the organization's goals and has hyperlinks to its newsletter and to a bulletin board. The Mid-South Sociological Association[7] also maintains a home page that provides hyperlinks to its membership directory, including many electronic mail addresses. This page also hyperlinks to sociology Web search engines (see Chapter 6) and to other sites of interest to sociologists. The Anabaptist Sociology and Anthropology Association (ASAA) home page[8] is for sociologists and anthropologists with a historical interest in the Anabaptist movement of the 16th century, including Mennonites, Amish, Hutterites, Church of the Brethren, Brethren Church, and Brethren in Christ. The New Zealand Sociological Association[9] is another sociological association with an Internet presence.

SOCIOLOGY HISTORY HYPERLINKS

Extensive searching of the Internet revealed few sources on the development of sociology and the sociological perspective. Other than in library searches and book references, the works of Durkheim, Weber, Mead, Cooley, Parsons, Mills, Pareto, Sorokin, and the other early giants in the field are almost nonexistent on the Internet. The principal exception is Karl Marx and his work. For example, the Marx and Engels On-line Library[10] maintains a gopher site with many of the original writings of these two theorists and directories related to their philosophies. We expect that similar Internet sources will appear covering other notable pioneers in sociology.

SOCIOLOGY DEPARTMENT HYPERLINKS

Most sociologists work in the academic community; thus, much Internet sociology is found through university sociology department home pages, gophers, and TELNET databases. Those on-line departments provide a good place to start inquiries about sociology and the training required to become a sociologist. Most department home pages contain hyperlinks to course offerings and to information about faculty research interests and electronic mail addresses. Such information is valuable to potential sociology students. Because the number of department home pages and gopher sites is growing rapidly, the list of department Internet sites below will quickly become dated. (We apologize in advance to any departments we may have missed. Please contact us if we did miss your department, and we will include your URLs on the Web server for this text and in the next edition.)

The University of Pennsylvania's Department of Sociology home page[11] provides department and faculty information (including electronic mail addresses) and a description of the department's programs. A valuable hyperlink at this site is its Population Studies Center, a research site in demography further described below in the "Demography" section. West Chester University's home page[12] provides general university information as well as information on its sociology department. Hyperlinks to research programs affiliated with the department, and to the joint WCU and California State University-Long Beach projects on small–group analysis, can also be found there. The Sociology Department of Queens College, CUNY, Web page[13] includes a mouse-clickable floor plan of the department. The page also includes hyperlinks for down-loading sociology software developed by the department. The University of Missouri-St. Louis Department of Sociology maintains both a home page[14] and a gopher[15] that offer information about the department. Duke University's Department of Sociology has a home page[16] with hyperlinks to other Duke University Web servers and gopher servers. Other sociology department pages are Brown University's Dept of Sociology[17] and Princeton University's Department of Sociology[18]. The Princeton sociology page provides an academic program description, a faculty directory, information on workshops and papers presented by the department faculty, and a hyperlink to their working papers. Moving overseas, Surrey University's Department of Sociology also offers both a Web site[19] and a gopher[20] that provide information about the university, a faculty electronic mail directory, research information, and other hyperlinks including the research electronic journal *Social Research Update*[21].

The number of on-line departments is sure to increase because of the ease of setting up gopher servers and Web pages. We expect that most departments will have such electronic access in the near future. Now we turn to servers dedicated to providing information on sociological.theories.

SOCIOLOGY THEORY HYPERLINKS

Social behavior and our social world is a very large area of study, but the days of grand, all-encompassing theories of society are past. In the latter half of the 20th–century, sociology has turned to the exploration of smaller units of the social world. Thus, sociologists today investigate the workings of diverse social institutions like families and communities. Or, they examine specific aspects of cultures such as power, status, aging, gender, crime, or unemployment. Sociology's emphasis today is on understanding these related processes, their meaning and their structures. Current sociological research is framed within one or more of the following theories: symbolic interactionism, functionalism, conflict theory, human ecology, exchange theory, and sociobiology. As you explore the Internet you will see that these various theories are not equally represented.

Symbolic Interactionism

Symbolic interactionism's presence on the Internet is limited. For instance, the Society for the Study of Symbolic Interaction has set up a Web page[22] devoted to qualitative, interactionist research. The page has hyperlinks to papers, member information, and conferences in the area of symbolic interactionism. Their gopher site[23] provides similar information.

Functionalism

As with symbolic interactionism, there is not a great deal of direct sociological work from the functionalist perspective available on the Internet, a surprise considering the amount of research that has been done within this approach. One rare example is The International Network for Social Network Analysis (INSNA) home page[24]. It provides information on using statistical analysis to understand the functions of social interaction. It also contains hyperlinks to other related sites. Another is the German site Network Visualization[25], which promotes efforts to visualize social structures. Its goal is to show how automatic procedures can be combined with aesthetics to understand unusually complex social phenomena. If you are unfamiliar with this approach, the site is worth a look.

Conflict Theory

Of the perspectives reviewed in this section, conflict theory is the best represented. The Progressive Sociology Network's gopher Authors[26] provides an alphabetical list of authors with hyperlinks to the text of their writings in progressive sociology. A related gopher, the Progressive Sociology Network Archives[27], allows you to study writings from conflict theory's perspective. The World-Systems Archive Home Page[28] provides information and hyperlinks exploring the functions world social systems. The Web site _Journal of World-Systems Research_[29] reviews current research and ideas in progressive sociology. The Institute for Global Communications's The Progressive Directory[30] Web page serves to expand and inspire movements for environmental sustainability, human and workers' rights, nonviolent conflict resolution, social and economic justice, and women's equality. Corresponding hyperlinks include EcoNet[31], P eaceNet[32], ConflictNet[33], LaborNet[34], and WomensNet[35]. Another related site is Conflict[36].

Exchange Theory

Little was found on exchange theory, a view that sees social behavior as a series of exchanges based on rewards and punishments. Those exchanges must be seen as beneficial by all parties for the social behavior to continue. A specific example example related to prostitution was found in the Institute for Advanced Techonology in the Humanities home page[37], however.

Sociobiology

Sociobiology is the study of the biological influences on social behavior, especially the role played by evolution in the formation of social structures. Though sites covering evolution in general can be easily located on the Internet, sociobiology itself does not have much of a presence. Exceptions include the Alt.Memetics Resource Page[38] and the Al t.Memetics Resources Page Archives[39], which contain a number of hyperlinks to texts and other hyperlinks in the field of memetics. They also provide hyperlinks to a few papers on the subject of sociobiology, for example; Rhonda Mahony's Web page[40] exploring the relationship between social memory, biology, and society; and sociobiology founder E.O. Wilson's Web page[41] . The Talk.Origins Archive page[42] introduces you to evolutionary biology and topics in sociobiology.

Human Ecology

Human ecology is the part of sociology that looks at the transactions between societies and their environments. Most of the sites on human ecology are not sociology sites, strictly speaking. Rather, they tend to be sites concerned with population problems and the effects of limited natural resources on society. An example of the latter concern is the Web site Humans and the Environment[43]. Another is the WWW Virtual Library Environment Civilization[44], which offers many hyperlinks to environmental and ecological sites. The home page for Communications for a Sustainable Future[45] explores large–scale ecological issues and speculates about our future from a human ecology point of view and how our culture will need to change if our environment is to continue to sustain society as we know it.

Another page that similarly explores the effects of building communities is the Eco-Hab home page[46] sponsored by Eco-Hab International (EHI), a group committed to promoting the organization, financing, planning, building, and management of environmentally sustainable, affordable communities. Its primary focus is on the inter-relationships between environment and development activities. A gopher site of the University of Virginia, EcoGopher Project[47], is designed "to facilitate access to environmental information."

So, using the Internet you can find information on social theories and their applications (e.g., strengthening families, urban planning, crime prevention, or building international understanding).

SOCIOLOGY ISSUES HYPERLINKS

Sociologists use theory and their general understanding of people and social structures, and apply this knowledge to studying specific issues. Below, we cover some of those major issues.

Culture

Culture is a broad topic that includes social behaviors like belief systems, traditions, customs, mores, art, and many other aspects of human interaction. Sociologists usually confine their studies to specific parts of culture. Some sites on the Internet have been designed to study culture.

The _Canadian Journal of Political and Social Theory_ sponsors Ctheory [48], an international electronic review of books on theory, technology, and culture. This Web page provides an on-line hyperlink to many articles, events, and book reviews relating to the study of contemporary culture. The electronic journal _Postmodern Culture_ [49] has hyperlinks to its articles and to concepts surrounding postmodernism. An on-line newsletter that reviews research in the field of ethnic studies is the Ethnomethodology Newsletter Index [50]. Another Web page is Native Web [51], with hyperlinks to information on many cultures. (See Chapter 14 for a longer list of sites for specific cultures.)

Differentiation and Stratification

The tasks and roles that go into creating and maintaining society must be divided up among its various members. The products that the society creates must be distributed among these same members. Seldom are such roles equivalent. When sociologists study how roles and tasks are determined and allocated, they are studying differentiation and stratification, a very complicated process in some instances. More specific topics in this area include social class, gender, age, race, and ethnicity.

Information on some of these societal characteristics can be found at the Web page Racial Religious EthnoNationalist Violence Studies[52] . This site reports on, investigates, and analyzes all types of violence related to ethnicity, religion, and other factors around the world. It also has mail archives on those subjects. The ERaM (Ethnicity, Racism and the Media) Programme[53] is a Web page dedicated to the study of ethnicity, racism, and the role of the media. The European Research Center on Migration and Ethnic Relations[54] bills itself as "the only university-based research institute devoted to the specialist study of these topics at the European level."

Age is another way in which societies often differentiate groups of persons. Wayne State University[55] offers a comprehensive index of hyperlinks to information sites on gerontology and the aging process, including biological, psychological, and sociological aspects. Another site concerned with the social aspects of aging is the Center on Aging[56], sponsored by the Institute of Business and Economic Research and funded by the National Institute on Aging. This site is not on-line at this time, but the news release you will see when you go to the site provides an electronic mail address by which the center can be contacted. At this time, the National Institute on Aging is not on-line either. Norris Medical Library of the University of Southern California maintains a gopher[57] that covers a wide range of issues concerning the aging process, including a path to the National Library of Medicine (NLM) Gopher[58].

Gender and the division of labor also differentiates societies. See the collection of listservers(see Chapter 3) covering the role of women and women's studies titled 12Menu[59].

Social Institutions

When sociologists study social institutions, they may look into the meanings and functions of informal and formal institutions. The Internet contains many examples of such institutions ranging from personal home pages with family geneologies to large governmental servers. Discussion of social institutions occurs on listservers and news groups. So, if you are interested in studying social institutions, you will find useful material nearly everywhere on the Internet. You should realize, however, that the Internet primarily reflects institutions in Western industrial countries, the main users of the Internet. Also, realize that the Internet sites listed below focus mostly on formal social institutions.

Religion.   The Internet has information on all major religions. The home page Religions of the World-Wide Web Virtual Library: Religion[60] offers information on the world's major religions. Hyperlinks from the home page take you to information specific to all of the major religions. You can also hyperlink to other sites covering religion, including news groups.

Government.   Government is another universal social institution, and its influence on society is profound. The Internet has information on many of the governments of the world. Much of the information on specific governments or governmental functions, including many of the "think tanks" responsible for data and research on governmental policy, are covered in Chapter 12. The Institute for Public Policy and Management, a part of the University of Washington's School of Public Affairs, has a home page[61] that focuses on the analysis of public policies. The University of Washington's School of Public Affairs has a similar home page at the Cascade Center for Public Service[62], but it concentrates on the relationship between government and public service.

Family.   The family as a social institution is of major concern to sociologists. A site that provides hyperlinks to many demographic trends relating to the family, including marriage, divorce, births, and abortions, is Youth Indicators 1993 - HOME : Demographics and Family Composition[63]. The Cooperative State Research, Education, and Extension Service (CSREES)[64] maintains a gopher with extensive hyperlinks in this area as well. Some of the state–level county extension services offer similar services. For instance, the Minnesota Extension Service gopher[65] has hyperlinks related to the study of families and family problems. The following sites may also prove useful. ChildCare[66] has information concerning child care needs and problems. The National Network for Family Resiliency (NNFR)[67] is a gopher that provides leadership for acquisition, development, and analysis of resources that foster family resiliency. A list of papers on the problems of families as related to governmental policy can be found at the gopher policy/Family[68]. The Kids Count Data Book 1994[69] contains the results of the Kids Count survey on economics, health, housing, births, and other family information. Another related gopher is Statistics: Population Statistics for Children, Youth and Family[70], which houses statistics for families and children and contains a searchable gopher page to the data from the Kids Count Data Book 1994. The Harvard Family Research Project[71] conducts and disseminates research concerning programs and policies to strengthen and support families, advance evaluation practices, and evaluate the impact of programs and policy development. If you wish to discuss the problems related to families further, you might want to look at the gopher server for FAMNET[72]. Famnet is an issues–based electronic mail group for professionals who work with children and their families.

Community.   The community is a natural focal point for sociological study. The Department for Rural and Urban Development, for example, has operated a home page[73] since January 1993 to aid both rural and urban communities in their natural process of development. The Community Development Society (CDS) runs a Web site[74] that promotes a "global perspective on community development."

Some sociologists direct their knowledge to improving the understanding and functioning of social institutions. One specific goal is directing that understanding to dealing with social problems. Key electronic sources[75] is a Web page listing of some of the major electronic sources on community development information resources. An Australian Web page, Integrating Environment and Development[76], has the goal of understanding the relationship between community development and environmental problems. CED-NET[77] is a Web page providing subscription information for an unmoderated discussion list. Various states in the U.S. have Web pages describing how the Internet can promote community development programs. An example of such a home page is the Tennessee Economic Development Center Internet Information Server[78]. Its self–described mission is to prepare Tennessee for competition in a global economy by supporting Tennessee communities and enterprises through community development initiatives.

Social Problems

Below are sites on the Internet that relate to the study of social problems. Sociologists spend much effort to determine the causes and meaning of and solutions to social problems. Note that the sites mentioned below constitute less than an exhaustive list and that Internet sites from other chapters (e.g., Chapter 11) will often apply. Also, be sure to check the URL listings by subject in Appendix A.

General.   The University of Michigan Go M-Link gopher[79] has hyperlinks to information about subjects such as aging, family issues, unemployment, and community issues and serves as a general pointer page for social problems.

Violence and Crime.   The gopher site for Partnerships Against Violence NETwork (PAVNET)[80] focuses on the major social issue of violence and its prevention. PAVNET represents the cooperative effort of several federal agencies to bring information on anti-violence programs to state and local officials quickly. For information about violence against children, see the National Data Archive on Child Abuse and Neglect gopher site[81], which links to data on child abuse and neglect.
       The Internet contains a great deal of information on the study of crime itself. For instance, Cecil Greek's Criminal Justice Page[82] covers topics such as law resources, juvenile crime, the death penalty, and prisons. It also has hyperlinks to resources on the O.J. Simpson case. The Internet Crime Archives[83] is a glitzy Web page that covers serial killers and mass murders and is not for the squeamish. The Department of Justice Statistics gopher[84] takes a more mainstream approach. It is a searchable gopher site with crime statistics and other crime information from various Department of Justice programs. The Department of Justice also maintains a gopher site[85] that is an index to statistics and other information. The gopher Criminology[86] brings more of a sociological flavor to crime studies with hyperlinks to many papers and articles on crime, criminology and other information sites, including a listing of computer bulletin boards related to criminology. The American Society of Criminology maintains a home page[87] with hyperlinks to the Department of Justice and other hyperlinks related to crime, sociology, and critical and radical criminology.

Urban Planning.   Urban planning and urban development resources are indexed on the home page UB SA&P Planning and Architecture Internet Resource Center[88]. This Web page lists many hyperlinks related to urban planning and policy. A similar site is the Web page Virginia Center for Housing Research][89], which provides research on housing data and community planning in the state of Virginia. <u>Housing and Household Economic Statistics Division of the U.S. Census</u>[90] is a Web page that contains census data on U.S. households ranging from poverty, health, and employment to the dynamics of economic well-being.

Health Care.   Health care is a social problem of concern to sociologists and others. The Internet contains much information on health care and related policies. The <u>National Institute of Health,</u> one of eight agencies of the Public Health Service, maintains a comprehensive Web server[91] and contains hyperlinks to 24 separate institutes, centers, and divisions.   The <u>Administration on Aging</u> maintains a gopher[92] for the Department of Health and Human Services that contains reports from the agency on issues of aging. The <u>Norris Medical Library</u> of the University of Southern California[93] has a gopher that indexes a large number of health-related organizations. We list more health-related hyperlinks in the chapters on social work (11), psychology (9), and political science (12).

If you wish to exchange information with others on how society should tackle social problems, you can subscribe to one of the problem-related listservers. The gopher <u>10menu</u>[94] provides addresses and instructions for many such listservers in the area of social problems.

RESEARCH HYPERLINKS

A major contribution of sociologists to our society is the research of our social world. If you are just starting to learn about sociological research and think you might have bitten off a bit more than you can chew, the Internet can be a great help. There is a great deal of research data currently on the Internet, and it is growing rapidly. In fact, research is one area in which there is so much information potentially useful to you that it may be difficult to find your way around at first. The larger data archives are easy to locate with a Web browser or with gopher. If you prefer to TELNET, you may find some of the better archives restricted to you. The larger data and information services will generally let you search abstracts; however, the downloading of actual documents or datasets may require a fee. Individual fees for students tend to be very modest. Some archives, such as Inter-University Consortium for Political and Social Research (ICPSR), require that your university be a member of their consortium. The university membership requirements can be located at their home page, listed below.

We now review Internet sites that offer hyperlinks to previously collected research data and to ongoing research data. These sites are useful to many of the social sciences, not just sociology. We placed them in this chapter because the bulk of the data appears to be sociological.

Large Archives

Those of you with access to graphical Web browsers should start with the Council of European Social Sciences Data Archives *Utenlandske dataarkiv*[95]. This Web site has a clickable map (there is a text version of the information found on the map) that will hyperlink you to many of the major social science research and data sites throughout the world. To access a site you simply click on the box that is connected to a point on the world map. Europe has an insert in the map to make locating the many archives on that continent easier. The map will also tell you which sites are accessed by Web browsers or gophers or via TELNET. This site is a good place to begin any literature or research review in social science. Another comprehensive site is run by the International Federation of Data Organizations (IFDO)[96]. It basically is a listing of member sites and is made available through the Swedish Social Science Data Service at Göteborg University. All the IFDO members that are on-line maintain extensive research archives in the social sciences. The hyperlinks available on this page overlap with *Utenlandske dataarkiv*. A mirror site is Australian National University's Social Science Data Archives[97]. Note that IFDO archives in Budapest and Jerusalem are only available via TELNET.

The South African Data Archive (SADA)[98] is another IFDO member that maintains a large data archive. This archive was established in 1993 by the Human Sciences Research Council (HSRC) to document the recent rapid changes in South Africa.

A source for Australian (and other) data is the Australian National University's Social Science Data Archives (SSDA)[99] . This site continually seeks new datasets to archive. The International Association for Social Science Service Information &Technology's home page[100] supplies information on archiving and managing social science data archives. The Consortium for International Earth Science Information Network (CIESIN) runs a Web site[101] at the University of Michigan. It contains datasets related to societal responses to environmental changes and hyperlinks to the CIESIN's Earth Science home page. The Norwegian Social Science Data Services (NSD)[102], an English version of their larger Norwegian version, contains datasets, publications, and other social research information. Another gopher site[103] is to a very diverse collection of data and institutions.

One of the largest on-line collections of sociological–research––related material is the Consortium of Sociological Research's gopher site[104], managed by University of Michigan's Consortium of Sociological Research. The corresponding Web site is the ICPSR - Home Page[105], run by the Inter-University Consortium for Political and Social Research (ICPSR). However, full on-line access to this vast archive requires that your university be a member of the consortium or that you pay a fee. You may search research abstracts free of charge, but a fee is required to download full-text files. Information on becoming a member and on services and related usage fees is given on the ICPSR home page.

The Economic and Social Research Council (ESRC) archive[106] is another very large collection of data in social research. It is maintained at the University of Essex. BIRON[107] is the archive's search tool that allows you to search the entire archive by index or key words. The Padstar Project[108] is a Web server for teaching and research in the social sciences. It also provides data searches from the ESRC data archive.

Web Index Pages

One of the index pages we have reviewed relating to sociology and the social sciences is Craig McKie's Social Science Research Engines[109]. This page consists of a very comprehensive list of sociological science search engines (see Chapter 6). Another useful index page is Sociology Resources[110]. It hyperlinks to research data sites for sociology and includes descriptions of the pages so you can review them before searching. The WWW Virtual Library in Sociology[111] also hyperlinks to other general sociology servers. The Berkeley Sociology Gopher[112] hyperlinks to the Directory for Social, Behavioral and Economic Sciences (NSF) and to the Social Scientist's Guidebook among other sites.

WAIS

The Australian National University Demography and Sociology Division, Research School of Social Sciences, maintains several WAIS servers (see Chapter 7) in demography and sociology. ANU's web page[113] allows you access to ANU's databases and many others. It is searchable by key words. If you are working with a Web browser like Netscape, you can use it to interface with WAIS directly and search those WAIS archives. The National Information Services and Systems's Web page[114] provides hyperlinks in the areas of social science, biology, and medicine, with access to over 700 resources.

Specific Research Topics

The number of possible URLs prevents us from listing every source of specific sociological data. Many are associated with sociology departments that have particular research interests. An example would be the WCU-CSULB Collaboration Class[115], a project that focuses on the use of sociometrics in small–group analysis at the sociology department of West

Chester University. This Web site consists of a list of research projects using the tool of sociometric evaluation. The World Bank's Social Indicators of Development[116] lets you search for information about national indicators of development. The World Bank also maintains a Web page for Trends in Developing Economies Database Search[117] that allows you to search for information on economic and social development trends for member countries.

Demographics

The Internet is a very good medium for finding demographic data. Some of the better and easier-to-use sites are related to the demographics of specific countries. For instance, the MIDAS Home Page[118] contains the 1991 United Kingdom's Census of Population statistics and provides information from other large ongoing surveys, macro-economic time series data banks, digital map datasets, spatial geo-referencing datasets, and scientific datasets. A similar server is the *Danish Data Archives* (DDA)[119]. European data can be found at the EURODATA Research Archive[120], a searchable archive that provides sociological data for the whole of Europe. A more general Web page in demography is CERN's Virtual Library index page in demography[121]. U.S. demography sources include the 1990 Census LOOKUP[122] and the Census Bureaus' Web page[123]. For quick access to population data on states and towns, use the UpClose Demographic Summaries 1994[124], a free demonstration page from UpClose Publishing that provides population summaries of states, counties, and towns with over 10,000 inhabitants. They will also mail you an in-depth demographic profile or send it to you via electronic mail, both for a small fee. Their home page is the UpClose Publishing Home Page[125]. The Louisiana Population Data Center[126] provides information concerning that state and hyperlinks to other demographic sites. One gopher[127] hyperlinks to databases and special servers in sociology. Another gopher, 11menu[128], identifies listservers in sociology research and demography. From this gopher, you can obtain subscription information for each of these discussion groups. Finally, you may find the discussion group (eram-research-list) useful because it provides a research network for social science professionals. The subscription address is

MAJORDOMO@BRADFORD.AC.UK

 Type the command "ERAM RESEARCH" in the body of the electronic mail message.

CONCLUSION

The most remarkable aspect of the Internet may be the fact that you can now connect to the society you are studying in a new way. The Internet enables you to inquire directly about people and their social structures. Even more remarkable is that the Internet itself is beginning to take on the aspects of a culture, developing traditions and social behaviors, and even struggling with morality and purpose. In the development of the Internet, sociologists have an opportunity to study the birth of a new culture. Similar technological births have occurred previously (e.g., the telephone). But the interactive aspects of the Internet will allow researchers to study its development in real time.

We began this chapter by suggesting that sociologists are in a unique professional relationship with the Internet. Sociologists can be both members of this electronic society and researchers into its workings and effects. The Internet is so young that there is little data on these types of sociologically interesting topics available at this time. Some groups are studying the subject of human-computer interactions (HCI). The QMW HCI Research Group Home[129] will hyperlink you to persons researching this question. Within this Web page is a hyperlink to the HCI Articles Archive . This archive is a searchable database that contains articles on the subject of human-computer interaction. A more in depth Web site is the Human-Computer Interaction[130], which will inform you about conferences and provide an information archive on the subject. It also has a hyperlink to job opportunities within HCI.

In a way, nothing has changed. Sociology has always been in the awkward position of having to struggle with the fact that sociologists themselves constitute a part of sociology's own subject matter. Technology has brought that old conumdrum once again into sociology's offices and research centers, making it harder than ever to separate researcher and subject.

NOTES

1.   http://www.itcs.com/elawley/bourdieu.html

2.   http://jefferson.village.virginia.edu/

3.   http://www.umsl.edu/~sociolog/theory.htm

4.   http://gpu.srv.ualberta.ca:8010/home1.htm

5.   http://www.w3.org/hypertext/DataSources/bySubject/Sociology/Overview.html

6.   http://www.qub.ac.uk/socsci/miller/esaintro.html

7.   http://www.uakron.edu/hefe/mssapage.html

8. http://www.hillsdale.edu/DepartmentalHomePages/Sociology
   /ASAAHomePage.html

9. gopher://csf.colorado.edu/11/psn/Marx

10. gopher://csf.colorado.edu/11/psn/Marx

11. http://www.ssc.upenn.edu/soc/Overview.html

12. http://albie.wcupa.edu/

13. http://www.soc.qc.edu/

14. http://www.umsl.edu/~sociolog/

15. gopher://umslvma.umsl.edu:71/11/gophers/so

16. http://www.soc.duke.edu:80/

17. http://www.brown.edu:80/Departments/Sociology/

18. http://www.princeton.edu:80/~sociolog/

19. http://www.soc.surrey.ac.uk/

20. gopher://boris.soc.surrey.ac.uk/

21. gopher://boris.soc.surrey.ac.uk/

22. http://sun.soci.niu.edu/~sssi/

23. gopher://gopher.niu.edu:70/11/acad_dept/col_of_las/dept_soci/SSSI

24. http://thecore.socy.scarolina.edu/insna.html

25. http://www.mpi-fg-koeln.mpg.de/~lk/netvis.html

26. gopher://csf.colorado.edu/11/psn/authors

27. gopher://csf.colorado.edu/11/psn/psn-archives/

28. http://csf.Colorado.EDU:80/wsystems/wsarch.html

29. http://csf.Colorado.EDU:80/wsystems/jwsr.html

30. http://www.igc.apc.org/

31. http://www.econet.apc.org/econet/

32. http://www.peacenet.org/peacenet/

33. http://www.igc.apc.org/conflictnet/

34. http://www.igc.apc.org/labornet/

35. http://www.igc.apc.org/womensnet/

36. gopher://gopher.igc.apc.org/11/conflict

37. http://jefferson.village.virginia.edu/pmc/issue.592/add-ext.592

38. http://www.xs4all.nl/~hingh/alt.memetics/index.html

39. http://www.xs4all.nl/~hingh/alt.memetics/index.html#archives

40. http://www-leland.stanford.edu/~rmahony/index.html

41.   http://www.envirohyperlink.org/orgs/wqed/e_o_wilson.html

42. http://rumba.ics.uci.edu:8080/faqs

43. http://kaos.erin.gov.au/human_env/human_env.html

44. http://ecosys.drdr.Virginia.EDU:80/civ.html

45. http://csf.Colorado.EDU:80/

46. http://www.panix.com/~urbanomi/ecohab.html

47. gopher://ecosys.drdr.virginia.edu/

48. http://www.ora.com:8080/johnl/e-zine-list/zines/ctheory.html

49. http://jefferson.village.virginia.edu/pmc/contents.all.html

50. http://www.comp.lancs.ac.uk/sociology/research/ethnonews/ethnon
     ewsindex.html

51. http://ukanaix.cc.ukans.edu/~marc/native_main.html

52. http://ukanaix.cc.ukans.edu/~marc/listserv/revs.html

53. http://www.brad.ac.uk/bradinfo/research/eram/eram.html#eramtop

54. http://www.ruu.nl/ercomer/index.html

55. http://www.iog.wayne.edu/IOGlinks.html

56. gopher://uclink.berkeley.edu:1605/00/News/Center_on_Aging

57. gopher://cwis.usc.edu:70/11/The_Health_Sciences_Campus/organizations

58. gopher://gopher.nlm.nih.gov:70/1

59. gopher://gopher.mid.net:7002/11/07menu/12menu

60. http://www.biologie.uni-freiburg.de/~amueller/religion/

61. http://www.gspa.washington.edu/IPPM_General.html

62. http://cases.pubaf.washington.edu/0c:/center.htm I /

63. http://www.ed.gov/pubs/YouthIndicators/Demographics.html

64. gopher://zeus.esusda.gov:70/11/

65. gopher://tinman.mes.umn.edu/

66. gopher://gopher-cyfernet.mes.umn.edu:4242/11/ChildCare

67. gopher://gopher-cyfernet.mes.umn.edu:4242/11/Family

68. gopher://cyfer.esusda.gov:70/11/CYFER-net/research/policy/Family

69. gopher://cyfer.esusda.gov:70/11/CYFER-net/statistics/Kids_Count

70. gopher://cyfer.esusda.gov:70/11/CYFER-net/statistics

71. gopher://hugse1.harvard.edu:70/11GOPHER_ROOT%3A%5B_hgse._p rojects._hfrp%5D

72. gopher://gopher-cyfernet.mes.umn.edu:4242/00/Family/famnet

73. http://www.macom.co.il/Jafi/communications/rural-urban-dept.html

74. http://www.infoanalytic.com/cds/

75. http://www.ids.ac.uk/eldis/key/key2.html

76. http://kaos.erin.gov.au/portfolio/esd/integ.html

77. http://titsoc.soc.titech.ac.jp/titsoc/higuchi-lab/icm/ced-net.html

78. http://www.usit.net/tedc.html

79. gopher://vienna.hh.lib.umich.edu:70/11/social

80. gopher://cyfer.esusda.gov:70/11/violence

81. //gopher.ndacan.cornell.edu/

82. http://www.stpt.usf.edu/~greek/cj.html

83. http://underground.net/Art/Crime/archives.html

84. gopher://justice2.usdoj.gov:70/1/ojp/bjs

85. gopher://corn.cso.niu.edu/11/acad_dept/col_of_las/dept_soci/CRIMINOLO-GY/moregopher

86. gopher://gopher.niu.edu:70/11/acad_dept/col_of_las/dept_soci/CRIMINOLO-GY

87. http://sun.soci.niu.edu/~critcrim/

88. http://arch.buffalo.edu:8001/internet/h_pa_resources.html

89. http://www.arch.vt.edu/vchr/vchr.html

90. http://www.census.gov/org/hhes/index.html

91.   http://www.nih.gov/icd/

92.   gopher://gopher.os.dhhs.gov:70/11/dhhs/aoa/aoa

93.   gopher://cwis.usc.edu:70/11/The_Health_Sciences_Campus/organizations

94.   gopher://gopher.mid.net:7002/11/07menu/10menu

95.   http://www.uib.no/nsd/diverse/utenland.htm

96.   http://www.ssd.gu.se/ifdotitel.html

97.   http://ssda.anu.edu.au/foreign.html

98.   http://www.hsrc.ac.za/sada.html

99.   http://ssda.anu.edu.au/

100. http://datalib.library.ualberta.ca:80/iassist/

101. http://www.ciesin.org/IC/SEDAC/SEDAC-home.html

102. http://www.uib.no/nsd/nsd-eng.html

103. gopher://unix1.utm.edu:70/11/departments/soc/int

104. gopher://icpsr.umich.edu/

105. http://www.icpsr.umich.edu/

106. http://dawww.essex.ac.uk/

107. http://www.ciesin.org/IC/esrc/biron.html

108. http://dasun3.essex.ac.uk/padstar.html

109. http://www.uakron.edu/hefe/mckie.html

110. http://sosig.esrc.bris.ac.uk/Subjects/sociol.html#family

111. http://www.w3.org/hypertext/DataSources/bySubject/Sociology/Ov
      erview.html

112. gopher://infolib.lib.berkeley.edu/11/resdbs/soci/

113. http://server.wais.com/cgi-bin/waisgate2?waisdocid=704012233
      +1&waisaction=retrieve

114. http://www.niss.ac.uk/subject/31menu.html

115. http://albie.wcupa.edu/ttreadwell/index.html

116. http://www.ciesin.org/IC/wbank/sid-home.html

117. http://quasar.poly.edu:9090/WorldBank/tides.html

118. http://midas.ac.uk/

119. http://www.dda.dk/dda.html

120. http://www.sowi.uni-mannheim.de/eurodata/eurodata.html

121. http://coombs.anu.edu.au/ResFacilities/DemographyPage.html

122. http://cedr.lbl.gov/cdrom/doc/lookup_doc.html

123. http://www.census.gov/cdrom/lookup

124. http://www.digimark.net/upclose/demomenu/demomenu.htm

125. http://www.digimark.net/upclose/

126. http://www.lapop.lsu.edu/

127. gopher://watserv2.uwaterloo.ca:70/11/facilities/University%20of%20Waterloo%20Library/finding/discipline/Sociology/further

128. gopher://gopher.mid.net:7002/11/07menu/11menu

129. http://www.dcs.qmw.ac.uk/research/hci/

130. http://www.ida.liu.se/labs/aslab/groups/um/hci/

11

Social Work

CHAPTER PREVIEW

Social work and the Internet should be perfectly matched because social work is a discipline that attempts to alleviate social problems and enhance quality of life by linking people to appropriate resources. The Internet is a tool whose very design lends itself to social work's goals. Old-fashioned networking is one of the most widely used techniques in social work practice. So, if your goal is to network people to resources, then the Internet can be a gold mine. Most of the Internet sites useful to social work are interactive, which promotes networking in the traditional social work sense of the term. Surprisingly, social work has yet to use the Internet as heavily as other disciplines, a paradox that may stem from social work's tendency to integrate social work practice into existing social structures, and not to develop new and independent social structures. Using the many governmental servers (listed below) that relate directly to understanding and alleviating social problems is a good example of how social work professionals and students could efficiently use the Internet. New and useful social work sites are still few in number, but a little creativity on your part can make many sites not specifically designed for social work very useful.

SOCIAL WORK DEPARTMENT HYPERLINKS

Possibly, you are thinking about an undergraduate major or a professional degree in social work. You might be taking an introductory course in social work or just be interested in enhancing quality of life or promoting the idea of empowerment. A good place to start your Internet exploring would be on the servers of the various university departments and schools of social work. There you will find definitions of social work and see the various philosophies surrounding the process of educating social workers.

Here are some schools of social work that have an Internet presence. The School of Social Work at the University of Illinois at Urbana[1] maintains a pointer page called Other Schools of Social Work[2] linking several on-line schools of social work. The University of Tennessee College of Social Work[3] also provides a hyperlink to schools both in the United States[4] and of international[5] sites. For example, the Department of Social Work at Humboldt State University[6], a well-executed Web page, provides an overview of social work and its history on its Social Work Profession[7] hyperlink. Other hyperlinks provide information about faculty, maps, and local communities. The Walter H. Richter Institute of Social Work[8] at Southwest Texas University also provides an overview of social work ethics and pictures of social workers when you click the A Profession of Many Faces [9] hyperlink. All of their social work faculty can be contacted by electronic mail with a mouse click on a Web browser. The University of Southern California School of Social Work[10] offers a unique gopher to testimonials and perspectives[11] on social work by social workers. An example of a social work student's home page is Rob's Page of Social Work[12]. This site was developed by a social work student at the University of Chicago[13] and has good information and some useful hyperlinks. His page is an example of the future of education and of the kind of work you may be called on to create. Of course, you may be creating your own home page right now. Let us know if you are!

If you are considering an undergraduate major or seeking an advanced degree in social work, realize that many universities offer catalogs and program descriptions on-line. For instance, the Rutgers University School of Social Work[14] on-line catalog has an excellent description of its social work curriculum. Another site maintained by a retired professor, not by the department, is the Social Work Home Page at the University of Windsor[15]. A useful hyperlink here is a countrywide list of electronic mail addresses of many Canadian social work faculty.

SOCIAL WORK HISTORY HYPERLINKS

Sites Related to Social Welfare

When exploring the Internet for documents and articles related to social work or social welfare, many of the sites already mentioned in Chapter 10 will be helpful. However, a few sites stand out as special stops for social work students interested in exploring the history of social work and the important issues surrounding the profession. Poor Relief [16] is an example of the many on-line papers that are available. Another example is the Online Wisconsin[17] Web page which discusses the debate over welfare reform among other topics. Using the search features on this page, you can find papers on many topics in the history of social work--a review of European historical perspectives on government and social programs and the poor, for example. Clicking on Intro[18] takes you to an excerpt from Linda Gordon's book on welfare and to a brief history of the Aid to Families With Dependent Children (AFDC) program. Social Security–A Brief History[19] covers the history of the Social Security Administration. The Social Security Administration's server[20] can provide historical perspective on its pioneering programs. For example, the history of the Work Project Administration (WPA) is part of the American Memory Project[21] server. The WPA[22] page depicts the works of African-American artists who were part of the WPA. Other hyperlinks examine the *zeitgeist* of the Great Depression through posters and fine art from the period. This Web page also demonstrates just how extensive an impact the WPA had on the United States and on individual states. One such state is Georgia, and the Web page WPA Projects in Georgia[23] documents the WPA's impact on an individual state struggling to assist its citizens during the Great Depression.

Other Sites

The Human Rights Home Page [24] discusses the development of the human rights movement and provides hyperlinks to copies of many of the famous documents that have shaped the human rights movement throughout history (e.g., the text of the *Magna Charta* and of Thomas Paine's *The Rights of Man*). A unique site regarding civil rights is the Web page Voices of the Civil Rights Era[25]. This site allows you to download audio recordings of some of the important speeches made during the civil rights movement.

SOCIAL WORK ISSUES HYPERLINKS

Ethics

Social work has developed many diverse perspectives and models that have guided the practice of the profession. A common set of values has emerged that express themselves in the ethics of the profession. The University of Maryland School of Social Work[26] has a hyperlink that provides an overview of the profession today, and when you click on the link for the school's history and ethics, you may access the hyperlinks Social Work Code of Ethics[27] and Assumptions Regarding The Practice Of Social Work[28]. The articles therein provide an overview of these issues. If you would like to pursue the issue of ethics a little further, The Institute

for Business & Professional Ethics [29] at De Paul University maintains a
server devoted to ethics in many fields.

Ecological Models and Systems Theory

The environment has served as a focal point for social work intervention
in nearly all major models of social work practice. That focus is the
natural product of viewing clients within a systems framework. Social
workers believe that changes in clients will change their environment, and
vice versa. Because of social work's emphasis on systems, social work
students should familiarize themselves with ecological models of social
work. We have not found specific Internet sites describing such models,
but several sites exist that cover ecological theories and social change
from a more general perspective. The principles of systems theory and
general systems theory are discussed at the home page What is Systems
Theory?[30]

On a planetary scale, the Web page PlanetKeepers[31] looks at
human integration with our environment. The page's concern is environmental crises and how to provide people with information about
environmental concerns. The 1994 National Environmental Scorecard[32]
and the International Political Economy Network[33] are two Web sites that
look at the political and economic influences of the environmental
movement.

Advocacy

Many social workers are involved in advocacy (e.g., helping clients solve
problems or supporting specific causes). A social work-sponsored site is
the Social Work Advocacy Network's SWAN—National Organizations[34].
Another advocacy site is The Activist Oasis–Research Center [35], a Web
page that provides links to many government and journalistic sites. The
site also provides key word searches of the AP wire service and links to
other news sources. A well-known advocacy group runs The American
Civil Liberties Union (ACLU) gopher[36], which provides a review of its
mission and services.

Problem Solving

The problem-solving process guides the social worker's interventions with
clients. The following sites are not really social–work specific sites, but
they may be of use to social workers even though they focus on problem
solving from a more abstract framework. The Web site Introduction to

21st Century Problem Solving[37] is directed toward mathematical problem solving. Describing particularly bad problem solving as counterexamples is the goal of the Web site Uncommon Sense[38]. However, there is still room on the Internet for sites relating to social work problem solving.

Psychology and Social Work

Early in the 20th century, the psychodynamic model of social work had a firm hold on the thinking of many social work practitioners, and this influence can be felt still. However, most social work practitioners today do not frame their interventions from a strictly psychodynamic perspective. But, for social workers interested in psychotherapy as a primary intervention technique, the following sites on the Net may be inte resting–Psychology Gateway[39] and PsychWeb[40]. Both serve as starting points for exploring psychological resources on the Internet. (For a more in-depth look at psychology and the Internet, see Chapter 9.)

Feminism

Women have been at the center of social work theoretical and professional development since the field's inception. Women have made major contributions to social work that can be traced back to Jane Addams, one of the profession's founders, and to Mary Richmond, who established the first professional school. Since then, many other women have also contributed to the development of social work as a field of study and practice.

Women have also been the largest group of clients for social work practice. Because a primary goal of the profession has always been empowerment of clients, social work has been a force in the empowerment of women and thus a force in the promotion of feminism. Within the past two decades, feminist models of social work practice have emerged. In those models, sexism is seen as a major force contributing to a loss of quality of life for female social work clients--as in the feminization of poverty.

Recently, women have used the Internet as a resource to educate and provide resources to professionals and to the public at large. For example, The National Organization for Women (NOW)[41] home page provides information about NOW's role in supporting women's causes. Two other sites to find information about the practice of social work from a woman's viewpoint are the Web page Feminism Resources[42] and the gopher Women's Resources[43]. Women's Leader Online[44] is a politically oriented Web site whose self-stated mission is to oppose the radical right and to provide a medium to communicate methods of political activity

within this cause. The page also provides a hyperlink to the discussion
list for feminist theory and social work FEMSW-L (see the list of social
work listservers at the end of the chapter for the address).

DEVELOPMENTAL STAGE HYPERLINKS

Social workers perceive their clients as people transacting in and adapting
to a constantly changing environment, and those transactions, in turn,
create changes in both clients and their environments. In that light,
developmental stages are viewed as both predictable and unpredictable
crises for clients and their environments. Social workers thus must
understand the nature of psychosocial development in their clients as
part of life's course. The Internet sites below will guide you to places
where you can explore concepts and issues surrounding lifespan
development.

Pregnancy, Prenatal Care, Birth, and Infancy

Pregnancy, prenatal care, and birth are the first transactions we have with
our environment. Traditionally, social workers assist couples who are
experiencing difficulty achieving conception, having problems with
pregnancy, or adopting. Social workers provide a diverse range of services
to clients including counseling, adoption services, family planning, genetic
counseling, and arranging for prenatal and postnatal care. After children
are born, families must make many adjustments to accommodate the
needs of infants. New parents may discover that new children trigger
economic problems, stress, or even child abuse. Newly pregnant women
and fathers-to-be may require education in parenting skills. Infertile
couples may need counseling or referral to adoption agencies or fertility
clinics. Social workers can keep current about services programs, projects,
and research that best serve their clients. The following sites on the
Internet are examples of the kinds of information available in this area.

   The International Food Information Council Foundation's[45] Web
server has a hyperlink on prenatal nutrition--Healthy Eating During
Pregnancy[46]. The University of Texas-Houston, Department of Obstetrics,
Gynecology & Reproductive Sciences[47] provides information about
obstetrics and gynecology, and their Women's Health Center Maternal
Fetal Medicine Department[48] describes services for high–risk pregnancies.

Childhood

Children spend most of their waking hours learning about their environment. Most of their learning is directed toward family, friends, and school. The result of their interactions with those groups and situations is physical, psychological, and social development. Social workers work to ensure that children's transactions follow an appropriate course so that children can develop to their full potential.

The Child Development[49] gopher site is part of the National Network for Child Care (NNCC) and offers a listing of developmental stages, both physical and social, of children from birth to 8 years of age. Additionally, the text is available in both Spanish and English. Pedinfo[50], a pediatrics Web server, provides medical information on children's health as well as links to children's hospitals and to university departments of pediatrics. Safte-T-Child Online[51] provides information on protecting children from abduction and harm, including how to rate your child's "street smarts," child product safety information, press releases, and other such information.

Adolescence

Adolescents expand their environment to the community and to the world at large. Adolescents begin to practice skills developed during childhood. Adolescents can easily find themselves overwhelmed by problems of identity, depression, crime, abuse, drugs, poverty, pregnancy, or mental illness. Social workers specializing in adolescence may be aided by the following sites.

The Web page Psychiatry On-Line Archives[52] contains a review paper on the crises of development in adolescent and adult years. Another Web page, Indiana Center for Adolescent Studies[53], contains studies on the adolescent stage. Two examples of sites covering specific adolescent problems, panic disorder and accidents, are Panic Disorders in Children and Adolescents[54] and Int. Soc. of Child and Adol. Acc. Prevention[55], respectively. Facts for Families[56] is an informational Web page on problems that concern parents about children and adolescents, such as eating disorders and depression. *Psychiatry Online's* article Crises of Development[57] discusses the role that crises play in developmental stages.

Marriage

Two Web sites devoted to this developmental milestone are <u>Marriage Encounter</u>[58] and <u>Jewish Marriage Enhancement</u>[59].

PRACTICE ENVIRONMENTS

Families

Most social workers see the family client system as fundamental to empowerment and therapeutic social change. Thus, understanding family structures, development, and processes are important to the practicing social worker. The family's place within larger communities is also important in understanding the work of the social worker with the family.

The Department of Health and Human Services gopher site <u>The Administration for Children and Families</u>[60] acts as an advocate for families for the purpose of empowerment. This site provides information on many programs available through the federal government and information on assisting families with problems.

Workplace

The <u>National Center for the Workplace</u>[61] is a gopher site maintained by the Department of Labor whose stated purpose is to help provide information on problems in the workplace created by recent societal changes. This site has on-line papers and publications as well as archives. A mailing list of employee assistance programs (EAPs) for employee assistance counselors is available.

Schools

Social workers find schools a primary practice environment, because schools are one of the key social institutions of our society. Schools, thus, are a major setting for the social work process. The Web page <u>Education Policy Analysis Archives</u>[62] and its similar <u>gopher</u>[63] provide electronic full–text articles focusing on improving schools and education. Another Web page, <u>CTI (Computers in Teaching Initiative)</u>[64], provides technological and computer assistance in the teaching of social services. Similarly, <u>ProCare</u>[65] is a CTI hyperlink that provides social work education software.

Health Care Settings

Social work in health care requires social workers to have a good understanding of how hospitals and other health care institutions function. The focus of health care social work goes well beyond the concept of illness or rehabilitation. Social work takes a holistic approach to health care, meaning health care social workers are concerned about access to and financing of health care and the patient recovery process. These social workers consider social, psychological, and biological factors involved in health care issues.

The Health Care Financing Administration's Web server Health Care Financing Administration (HCFA)[66] provides links to many data sites on health care and health care facilities. Another server that contains information on health–related issues, including a wealth of health statistics, is HyperDoc[67]. The Health and Social Work Homepage[68] is a Web site for social work in health care. The Association of Teachers of Preventive Medicine[69] maintains a Web page for those interested in the issue of primary prevention. The Public Health Service[70] maintains a gopher containing an extensive menu of on-line resources and articles as a hyperlink of the U.S. Department of Health and Human Services[71] Web page. For international data on health care, the United Nations offers Web resources like Unicef gopher[72] site and the World Health Organization (WHO) Home Page[73].

Mental Health Facilities

Social workers provide more mental health services than any other professional group, and social workers are trained in various methods of psychotherapy, family therapy, and psychiatric casework. Further, social workers often provide primary psychotherapy services in mental health clinics and psychiatric hospitals. Social workers may also become licensed, which allows them to provide psychotherapy and other clinical services through a private practice.

Mental Health Resources[74] lists mental health services and is available to clinical social workers who are on-line. Jason Aronson Publishers[75] maintains a Web page that provides interesting interviews with authors in the field of mental health and therapy. Psychiatry On-Line[76] is a provider of psychiatric information, and the Grohol Mental Health Psychology Web Pointer [77] will connect you to many mental health sites.

Neighborhoods and Communities

Another objective of social workers is to improve their clients' quality of
life. Clients are often a couple or a family, and those clients' larger
systems may include small groups, organizations, the community, or even
society at large. So, to improve their clients' quality of life, social workers
may target those systems that overlap with their clients. Often, neighborhoods and communities become the arena for social work.

      The Internet can provide information on successful community
programs. For instance, the Web page Hands on Atlanta, Inc.[78] is an on-
line volunteer service that maintains several programs emphasing citizen
participation. The Carter Center's Web page Because There Is Hope[79] also
describes the structure and philosophy of the Atlanta project noted
above. For information on other community projects around the U.S., the
National Civic League[80] offers a home page that lists community project
information, including photographs of the people involved in the various
community projects, and a searchable database. Neighborhoods Online:
National[81] is another Web server dedicated to community organization
and empowerment and to strengthening neighborhoods. A hyperlinked
local example is Neighborhoods Online: The City of Philadelphia[82], which
also has many links to other sites on local empowerment and maps linked
to the neighborhoods via census data. Other communities, too, are using
the Internet to organize their resources and make them more accessible to
their citizens. Fort Collins, Colorado's, Fortnet[83] is an example of this
style of Internet community organization.

Bureaucracy

Social work has a tradition of providing professional services via social
service agencies. In fact, many social workers once believed that services
provided outside of social service agencies were not social work. This
belief was most pronounced in the functionalist model of practice. Most
social workers no longer see their services as limited to agency settings,
but those agencies are still common vehicles for the delivery of social work
services.

      For social workers practicing within an agency setting, the Internet
can be a powerful resource. For example, the Web page Internet Resources
for Nonprofit Public Service Organizations[84] provides a good starting
point for useful information on how agencies can serve their clients. For a
listing of nonprofit agencies that maintain home pages on the Internet, see
Select Nonprofit Organizations on the Internet[85]. Or, for handy URLs,
electronic mail addresses, and telephone numbers, see Resources for Not -
For-Profits in Housing, Health and Human Services[86]. For another large
Web server with hyperlinks to sites with a broad range of social welfare

concerns, try the Meta-Index for Non-Profit Organizations[87]. To see the Internet presence of large state and national bureaucracies, hyperlink to the Texas Department of Mental Health and MentalRetardation[88], Florida Mental Health Institute Home Page[89], California State Government Network (CSGnet)[90], or U.S. Department of Health and Human Services[91]. Finally, for an international viewpoint, look at the Web server Social Services From Spain[92].

Religious Institutions

A relationship between religious ministries and social work can exist. Conference papers from a meeting on welfare reform and theological concerns, hosted by the Covenant Presbyterian Church in Oak Ridge, Tennessee, can be found on the Web page Welfare Reformed: A Compassionate Approach[93]. An example of an on-line ministry is the Bay Area Volunteer Information Center[94] home page. The page has a hyperlink to the Urban Ministry of Palo Alto[95], a group that describes itself as "a spiritually-centered community of people who care about each other. Our community includes unemployed people, homeless people, local church congregations, people on disability, people in crisis and over 200 volunteers." Similarly, the Episcopal Diocese of Newark, New Jersey's, Oasis[96] is a mission and ministry for gays and lesbians and their families and friends. A large index page is the Christian Organizations and Churches[97] home page. This page hyperlinks to home pages of a large number of churches, including some overseas. Three Essential Elements of Biblical Charity: Faith, Family, and Work[98] is a discussion of the Christian obligation to the poor, originally published in *Premise*.

Criminal Justice

Criminal justice covers a large section of the Internet. Several different home pages are hyperlinked through the Web server at the Department of Justice[99]. Federal Bureau of Prisons director Kathleen M. Hawk's Federal Bureau of Prisons mission statement[100] is one hyperlink from that page. Another home page is Investigatory and Law Enforcement Offices[101], which includes a hyperlink to the home page of the FBI[102]. Another hyperlink there is the Drug Demand Reduction Program/Community Outreach Program[103]. The Department of the Treasury's Bureaus[104] home page provides access to the Secret Service; Bureau of Alcohol, Tobacco, and Firearms; United States Customs Service; Federal Law Enforcement Training Center; and Financial Crimes Enforcement Network. The Albany gopher menu[105] hyperlinks many crime prevention and law enforcement agencies.

Policy and Legislation Development

Practicing social workers are often too busy providing services to their clients to have time for more than a cursory review of legislation and policy. The Internet can change that because legislation can be easily accessed on-line, and electronic mail extends social workers' access to policymakers.

Rand[106] is a nonprofit think tank for the development of public policy. Its server contains an extensive listing of research in public policy, with electronic mail delivery of documents. A hyperlink from the Rand server is Hot Topics[107], a list of on-line papers concerning policy planning and research findings. The Brookings Institute[108] also maintains a Web server offering policy analysis. The Humphrey Institute of Public Affairs[109] makes available an archive on listservers in the area of public policy. The archive allows you look at the ongoing discussions and make key word searches. PUBPOL-D[110] is the archive itself. UniPress's Web server Will T. Bill [111] is a search engine that will enable you to search for all legislation in the 103rd and 104th congresses. Main Street On-Line's Government Mailroom[112] helps you to easily find your senator or representative's electronic mail address and then send a message. Alerts link[113] posts current legislation and government policy and hyperlinks to other, similar sites. The Cato Institute[114] is another policy think tank, but with a libertarian point of view, that runs a Web server. Many of its studies are on the relationship between government and social problems, including health and welfare. Some studies are accessible on-line through the Cato Institute Research Areas[115], and all publications can be searched by key words and type of publication[116]. The Hoover Institute on War, Revolution and Peace[117] is a conservative think tank, and its newsletter Hoover Newsletter[118] is also on-line. The Texas government gopher[119] is one of several ways to search the *Congressional Record* and the *Federal Register*.

DIVERSITY

In the diversity of society, social work sees the resources and strengths needed to improve the quality of life for all. At the same time, social workers' clients may represent very diverse groups of people. For both of these reasons, social workers must be aware of cultural differences and how these cultural differences influence the problem-solving process. Because cultural differences stem from a number of factors, social workers should be able to work with clients regardless of their ethnicity, race, religion, sexual orientation, or mental and physical challenges. Social workers must approach clients non-judgmentally view if they are to be successful. The URLs listed below are not a complete list, but they should give you a sample of diversity resources on the Internet.

Race and Ethnicity

A diversity starting point is the index page <u>American Studies: Race and Ethnicity</u>[120]. Others are the <u>African American Homepage</u>[121] and <u>The African-American Mosaic: A Library of Congress Resource Guide for the Study of Black History and Culture</u>[122]. Language diversity is the focus of <u>The National Center for Research on Cultural Diversity and Second Language Learning</u>[123]. Hyperlinks of this server, the Web page <u>Project Briefs</u>[124] and <u>gopher link</u>[125], look at the roles of the community and home in cultural diversity. The Ethnic Studies department of the University of Southern California provides some diversity hyperlinks through the university's library resources. One example is <u>Asian American magazines and periodicals</u>[126], which provides on-line documents and lists of bibliographies by ethnic group. The Black Graduate Students group at the Georgia Institute of Technology has put together a large index page, the <u>Universal Black Pages</u>[127], an attempt to hyperlink all pan-African home pages. <u>*Meanderings*</u>[128] is an on-line magazine with an African-American perspective on politics and current issues. Finally, a social work-specific site, <u>Internationalizing Social Work Education</u>[129], looks at social work from the perspective of other cultures.

Disabilities

Persons with disabilities seek services that allow them to achieve their full potential. Social workers must understand and empathize with the disabled and with their quest for full membership in society. Advocates for the physically challenged are active on the Internet.

Again, the Internet provides social workers with a way to access such information. Some sites are <u>disABILITY Resources on the Internet</u>[130] and <u>Cornucopia of Disability Information</u>[131]. Also, <u>Galaxynet</u>[132] maintains a searchable index page for easy access to information concerning specific disabilities. Another gopher[133] offers downloadable text files on a wide range of disabilities.

Gender and Aging

WomensNet[134] is the home page of a Web site providing information about resources for women. Also see the section "Feminism" above. Two sites to find information on aging are the University of Toronto Center for Studies of Aging [135] and The Medicare Handbook[136].

RESEARCH AND PRACTICE HYPERLINKS

Solutions to social problems may require social workers to intervene in the lives of others. Such interventions ultimately must be evaluated for effectiveness, and that activity constitutes the research component of social work. The practice component adds issues of values and ethics to simple effectiveness analyses, making the practice of social work a delicate balance between science and humanism. Social workers in the field are usually so severely constrained by time that they find it difficult to keep up with the latest research. Here is where the Internet can help those social workers by making it easier for them to economically (in terms of both time and money) access the latest data pertinent to their practices. The Internet can be a link between social work researchers and social work practitioners, assisting social workers in choosing the best intervention at the proper systems level for a particular client. The sites below link data, research, professional discussions, and other information about specific social problems and may help you more easily find the information you need to be an effective social worker.

General Hyperlinks

Yahoo Inc. provides a general pointer page of Public Interest Organizations[137] that can serve as a hyperlink to many organizations involved in alleviating particular problems. The Consortium for International Earth Science Information Network's Dataset Guides[138] review a wide range of datasets on many topics of concern. These datasets can also be accessed through the Gateway[139] page.

Census information is one of the best tools for researching social problems and the Internet makes census searches easy. The Census Look Up Home Page[140] hyperlinks to Lawrence Berkeley Laboratory #1[141], Lawrence Berkeley Laboratory #2[142], and the U.S. Bureau of the Census[143]. That on-line information covers a wide range of data about poverty, housing, education, family demographics, culture, ethnicity, child care, economic patterns, and much more. Census data can be retrieved at several different geographic levels including state, county, town, and census tract. With a little practice you can even gather information about specific neighborhoods easily. The days of laboriously reviewing census datasets in library stacks are over. Using the Internet, you can quickly put together a demographic profile of any community.

Other sources of general information include the University of Windsor's Social Work News and Announcements[144] and Web Servers for Social Workers[145]. Computer Uses in Social Work[146], a web page presented by Beena Choksi at the University of Illinois at Urbana-Champaign, discusses the role of computers in the practice of social work.

Crime

The Bureau of Justice Statistics Files[147] is a gopher with a large selection of resource files and papers on crime and the criminal justice system. Davis Police On-Line[148] is a municipal police department link to the community through the Internet. This site shows community crime statistics, citizen alerts, and other crime-prevention information. Deterrence is the focus of the on-line article The Value of Civilian Arms Possession as Deterrent to Crime or Defense Against Crime[149]. The Assault Prevention Information Network[150] includes hyperlinks to U.S. Justice Department statistics, the Partners Against Violence program, and the full text of the recent crime bill. Another law, the Violent Crime Control and Law Enforcement Act of 1994[151], can be viewed on-line, too. An electronic newsletter, Criminal Justice–The Americas[152], can keep you informed about criminal justice. An example of neighborhood information on crime prevention is the Maryland Community Crime Prevention Institute World Wide Web Information Source[153].

Domestic Violence

Domestic violence is a serious social work problem as reflected by the recent dramatic increases in reports of child abuse and other domestic violence. Internet resources available to social workers dealing with this problem include the Web pages National Child Rights Alliance[154], Child Quest International[155] (to assist in locating missing children), the Kempe National Center for the Prevention and Treatment of Child Abuse and Neglect[156], and Safety Net: Domestic Violence Resources[157].

Inadequate Housing

Safe housing and neighborhoods are fundamental requirements for
increasing quality of life. Many Internet sites address this need. For
instance, the <u>Community and Urban Development Descriptions</u>[158] Web
page hyperlinks to resources and listservers in this area. Information
about homelessness and ways to help the homeless can be found on the
page <u>54 Ways You Can Help The Homeless</u>[159]. Community services block
grant information can be found at the server <u>Search the Community
Services Block Grant</u>[160]. An innovative approach to housing can be
reviewed at the gopher <u>The Cohousing Archives</u>[161]. The gopher site
<u>Institute for the Study of Civic Values</u>[162] looks into the requirements for
building communities and highlights successful examples of such projects.
The Department of Housing and Urban Development (HUD) maintains a
gopher <u>Housing and Urban Development</u>[163]. The Web page <u>Empowerment
Zones and Enterprise Communities</u> [164] is another source of information for
both rural and urban communities. HUD also has a <u>searchable data-
base</u>[165] for agency information, grants, and procurements. The <u>Low
Income Home Energy Assistance</u> (LIHEAP)[166] gopher site explains and
offers information about the program.

Poverty

Poverty has always been one of the chief concerns of social work. The
Internet provides a great deal of information on the causes and effects of
poverty. One place to start is the <u>Poverty and Welfare gopher</u>[167], which
provides documents on the impact of poverty on people's lives. <u>The
Green Book</u>[168] is an electronic book-sized collection of data about a wide
range of government entitlement programs including welfare, child
support, social security, and others. The *Green Book* is published under the
jurisdiction of the Committee on Ways and Means of the House of
Representatives. The data are also available through a Department of
Health and Human Services <u>FTP</u>[169] site.

The <u>Goodwill Industries of Southeast Wisconsin, Inc.</u>[170] is an
example of a well-known community agency that has gone on-line to
provide information about its services. The home page <u>HungerWeb</u>[171]
addresses hunger and poverty, including methods for reducing those
problems. The home page <u>Human Factor</u>[172] focuses on how it will create
an Internet presence for other social service agencies for a fee.

Child Care

The gopher <u>National Network for Child Care</u> (NNCC) [173] provides access to information on research, discussions, and programs to enhance child care environments. The Web page <u>A Place for the Whole Family to Heal</u>[174] is an example of a multipurpose family resource center. The <u>Children, Youth and Family Consortium</u>[175] gopher is a searchable site for research on families, their problems, and relevant programs. This site includes an archive of postings from related discussion groups, newsletters, papers, and presentations. The <u>Fathernet</u>[176] and <u>Fatherhood and Fatherlessness</u>[177] pages provide research on the care roles of fathers. The <u>Head Start</u>[178] gopher describes project Head Start and is searchable. <u>At-Risk Child Care</u>[179] and <u>Aid to Families With Dependent Children</u>[180] gophers are also searchable. <u>Parents Helping Parents</u>[181] is a home page that links parents to many useful resources and discussions on issues that concern parents and children. The <u>Bay Area Single Parents Club</u>[182] is a Web page set up for single parents to meet other adults for dating and social events.

Mental Health

Social workers' roles in mental health settings vary--therapist, advocate, and manager of resources.The following hyperlinks are starting points for exploring the issue of mental health.

The Web site <u>All About Personal Growth</u>[183] provides information on neurolinguistic programming, hypnosis, and time line therapy. The Web page <u>Cognitive Therapy</u>[184], whose author was motivated by a friend's condition, reviews therapeutic approaches in cognitive therapy. Another Web page, <u>Psychlink</u>[185], provides information on some of the more common psychopathologies. The <u>Human Services Research Institute</u>[186] maintains a gopher site dedicated to archiving postings from listservers related to research information on mental health systems, papers, and hyperlinks to other servers. This site focuses on the area of health care reform, and the criminal justice system as they relate to mental health. Its archives also contains sections on outcome research in mental health as well as assistance in research design and implementation.

Drug Abuse and Chemical Dependency

Drug abuse and chemical dependency are two common problems that social workers face in their practices. The Internet offers many resources for drug abuse and chemical dependency. For instance, <u>Al-Anon andAlateen</u>[187] have a Web site that provides an overview of these self-help programs. The Big Book[188] is now on-line. Many consider the principles outlined in its pages to be the most effective recovery program ever designed for chemical dependency. The Friends of Bill W's[189] Web page offers a perspective on Alcoholics Anonymous. Cocaine Anonymous[190] maintains a home page that links to both an assessment of addiction and a large list of telephone numbers for help in recovery. The state of Texas has a human services site, the Substance Abuse Resource Directory[191]. The well-known treatment resource Phoenix House[192] maintains a home page. It also provides an automatic electronic mail service for service information requests, a photo display, and a way to make donations.

Discrimination

The National Empowerment Center[193] maintains a gopher site with FTP access to all of its text data over a wide range of empowerment difficulties including housing, employment, disabilities, and mental health. It also has a listing of (800) telephone numbers for information on and assistance in these and many other areas. On-line papers reviewing discrimination in housing as well as the role played by Housing and Urban Development Department programs can be found at HandsNet Weekly Digest[194]. The searchable gopher of the Administration for Native Americans (ANA)[195] provides information about the agency that directs governmental efforts to increase economic well-being in the Native American community. To encourage full participation by women in society, the Global Fund for Women[196] makes grant resources available to women. The Human Rights Web Home Page[197] is a resource for those interested in promoting human rights. For a list of books categorized by types of discrimination and history, see Racial Discrimination & Prejudice[198].

Illness and Death

Traditionally, hospitals hired social workers to assist in the care of patients because hospital stays and recuperation periods could be very lengthy, and long readjustment periods were required. Today, social workers practicing in health care are more focused on prevention, delivery of services, and health care financing reform. The following sites reflect social work's contemporary interests in this field. Preventing HIV and AIDS: What You Can Do[199] is a site that gives information on AIDS prevention at the individual level as well as news. The Centers for Disease Control[200] and the National Health Information Center[201] are statistical and informational sites concerned with the nation's health.

Emotional Support Resources [202] is an extensive Web page listing support resources based on specific health care issues. Health Care[203] is a similar site, but it is gopher–based. Medicine, Western Hemisphere [204] is lengthy, too, and will hyperlink you to medical schools and other health centers. The Columbia University Health Service[205] Web page has a searchable archive of health care advice, Go Ask Alice[206].

The Zen Hospice Project[207] explores the process of death and dying and offers information and hyperlinks to other, similar sites, including the Crisis Brings Grief[208] Web page.

Disabilities

Internet resources for understanding the needs of persons with disabilities is a rapidly growing area of the Internet. For instance, Evan Kemp Associates, Inc.[209] is a commercial Web site that offers general information, consumer information, and a newsletter for the physically challenged. Michigan State University's Deaf Gopher [210] makes on-line journals, resources, and information available. Gallaudet University Information Server[211] provides similar services. An Equal Access to Software and Information[212] is another gopher and is dedicated to promoting accessible computers and computing. Canine Companions for Independence[213] is an example of a nonprofit center explaining how to apply for its services. The Trace Center[214] is a gopher site of a group working in the area of technology and disabilities that makes available research, publications, and computer information for the challenged. The WIDnet List of Disability Listservs[215] is a gopher site that provides addresses of many discussion groups related to issues of the challenged.

SOCIAL WORK LISTSERVERS

The following is an alphabetical list of listservers providing discussions specific to social work. Please see Chapter 3 for information about listservers and how to subscribe to mailing lists. See also THE LIST: Discussion Lists for Social Workers[216], a Web page of social work discussion lists.

ABUSE-L
Family violence
listserv@ubvm.cc.buffalo.edu

AMERICANS WITH DISABILITIES ACT LIST (ADA)
Discussion of ADA
Majordomo@counterpoint.com

CJUST-L
Criminal justice
listserv@cunyvm.cuny.edu

COHOUSING-L
Discussion group for the issue of cohousing
listserv@uci.com

COMMUNITY ECONOMIC DEVELOPMENT DISCUSSION LIST (CED-NET)
Community economic development
majordomo@sfu.ca

CSOCWORK
Canadian Social Workers
listserv@pdomain.uwindsor.ca

CUSSNET-LIST
Computer use in social sciences
listserv@stat.com

DEAF-MAGAZINE
Weekly magazine for deaf persons
listserv@listserv.deaf-magazine.org

EAP
Employee assistance programs
majordomo@utopia.pinsight.com

EJINTVIO
Intimate violence
listserv@uriacc.uri.edu

EVALTEN
Evaluation methodology and statistics discussion list
listserv@sjuvm.stjohns.edu

FEMISA
Feminism
listproc@cfs.colorado.edu

FEMSW-L
Feminist social work
listproc@moose.uvm.edu

HEALTHRE
Health care reform
listserv@ukcc.uky.edu

HOMELESS
Needs of the homeless
listproc@csf.colorado.edu

INTSOCWORK
International social work
list@nisw.org.uk

OUTCOMETEN
Outcomes of mental health intervention
listsersv@sjuvm.stjohns.edu

METHODS-L
Computer use in the social sciences
listserv@stat.Com

PSYCHO-THERAPY
Psychotherapy
majordomo@netcom.com

SCIOFSLW
Philosophy of social work
istproc@lists.vcu.edu

SCWK-L
Social work students
maiser@ist01.ferris.edu

SWMG-LIST
Measurements
listserv@stat.com

TRAVABLE
Travel for disabled persons
listserv@sjuvm.stjohns.edu

UNCJIN
United Nations criminal justice information network
listserv@albany.edu

CONCLUSION

We stated at the beginning of this chapter that the potential of social work to use the Internet to further its goals has not been fully realized. In the future, social work's involvement with the Internet will grow. An extensive social work virtual community will develop and hyperlink. Questions still remain, however. How will technology affect clients? Will technology make social work more caring and humane? Or will clients become lost in a virtual bureaucracy the way some clients are in paper bureaucracies? Will computers increase or decrease the empathic social work change process? Will computers give social workers more or less time for face-to-face interaction with clients? One answer to all of these questions is the same as for older questions in social work. Namely, the use of the Internet in social work research and practice must fall under the guidance of the tried–and–true values and ethics that have guided the profession since its start.

NOTES

1.   http://www.social.uiuc.edu/

2.   http://www.social.uiuc.edu/home/outside/swschool.htm

3.   http://www.csw.utk.edu/

4.   http://www.csw.utk.edu/us-sch.html

5.   http://www.csw.utk.edu/intl-sch.html

6.   http://mathcat.cnrs.humboldt.edu/sw/swhome.html

7.   http://mathcat.cnrs.humboldt.edu/sw/aboutsw/profession2.html

8.   http://www.health.swt.edu/SOWK.html

9.   http://www.health.swt.edu/SOWKProfession.html

10.   http://cwis.usc.edu/Univ/entries/socialwork.html

11.   gopher://cwis.usc.edu:70/00/University_Information/Academic_Departments/Social_Work/School_of_Social_Work_1994-1996/quotes

12.   http://http.bsd.uchicago.edu/~r-tell/socwork.html

13.   http://www-college.uchicago.edu/

14. http://info.rutgers.edu/Academics/Catalogs/socialwork/volume.4.shtml

15. http://www.uwindsor.ca/faculty/socsci/socwk/index.html

16. gopher://english.hss.cmu.edu/0F-2%3A1255%3AAdams-Poor%20Relief%20

17. http://fount.journalism.wisc.edu/olw/welfare/welfare.html

18. http://fount.journalism.wisc.edu/olw/welfare/gordon.html

19. http://www.ssa.gov/history/history.html

20. http://www.ssa.gov/

21. http://lcweb2.loc.gov/amhome.html

22. http://lcweb.loc.gov/exhibits/African.American/wpa.html

23. http://scarlett.libs.uga.edu/darchive/hargrett/wpa/wpa.html

24. http://www.traveller.com/~hrweb/history.html

25. http://webcorp.com/civilrights/index.htm

26. http://ssw01.ab.umd.edu/welcome.htm

27. http://ssw01.ab.umd.edu/ethics.htm

28. http://ssw01.ab.umd.edu/comm-ass.htm

29. http://falcon.depaul.edu:80/ethics/

30. http://134.184.35.101/SYSTHEOR.html

31. http://galaxy.einet.net/galaxy/Community/Environment/Environmental-
     Activism/wayne-pendley/plankeep.html

32. http://www.econet.apc.org/lcv/scorecard.html

33. http://csf.colorado.edu/ipe/index.ht

34. http://falcon.cc.ukans.edu/~pthomas/national.html

35. http://www.matisse.net/politics/activist/activist.html

36. gopher://aclu.org:6601/

37. http://www2.hawaii.edu/suremath/howTo.html

38. http://www.interaccess.com/users/edmc/

39. http://www.lafayette.edu/allanr/gateway.html

40. http://www.gasou.edu/psychweb/psychweb.htm

41. http://now.org/now/home.html

42. http://sosig.esrc.bris.ac.uk/Subjects/feminism.html

43. http://sunsite.unc.edu/cheryb/women/wshome.html

44. http://worcester.lm.com/women/women.html

45. http://ificinfo.health.org/homepage.htm

46. http://ificinfo.health.org/eatpreg.htm

47. http://obg.med.uth.tmc.edu/home.html

48. http://obg.med.uth.tmc.edu/maternal/mat.htm

49. gopher://tinman.mes.umn.edu.:4242/11/ChildCare/ChildDevel

50. http://pedinfo.wustl.edu/PEDINFO_WWW:index.html

51. http://yellodino.safe-t-child.com/

52. http://www.cityscape.co.uk/users/ad88/arch.htm

53. http://education.indiana.edu/cas/cashmpg.html

54. http://www.med.umich.edu/aacap/panic.disorders.html

55. http://weber.u.washington.edu/hiprc/iscaip2.html

56. http://www.med.umich.edu/aacap/facts.index.html

57. http://www.cityscape.co.uk/users/ad88/crises.htm

58. http://freenet3.scri.fsu.edu:81/ht-free/wwme.html

59. http://peewee.chinalake.navy.mil:80/computational_sciences/staff/carey/JME/index.html

60. gopher://gopher.acf.dhhs.gov:70/1

61. gopher://uclink.berkeley.edu:3030/

62. http://info.asu.edu/asu-cwis/epaa/welcome.html

63. gopher://info.asu.edu:70/11/asu-cwis/epaa/archives

64. http://ilc.ecs.soton.ac.uk/chst/ctiinf.htm

65. http://ilc.ecs.soton.ac.uk/chst/procare.htm

66. http://www.ssa.gov/hcfa/hcfahp2.html

67. http://www.nlm.nih.gov/

68. http://www-hsw.anglia.ac.uk/

69. http://hinet.medlib.arizona.edu/~teytan/ATPM.html

70. gopher://gopher.os.dhhs.gov:70/11/dhhs/phs

71. http://www.os.dhhs.gov/

72. gopher://csf.Colorado.EDU:70/00/psn/ppn-archives/childrens-health.unicef-94

73. http://www.who.ch/

74. http://www.cityscape.co.uk/users/ad88/resuk.htm

75. http://www.aronson.com/clients/aronson/Int/psychints.html

76. http://www.cityscape.co.uk/users/ad88/psych.htm

77. http://csbh.mhv.net/%7Egrohol/web.htm

78. http://www.mindspring.com/~rtbrain/hands.html

79. http://www.emory.edu/CARTER_CENTER/hope.htm

80. http://www.csn.net:80/ncl/

81. http://www.libertynet.org/community/phila/natl.html

82. http://www.libertynet.org/community/phila/nol.html

83. http://www.fortnet.org/FORTNET/index_g.html

84. http://asa.ugl.lib.umich.edu/chdocs/nonprofits/nonprofits.html#toc

85. http://www.ai.mit.edu/people/ellens/non.html

86. http://www.ai.mit.edu/people/ellens/Non/online.html

87. http://www.ai.mit.edu/people/ellens/non-meta.html

88. http://www.mhmr.texas.gov/

89. http://hal.fmhi.usf.edu/

90. http://www.ca.gov/

91. http://www.os.dhhs.gov/

92. http://www.civeng.carleton.ca/SiSpain/social/menu.html

93. http://www.usit.net/public/CAPO/wrfullab.html

94. http://www.meer.net/users/taylor/index.htm

95. http://www.meer.net/users/taylor/urbanmin.htm

96. http://www.princeton.edu/~meneghin/oasis/oasis.html

97. http://saturn.colorado.edu:8080/Christian/Churches/churches.html

98. http://www.usit.net/public/capo/premise/95/feb/grnt1.html

99. http://justice2.usdoj.gov/

100. http://gopher.usdoj.gov/bureaus/bop.html

101. http://gopher.usdoj.gov/bureaus/bureaus.html

102. http://www.usdoj.gov/fbi/fbi.html

103. http://www.usdoj.gov/fbi/programs.html

104. http://www.ustreas.gov/treasury/bureaus/bureaus.html

105. gopher://uacsc2.albany.edu/11/newman

106. http://www.rand.org/

107. http://www.rand.org/hot/

108. gopher://gopher.brook.edu/

109. http://www.hhh.umn.edu/

110. http://www.hhh.umn.edu/Archives/archives.html

111. http://policy.net/capweb/congress.html

112. http://main.street.net/government/gov-gate.html

113. http://policy.net/policy/alerts.html

114. http://www.cato.org/main/

115. http://www.cato.org/main/programs.html

116. http://www.cato.org/main/search.html

117. http://hoover.stanford.edu/www/Welcome.html

118. http://hoover.stanford.edu/www/newsWin1995.html

119. gopher://link.tsl.texas.gov:70/11/.dir/

120. http://minerva.cis.yale.edu/~davidp/race.html

121. http://www.lainet.com/~joejones/index.htm

122. http://lcweb.loc.gov/exhibits/African.American/Intro.html

123. http://zzyx.ucsc.edu/Cntr/cntr.html

124. http://zzyx.ucsc.edu/Cntr/cntr.projects.html

125. gopher://lmrinet.gse.ucsb.edu:70/11/natcnt/Research%20reports

126. http://www.usc.edu/users/help/flick/Reference/asian_amer_mag.html

127. http://www.gatech.edu/bgsa/blackpages/info.html

128. http://www.webcom.com/~sppg/meanderings/me.shtml

129. http://caster.ssw.upenn.edu/~restes/intl.html

130. http://www.eskimo.com/~jlubin/disabled

131. gopher://val-dor.cc.buffalo.edu/1

132. http://galaxy.einet.net/GJ/disabilities.html

133. gopher://handicap.shel.isc-br.com:70/11/ftp/pub

134. gopher://gopher.igc.apc.org:70/11/women

135. http://library.utoronto.ca/www/aging/depthome.html

136. http://www.ssa.gov/hcfa/handbook/hndbk.html

137. http://www.yahoo.com/Economy/Organizations/Public_Interest_Groups/

138. http://www.ciesin.org/DS/dataset-home.html

139. http://www.ciesin.org/gateway/gw-home.html

140. http://cedr.lbl.gov/cdrom/doc/lookup_doc.html

141. http://cedr.lbl.gov/cdrom/lookup

142. http://bigsur.lbl.gov/cdrom/lookup

143. http://www.census.gov/cdrom/lookup

144. http://server.uwindsor.ca:8000/~bobgc/news.html

145. http://server.uwindsor.ca:8000/~bobgc/webs.html

146. http://www.ed.uiuc.edu/edpsy-387/beena-choksi/cswfin.html

147. gopher://justice2.usdoj.gov/1/ojp/bjs

148. http://wheel.dcn.davis.ca.us/~dpd/homepage.html

149. http://www.cs.cmu.edu/~karl/firearms/crime-deterrent.html

150. gopher://mlink.hh.lib.umich.edu:70/11/social/Crime

151. http://gopher.usdoj.gov/crime/crime.html

152. http://www.acsp.uic.edu/oicj/pubs.htm

153. http://midget.towson.edu:8001/MDCP.HTML

154. http://www.ai.mit.edu/people/ellens/NCRA/ncra.html

155. http://www.omega.com/adima/bands/child_quest/cqmain.html

156. http://nhicnt.health.org/htmlgen/htmlgen.exe/Entry?HRCode='HR1106'

157. http://www.interport.net/~asherman/dv.html

158. http://asa.ugl.lib.umich.edu/chdocs/nonprofits/urbandev.html#cednet

159. http://ecosys.drdr.virginia.edu/ways/54.html

160. gopher://spike.acf.dhhs.gov:70/11/ACFPrograms/CSBG

161. gopher://garnet.berkeley.edu:1250/11/.welfare/.housing

162. gopher://hey.Internet.com:2400/11/cdiscv/

163. gopher://gopher.hud.gov/

164. gopher://cyfer.esusda.gov:70/11/ace/ezec

165. http://web.fie.com/web/fed/hud/#search

166. gopher://spike.acf.dhhs.gov:70/11/ACFPrograms/LIHEAP

167. gopher://garnet.berkeley.edu:1250/11/.welfare/.poverty

168. http://www.os.dhhs.gov/0/aspe/green_book/gbpage.html

169. ftp://ftp.os.dhhs.gov/pub/

170. http://www.spectracom.com/goodwill/

171. http://netspace.org/hungerweb/WHP/browsers.html

172. http://www.human.com/services.html

173. gopher://tinman.mes.umn.edu.:4242/11/ChildCare

174. http://nisus.sfusd.k12.ca.us/community/rmcback.html

175. gopher://gopher-cec.mes.umn.edu:80/11/

176. http://www.npr.gov/NPR/html_NPR/icsn.html

177. http://www.vix.com/pub/men/nofather/nodad.html

178. gopher://spike.acf.dhhs.gov:70/11/ACFPrograms/HeadStart

179. gopher://spike.acf.dhhs.gov:70/11/ACFPrograms/At-RiskChildCare

180. http://www.lao.ca.gov/chc5180.html

181. http://www.portal.com/~cbntmkr/php.html

182. http://www.apk.net/cupid/baspc/index.html

183. http://www.aloha.com/~mind/index.html

184. http://baby.indstate.edu:80/msattler/sci-tech/med/psych/cognitive-therapy.html

185. http://www.realtime.net/~mmjw/

186. gopher://ftp.std.com/11/nonprofits/hsri

187. http://solar.rtd.utk.edu/~al-anon/

188. http://uts.cc.utexas.edu/~clyde/BillW/BB_Introduction.html

189. http://uts.cc.utexas.edu/~clyde/BillW/Intro.html

190. http://www.ca.org/index.html

191. gopher://link.tsl.texas.gov:70/11/.dir/drugal94.dir

192. http://www.riverhope.org/phoenix/

193. gopher://gopher.std.com:70/11/nonprofits/empowerment-ctr

194. http://www.igc.apc.org/handsnet/hn.weekly.digest/index.html

195. gopher://spike.acf.dhhs.gov:70/00/ACFPrograms/ANA/ana.txt

196. http://www.ai.mit.edu/people/ellens/gfw.html

197. http://www.traveller.com/~hrweb/hrweb.html

198. http://www.usc.edu/users/help/flick/Reference/race_discrim_main.html

199. http://bianca.com/lolla/politics/aids/aids.html

200. http://www.cdc.gov/

201. http://nhic-nt.health.org/odphp.htm

202. http://asa.ugl.lib.umich.edu/chdocs/support/emotion.html

203. gopher://zeus.esusda.gov:70/11/initiatives/dfh

204. http://sprawl.sensemedia.net:8080/people/scott/036.htm

205. http://www.cc.columbia.edu:80/cu/healthwise/

206. http://www.cc.columbia.edu:80/cu/healthwise/

207. http://www.well.com/user/devaraja/Links.html

208. http://www.dgsys.com/~tgolden/1grief.html

209. http://disability.com/

210. gopher://burrow.cl.msu.edu:70/11/msu/dept/deaf

211. gopher://gallux.gallaudet.edu:70/1

212. gopher://sjuvm.stjohns.edu:70/11/disabled/easi

213. http://grunt.berkeley.edu/cci.html

214. gopher://trace.waisman.wisc.edu/

215. gopher://sjuvm.stjohns.edu:70/11/disabled/widlist/wid-dis

216. http://lamar.colostate.edu/~mcmurray/lists.html

12

Political Science

CHAPTER PREVIEW

The Internet is changing how all the social sciences conduct research and study. Political science, the study of political processes and governing, is where that change has been most pronounced. As this chapter shows, political scientists now have access to a tremendous number of on-line resources, including legislation tracking, governmental services, and political parties, plus the usual assortment of list servers and news groups.

If democracy functions best with open information exchange, communication, and debate, then the future of democracy should be assured. The Jacksonian model of democracy, whereby individual citizens have a stronger voice, may at last be upon us. Cheaper and more powerful computers, friendlier software, and more widespread Internet access have made it possible for nearly anyone to join national political debates. Indeed, the Internet itself has become a new political medium.

POLITICAL SCIENCE AND THE INTERNET

Several Internet sites exist where the relationship between politics and the Internet are discussed, and they make a good introduction to this chapter. See, for instance, The Political Scientist's Guide to the Internet[1], a review of the relationship between political scientists and the Internet. The page also contains hyperlinks to on-line commentaries like "Why It Is Important for Political Scientists to Use Internet Resources" and to research sites. The changes in political processes caused by the Internet are discussed in an on-line article by Mark Poster[2]. One page, The Berman Senate Judiciary Testimony May 1[3], concerns the issue of freedom of speech on the Internet and raises some constitutional questions. Another Web page of interest here is the The Political Participation Project[4], which studies how computer networks are affecting political participation in the United States. Clearly, politics are influencing the Internet and vice versa.

GENERAL POLITICAL SCIENCE HYPERLINKS

The Web page The World-Wide Web Virtual Library: Research Resources[5] is a list of general hyperlinks in political science. Northwestern University's 1[6] is a gopher serving practically the same purpose. Another page, divided into areas of political interest, is Government/Law/Politics[7], which serves as a general index to politics and to government Internet resources. The Christian Coalition's Web page[8] provides another list of political science hyperlinks. The American Political Science Association maintains a gopher[9] with many hyperlinks to political science resources. Finally, the on-line journal JPAM[10] may prove useful as a starting point for your searches.

POLITICAL SCIENCE DEPARTMENT HYPERLINKS

The Web page POLS Guide: Political Science Departments[11] is a list of on-line political science departments throughout the U.S. This page is interactive in that it allows you to complete a form in order to add unlisted departments. A related page, POLS Guide: Research Institutions[12], allows you to find research institutes in political science. The PSA Home Page[13] of the Political Science Association lists departments of politics and political science in the United Kingdom and the U.S. The Canadian Political Science Association[14] has also recently begun to publish a Web page. The American Political Science Association maintains a gopher[15].

POLITICAL SCIENCE SUBFIELD HYPERLINKS

Political Theory

Political theory focuses on why certain forms of government arise and serves to connect political science to history and philosophy. The Web page POLS Guide: On-line Documents[16] contains the text of many of the political writings of Thomas Jefferson, Plato, Karl Marx, and others. A gopher serving the same function is the American Political Theory[17] with hyperlinks to historical texts, documents, laws, and other resources. A Web page[18] lists articles like McCutchen's "Mistakes, Precedent, and the Rise of the Administrative State: Toward a Constitutional Theory of the Second Best," a discussion about the role of administrative agencies in government.

Politics and Political Behavior

Resources on politics and the mechanics of government are a rapidly expanding part of the Internet. For U.S. Politics, see Yahoo–Government:Politics:Parties and Groups[19], a list of Web pages for American political parties of all sizes. The Right Side of the Web[20] and The Left Side of the Web[21] specialize in conservative and liberal political philosophies, respectively. The Republican Web Central Home Page[22] and the Democratic Party Web Page[23] will each allow you to explore information from the two main political parties. The Democratic National Committee[24] also has a Web page that will provide information on that party's platform and stance on issues. Information on third parties and other lesser–known political movements is more easily found on the Internet than elsewhere. Examples include United We Stand America[25], Libertarian Republicans[26], Republican Liberty Caucus[27], and Libertarian Party[28]. Politics Story[29] provides a Web page discussing the Internet and how political parties interact with it. It also contains hyperlinks to other pages on politics. C-SPAN's Public Affairs Servers Hotlinks[30] covers the spectrum of politics and has hyperlinks to presidential campaign organizations.

For information on political parties outside the U.S. hyperlink to Political Parties Around the World[31], a page that will connect you to several international political parties and movements.

Public Policy and Administration

The on-line journal JPAM[32] is a good place to begin searches on public policy and administration. The Policy Analysis and Management (APPAM) gopher[33] is a professional organization dedicated to blending the talents of political science for analysis bearing on public concerns. The Institute for Policy Innovation[34] is a nonpartisan organization seeking solutions to today's public policy problems. The Quaker–sponsored site Peaceweb[35] is a peace activist Web site.

Comparative Government

Comparative government experts usually focus on the comparison of national governments. No specific Internet sites dedicated to comparative government were found. But primary information can be found at sites like the International Relations Association[36], an on-line institute for the study of international politics, law, conventions, and bodies of government. A similar site is the gopher Other International[37], which lists gopher sites maintained by international governmental organizations. The

International Open Government on WWW[38] page connects you to international governmental sites listed by country. See, for example, the French Presidential Election: 1995[39], which provides information on that political campaign. Another such page is the Banque de Données Socio-Politiques (BDSP)[40], whose goals are to store data on French political science, sociology, and history.

UNITED STATES GOVERNMENT

General Searches

Much of the government of the United States is on-line, thus providing easy access for citizens with Internet connections. The complexity of the federal government can make for difficult searching, but some sites help simplify the search task. For instance, the FedWorld Home Page[41] provides hyperlinks to large areas of the federal government through an alphabetical list of subjects. Another more specialized server is the Federal Information Center - United States Government[42], a Web page that primarily directs requests for information concerning the federal government to toll-free telephone numbers. Home Page Washington's General Government Index[43] is a general hyperlink to both the government in Washington state and the federal bureaucracy. The Web page of the Office of Technology Assessment[44] is of particular interest because this office is responsible for understanding the Internet and its uses in government. However, Congress may eliminate that office in order to trim the federal budget.

Branches of Government

Executive Branch.   A good starting point for executive branch searches is the Web page Executive Branch Agencies - The President's Cabinet[45], which hyperlinks to all the cabinet departments and to more specific areas. Another Web page hyperlinks to the Independent Federal Agencies and Commissions[46] and is also a good place to find a wide selection of governmental information from within the executive branch. For example, Welcome to GSA[47] is the home page of the General Services Administration. The White House itself maintains a home page, Welcome to the White House[48].

Legislative Branch.   Congress is also on-line, but more spottily so than the executive branch. Some senators, representatives, and even congressional committees have their own Web pages. Soon, you may regularly participate in "town meetings" with your legislators on-line.

For Senate information, see the main <u>Senate gopher</u>[49]. If you know the Senate committee you are seeking, try the index gopher <u>Committee</u>[50].

The House of Representatives appears to offer more on-line services than the Senate, with numerous committees maintaining their own servers. The House of Representatives's home page, <u>U.S. House Of Representatives - Home Page</u>[51], hyperlinks to other House Web pages and to gopher servers for committees. Another <u>gopher</u>[52] lists the on-line House committees and subcommittees. For example, the <u>Web page</u>[53] is the home page for the House transportation committee. Other committees on-line include the <u>House Committee on Resources</u>[54], the <u>House Committee on Government Reform & Oversight</u>[55], and the <u>Judiciary Committee</u>[56]. To track legislation as it relates to particular states, see this <u>searchable gopher</u>[57]. To find the electronic mail addresses or other directory information for specific House members or committees, use the Web page <u>U.S. House of Representatives - Who's Who</u>[58].

Judicial Branch.   The third branch of government, the judiciary, has a much smaller Internet presence, befitting its smaller size. Supreme Court decisions can be found on the gopher <u>Judiciary</u>[59], which hyperlinks to court decisions and the U.S. Judicial code and is searchable.

International Affairs

International affairs–related servers are well represented on the Internet. The Internet has the potential to change the nature of international relations by putting citizens of every country in direct communication with each other. This type of activity will only increase as the Internet becomes more global and culturally diverse.

The United Nations' home page, <u>United Nations</u>[60], provides information on current U.N. activities. The <u>IANWeb -- International Affairs Network Web</u>[61] is dedicated to the study of international affairs. The <u>World-Wide Web Virtual Library: Research Resources</u>[62] is an international affairs index with hyperlinks listed by subject. An example of a specialized resource is the <u>Norwegian Institute of International Affairs'</u>[63] gopher, which tracks international issues of interest to Norway.

Security and Defense.   International security is the focus of the gopher <u>SD Security Dialogs</u>[64], which includes access to the electronic journal *Security Dialogs*. The <u>Marshall Center's</u>[65] goal is to assist new European democracies in the areas of security and defense. Another view on the subject of international defense comes from the <u>Commission on</u>

Global Governance–Hosted by DEFSEC-Net[66], which authors the *Report of the Commission on Global Governance.*

Economic Policy.   Economic policy is a major concern in international affairs. Internet sites for economic policy include the International Political Economy Network[67], which studies the workings of the global economy. The Web sites Economics[68] and Trade[69] both deal with international policies in economics. The searchable Web site Multilaterals Project[70] makes available the texts and other instruments from international multilateral conventions. Another gopher[71] provides hyperlinks to sites concerning the study of global systems.

POLITICAL SCIENCE APPLICATIONS

Most of the URLs presented in this chapter thus far already relate to the application of political science. The following links contain data or hyperlinks that lead to more specific information on applying political science.
        Harvard University's Kennedy School of Government's CaseNet: Active Learning in International Affairs[72] was developed to teach political science through actual case studies. The site provides cases for instruction and instructional aids for teachers. SIPRI[73], an institute for the study of peace and military activity, demonstrates applications of political science. The North Atlantic Treaty Organization's gopher[74] is a European applications site. Interactive Democracy[75] can help you get involved in influencing political change directly because it makes it possible to send electronic mail to political and media leaders.

RESEARCH HYPERLINKS

General

The POLS Guide: Political Science Research[76] is a guide to on-line research in political science. It hyperlinks to libraries, academic departments, and political research institutes, and can be considered as a general index of research sites. More specific types of research sites are reviewed below.

Research Institutes

There exists a wide spectrum of think tanks for researching policy from various political perspectives. Some of the more influential institutes that are on-line include The Cato Institute[77], which conducts research from the libertarian political perspective, reviews research done by the institute, and lists on-line papers produced under its auspices. A conservative think tank, the Hoover Institute has a Web page[78] that hyperlinks to its newsletter and to other information about the institute and its research projects. Three other institutes that are on-line and offer data from their particular perspectives are The Hubert H. Humphrey Institute of Public Affairs[79], The Brookings Institute[80], and The Carter Center[81]. Still another such site is the Rand Corporation's RAND Home Page[82], which specializes in the study of defense and technology policy issues.

Archives

Many of the archives listed throughout this book can also apply to the work of political scientists. Here are some archives not cited elsewhere in this text. CLIO: The National Archives Information Server[83] provides much data about the history of the government, and some of the data is searchable. The House of Representatives Law Library can be accessed through the home page The House of Representatives–Internet Law Library - Welcome![84]. This site is divided into many parts, including The House of Representatives–Internet Law Library–Civil Liberties and Civil Rights[85], and The House of Representatives–Internet Law Library–Education and the Law[86].

Another general political science archive is the searchable gopher Political Data Archive[87]. To research government documents, try either the On-line Documents & Texts[88] or the National Archives Online Exhibit Hall[89].

Specialized Political Science Searches

Specialized political science searches are another way to find information. THOMAS: Legislative Information on the Internet[90] is a Web server that tracks legislation and also offers a tutorial on how laws are made. UniPress's W3's Will T. Bill[91] is a WAIS search tool for tracking legislation. Both of these sites will let you locate legislation by searching for key words, bill number, or author. Other congressional information can be tracked through a congressional information gopher[92]. All Things Political Sep 2[93] is a Web page that provides a variety of hyperlinks to politics, e-mail, polls, searches, and news groups.

OTHER POLITICAL SCIENCE RESOURCES

The *Congressional Quarterly*[94] gopher is the electronic version of the print publication of the same name. Discussion groups and news groups are heavily used in political science. The <u>Online Political Information Network</u>[95] is an index page to discussion and news groups. Political science listservers, organized by topic, can be found at another gopher[96]. <u>Vote Smart Web</u>[97] is an interesting and comprehensive page designed to help U.S. voters obtain information easily about candidates for political office.

CONCLUSION

The Internet is playing and will continue to play a major role in influencing politics and government functions. How will this influence grow? What roles should governments play? Will the Internet be regulated, censored, or restricted? Or should the Internet be totally free of governmental restrictions? These questions and others will be debated in the coming years, and the answers will be arrived at through public policy debates. Complicating the picture is the Internet's international scope. Regulating the Internet would require complex, difficult–to–enforce international agreements. We can safely predict that political scientists will continue to use the Internet as both a research tool and a place to conduct research. What we cannot forsee is how closely the future Internet will resemble the present one.

NOTES

1.   http://www.trincoll.edu/pols/home.html

2.   http://www.humanities.uci.edu/~human/history/faculty/poster_mark/writ-ings/democ.html

3.   http://www.cdt.org/policy/terrorism/internet_bomb.test.html

4.   http://www.ai.mit.edu:80/projects/ppp/home.html

5.   http://www.pitt.edu/~ian/ianres.html

6.   gopher://toby.scott.nwu.edu:70/1

7.   http://execpc.com/~dboals/govt.html

8.   http://cc.org/

9.   gopher://apsa.trenton.edu:70/11/

10.   gopher://cspo.queensu.ca:7070/11/APPAM/JPAM

11.   http://www.trincoll.edu/pols/research/departments.html

12.   http://www.trincoll.edu/pols/research/institutions.html

13.   http://www.lgu.ac.uk/psa/psa.html

14.   http://www.sfu.ca/igs/CPSA.html

15.   gopher://apsa.trenton.edu/

16.   http://www.trincoll.edu/pols/research/documents.html

17.   gopher://apsa.trenton.edu:70/11/

18.   http://www.law.cornell.edu/clr/mcc.htm

19.   http://www.yahoo.com/text/Government/Politics/Parties_and_Groups/

20.   http://www.clark.net/pub/jeffd/index.html

21.   http://paul.spu.edu/~sinnfein/progressive.html

22.   http://republicans.vt.com/

23.   http://www.webcom.com/~digitals/

24.   http://www.democrats.org/

25.   http://www.uwsa.org/

26.   http://www.colum.edu/user/bxl000/www/pyr/pyrdir.html

27.   http://w3.ag.uiuc.edu:80/liberty/rlc/index.html

28.   http://www.lp.org/lp/

29.   http://www.dgsys.com/~editors/politics.html

30.   http://www.c-span.org/congress/hotlinks.htm

31.   http://www.luna.nl/~benne/politics/parties.html

32.   gopher://apsa.trenton.edu:70/00/directory

33.   gopher://cspo.queensu.ca:7070/00/APPAM/vision.stmt

34.   http://ipi.metronet.com/

35.   http://www.ottawa.net/~peaceweb/

36.   http://www.acs.appstate.edu/dept/ira/

37.   gopher://marvin.stc.nato.int:70/11/Other_International

38.   http://www.lgu.ac.uk/lgudocs/psa/intgovt.html

39.   http://solcidsp.grenet.fr:8001/gbpres1.html

40. http://solcidsp.grenet.fr:8001/gbbdsp.html

41. http://www.fedworld.gov/

42. http://www.gsa.gov/et/fic-firs/fichome.htm

43. http://olympus.dis.wa.gov/www/gov.html

44. http://www.ota.gov/

45. http://www.whitehouse.gov/White_House/Cabinet/html/cabinet_links.html

46. http://www.whitehouse.gov/White_House/Independent_Agencies/html/independent_links.html

47. http://www.gsa.gov/default.htm

48. http://www.whitehouse.gov/

49. gopher://gopher.senate.gov/

50. gopher://ftp.senate.gov:70/11/committee

51. http://www.house.gov/

52. gopher://gopher.house.gov:70/1D-1%3A768%3AHouse%20Committee%20Information

53. http://www.house.gov/transportation/welcome.html

54. http://www.house.gov/resources/welcome.html

55. http://www.house.gov/reform/welcome.html

56. http://www.house.gov/judiciary/welcome.html

57. gopher://toby.scott.nwu.edu:70/1D-1%3A5799%3Astates

58. http://www.house.gov/Whoswho.html

59. gopher://marvel.loc.gov/11/federal/fedinfo/byagency/judiciary

60. http://www.un.org/

61. http://www.pitt.edu/~ian/

62. http://www.trincoll.edu/pols/research/documents.html

63. gopher://gopher.nato.int/11/secdef/nupi

64. gopher://marvin.stc.nato.int:70/11/secdef/prio/SD

65. http://www.marshall.adsn.int/marshall.html

66. http://www.fsk.ethz.ch/D-REOK/fsk/cgg/cgg_home.html

67. http://csf.Colorado.EDU:80/ipe/

68. gopher://cesar.unicamp.br/11/Papers/Economics

69.   http://ananse.irv.uit.no/trade_law/nav/trade.html

70.   http://www.tufts.edu/fletcher/multilaterals.html

71.   gopher://csf.colorado.edu/11/wsystems

72.   http://csf.Colorado.EDU/CaseNet/index.html

73.   http://www.sipri.se/

74.   gopher://gopher.nato.int/

75.   http://www.teleport.com:80/~pcllgn/id.html

76.   http://www.trincoll.edu/pols/research/research.html

77.   http://w3.ag.uiuc.edu/liberty/cato/index.html

78.   http://hoover.stanford.edu/

79.   http://www.hhh.umn.edu/

80.   gopher://gopher.brook.edu/

81.   http://www.emory.edu/CARTER_CENTER/homepage.htm

82.   http://www.rand.org/

83.   http://www.nara.gov/

84.   http://www.pls.com:8001/his/1.htm

85.   http://www.pls.com:8001/d2/kelli/httpd/htdocs/his/93.GBM

86.   http://www.pls.com:8001/d2/kelli/httpd/htdocs/his/99.GBM

87.   gopher://burrow.cl.msu.edu:70/11/internet/msu/pda

88.   http://www.trincoll.edu/pols/research/documents.html

89.   http://gopher.nara.gov:70/0/exhall/exhibits.html

90.   http://thomas.loc.gov/

91.   http://www.unipress.com/will-t-bill.html

92.   gopher://una.hh.lib.umich.edu:70/11/socsci/poliscilaw/uslegi

93.   http://dolphin.gulf.net/Political.html

94.   gopher://gopher.cqalert.com/

95.   http://www.ai.mit.edu/projects/ppp/news.html

96.   gopher://gopher.mid.net:7002/11/07menu/07menu

97.   http://www.vote-smart.org/

13

Geography

CHAPTER PREVIEW

Geography is the scientific study of the living and nonliving features of the Earth. Geographers attempt to explain the relationships between geographical entities, their locations and distribution patterns, or the reasons specific places developed in the manner they did. Physical geographers study the earth's nonliving features. Human geographers study people and their relationships to the physical environment. Human ecology is a related subfield. Regional geographers look at specific living and nonliving distribution patterns within specific, definable spaces. Geography and cartography, the making of maps, have an old and intimate relationship. In this chapter, we show how the Internet assists geographers, highlight specific subfields, demonstrate applications of geography, and list areas of research. Unlike some other social science disciplines, geographers have used traditional multimedia (e.g., maps, and globes) to explain and to present research findings. Geographers are well acquainted with the use of text, graphical elements, and three-dimensional visual tools. Thus, the shift from traditional multimedia to newer formats was not as great a step in geography as it was in some other social science disciplines. To most geographers, computers and the Internet are just newer and better tools than some of their older ones. You will need a Web browser with graphical capabilities to best use most of sites listed below.

THE GEOGRAPHY OF THE INTERNET

Before we begin our look at Internet geography, we want to consider the geography of the Internet itself. The Internet has altered traditional ideas about time and space, and you may have already experienced how the Internet alters your perception of both. The Internet is a real place, and the information stored within it has a physical location. As you search for that information, you may traverse geographic boundaries and conquer long distances with the click of a mouse. So, early on in your Internet experiences, you may find the Internet's own internal geography a difficult concept to grasp. For example, you can cross nearly any old-fashioned physical or political boundary, provided the Internet has already reached that location. You may hyperlink to any such country at any time with little effort. Through such virtual travel, you can truly explore the world in new ways. Who knows how such travel will change our perceptions of geography? However, we already know that the Internet is a marvelous tool for instruction and research in geography. In this light, our first URL is The Virtual Tourist World Map[1], a map of servers on the Internet. On it, you can travel this virtual world and still maintain your original conceptions of the accompanying physical locations of the Internet sites you are visiting. This site can help you understand the Internet's basic geography. A companion to The Virtual Tourist is the City–Net World Map[2] , an on-line geographic server that provides information about the real places found on the Virtual Tourist home page. We now turn to the actual information concerning geography available on the Internet.

GENERAL GEOGRAPHY HYPERLINKS

Like the other disciplines already covered in this book, geography has many Internet sites consisting of lists of general hyperlinks. For instance, the World-Wide Web Virtual Library[3] has a list of geographic hyperlinks, as does Yahoo–Science:Geography[4] . Yahoo maintains another list, Geographic Institutes Science:Geography:Institutes[5]. Geographic institutes worldwide can also be located through a list of hyperlinks at UCL /GEOG - Geographic Institutes around the World[6]. The University of Lund[7] maintains a gopher with hyperlinks to geography resources. This gopher also contains several WAIS (see Chapter 7) interfaces to the Australian National University. A useful Web page is World Flags[8], a collection of past and present flags of places in the world.

PROFESSIONAL GEOGRAPHY GROUP HYPERLINKS

You can contact many professional geographers through a Web page at the University of Buffalo's Geographers's AAG Member Email Address-es[9], a complete list of the association's 7200 members. The Association of American Geographers Home Page[10] identifies officers and their directory information and has hyperlinks to regional and specialty groups.

GEOGRAPHY DEPARTMENT HYPERLINKS

The Sensitive Map of Geography Departments[11] is a Web page with a clickable map for locating schools with on-line geography departments. You can click on an area of the world and get a map with the location of departments of geography that you can access. Information about geography departments in universities around the world can also be found on the Web page Geography Departments[12], a listing of on-line geography departments from many countries.

      Here are two specific departments to which you can hyperlink. Arizona State University Department of Geography[13] contains a message from the chair of the department and a listing of its faculty and staff. The Geography Department at the University of Buffalo - Home Page[14] lists graduates and shows where they now work. This page also has a hyperlink to the department's Geographic Information and Analysis Lab (GIAL)[15].

GEOGRAPHY SUBFIELD HYPERLINKS

Geographers tap concepts of spatial relationships and their general understanding of people and social structures and apply this knowledge to study specific issues. Below, we cover some of the major subfields in geography.

Physical Geography

Physical Geography Resources[16] is a Web page that contains a long list of general sites of hyperlinks to physical geography. Within the subfield of physical geography are additional subfields, including climatology, oceanography, and geomorphology.

Climatotology. Climatology is a familiar subfield of geography. Arizona State University's Web page The Office of Climatology (OoC)[17] provides climatological research, education, and services to the public. This site also has hyperlinks to publications and research projects connected with the OoC. The University of Illinois's Web page Welcome to Weather World[18] provides a collection of satellite images, both current and archived, that can be viewed on-line. This site has hyperlinks to other general and specific items. Examples include WXMAPS (warning maps), surface maps, and animations of those maps from the last several hours. Now you can forecast the weather on your own or view the weather as it happens.

Oceanography.   An exhibit featuring the study of the oceans can be found at the Ocean Planet Homepage[19], a Web page maintained through the Smithsonian Institution's National Museum of Natural History. The Woods Hole Oceanographic Institution[20] also has a Web server for oceanography.

Geomorphology.   Geomorphology is the subdiscipline of geography concerned with solid–land formations. Geomorphologists measure these formations and study their evolution and dynamics. The Johns Hopkins University Applied Physics Lab maintains the JHU/APL Digital Relief Map of the US (Composites Browser)[21] which provides relief maps of the United States. This server can locate features through a clickable map where each click enlarges the area shown. Another Web page, The National Geophysical Data Center[22], links to geographic archives, including Solid Earth Geophysics, Solar-Terrestrial Physics, Marine Geology, and Geophysics DMSP Satellite Data Archive among others. The Topographic Map Service[23] provides Canadian maps.

Human Geography and Human Ecology

Human geography examines the location of human populations, their relationship to the surrounding environment, and their spatial distribution patterns. We have combined human geography and ecology sites because of their similarity. The Web page Landscapes[24] contains a list of human ecology and biogeography sites and provides information about mapping services and instructions on how to use them. Those mapping services offer a way of integrating U.S. and other census data into maps. A downloadable tutorial is also available. The U.S. Census Bureau's TIGER Mapping Service[25] allows you to request custom on-line maps and combine them with census data easily. The U.S. Gazetteer[26] is still another way of accessing maps related to the census. Geography[27] is a gopher listing geography sites, and it includes demographic hyperlinks.

Cartography

When most of us think of geography, we think of maps. Cartography is the science of mapmaking. Cartography resources are available on the Internet. For instance, The World in Peters Projection[28] is a collection of world maps that can be viewed on-line. Another resource is the USGS Mapping Information: Home Page[29], the home page of the National Mapping Program of the United States Geological Survey (USGS). This federal program provides accurate and up-to-date cartographic data and information for the United States. You may download mapping software from their site, <u>The USGS Mapping Information: Mapping Science Software</u>[30].

APPLICATIONS HYPERLINKS

The synergy between geographic data and computers has resulted in new methods of analyzing geographic information and has led to the birth of Geographic Information Systems (GIS), a new method of using spatial data that has spawned many new applications. For more information on GIS, see <u>Geographic Information Systems - GIS</u>[31], the home page for a tutorial on GIS. The Web page <u>Analysis and ModelingGIS</u>[32] shows that some of the prime values of GIS lie not in map storage, presentation, or telecommunication, but in the use of geolocation for coincidence tabulation and for complex modeling to demonstrate how geographic change occurs. A similar page, <u>REGIS: Environmental Planning GIS at Berkeley</u>[33], comes from a research program with the goal of developing GIS tools and applying them in environmental planning, management, research, and teaching applications. The <u>FireNet Information Network</u>[34] is a specialized list of sites that connects geography to the management of wildfires. The page <u>GRASS info</u>[35] (short for the Geographic Resources Analysis Support System) is a management tool for Army environmental planners and land managers. GRASS is also used in civilian project planning and design. <u>USGS Fact Sheets</u>[36] is a page containing hyperlinks to USGS projects and to geographic reports by state.

RESEARCH HYPERLINKS

General Information Lists

<u>The U.S. Geological Survey - Index of USGS Servers</u>[37] is a list of the servers maintained by the USGS by subject. It is an excellent starting point for any study in geography. For specific places around the world, start with <u>The World Factbook 1994</u>[38], a page that will link you to a geographic summary of any country in the world.

Archives

Geography has Internet archives like the other disciplines reviewed earlier. Some specific geography archives you could look at include the <u>JPL Image/Information Archives</u>[39], the searchable <u>Gopher Index</u>[40], the <u>Global</u>

Land Information System (GLIS)[41], a USGS interactive computer system, or theDigital Data Series[42].

A clearinghouse page, the USGS Node of National Geospatial Data Clearinghouse[43], has geospacial data the public can purchase from the USGS. The National Center for Geographic Information and Analysis (NCGIA) at the University at Buffalo[44] is engaged in research with computer technologies that will enable scientists and policymakers to visualize geographic problems through maps, images, and other data. Another searchable page is the Query Interface to the USGS Internet Servers Broker[45]. It allows you to conduct searches of all USGS servers using a powerful search engine. The gopher 1[46] is a searchable gopher of the USGS/GNIS database listed by state. Another site of interest is theUSGS 's Geo Data[47], an FTP site for downloading geographic data including Digital Elevation Models (DEMs). The Earth Moon Menu[48] offers images of the Earth–Moon system and other hyperlinks such as a graphic of the ozone depletion in the atmosphere. Earth[49] is a page that provides hyperlinks to high-resolution satellite images of the Earth. Earth Introduction[50] is a Web page that provides maps and views of the Earth. Some of the maps hyperlinked from this page are multiscale maps, meaning that you can select the image area and resolution and the computer will then generate the map according to your specifications. Another archived map collection is the PCL Map Collection[51], a part of the Perry-Castañeda Library Map Collection from the University of Texas at Austin. Other useful archives include the USGS NSDI Clearinghouse - Aerial Photographs and Satellite Photographs[52], which displays on-line satellite images of various points on the Earth. The Declassified Satellite Photographs[53] Web page shows sample photographs of places taken from reconnaissance satellites during the Cold War.

Software

Software specific to the study of geography is available for downloading through the Internet. See the SOEST Anonymous FTP Offerings[54] for a page with hyperlinks to Graphical Information Systems (GIS) software.

CONCLUSION

A basic premise of geography is to study and understand the world around us. Virtual travel will never take the place of actual travel. But virtual travel will provide you with a powerful method of visualizing faraway places. Soon, you may be able to access real-time images from all over the world. See The Trojan Room[55] for the history of one the first examples of real-time imagery on the Internet, the state of a shared coffee pot in a Cambridge University computer lab. Geographers have already begun to use the Internet in new and innovative ways, and we cannot yet imagine the many future uses that will evolve. But is fitting for a social science discipline with such a long history of using multimedia to already have developed so many innovative uses for the Internet.

NOTES

1.   http://wings.buffalo.edu/world/

2.   http://wings.buffalo.edu/world/vt2/

3.   http://hpb1.hwc.ca:10002/WWW_VL_Geography.html

4.   http://www.yahoo.com/Science/Geography/

5.   http://www.yahoo.com/Science/Geography/Institutes/

6.   http://www.utexas.edu/depts/grg/virtdept/resources/depts.html

7.   //gopher.ub2.lu.se:70/11/resources/bysubject/geography/geogr

8.   http://www.adfa.oz.au/CS/flg/

9.   http://www.geog.buffalo.edu/geog/aag_email.html

10. http://www.aag.org/

11. http://lorax.geog.sc.edu/geogdocs/otherdocs/academic.html

12. http://www.utexas.edu/depts/grg/virtdept/resources/depts.html

13. http://aspin.asu.edu:80/provider/geography/

14. http://www.geog.buffalo.edu:80/

15. http://www.geog.buffalo.edu//GIAL/welcome.html

16. http://feature.geography.wisc.edu/phys.htm

17. http://aspin.asu.edu:80/provider/geography/climate/index.html

18. http://www.atmos.uiuc.edu/wxworld/html/top.html

19. http://seawifs.gsfc.nasa.gov/ocean_planet.html

20. http://www.whoi.edu/

21. http://www.zilker.net:80/~hal/apl-us//

22. http://web.ngdc.noaa.gov/ngdc.html

23. http://www.geocan.nrcan.gc.ca/topo/index.html

24. http://life.anu.edu.au:80/landscape_ecology/landscape.html

25. http://tiger.census.gov/instruct.html

26. http://tiger.census.gov/cgi-bin/gazetteer

27. gopher://ukoln.bath.ac.uk:7070/11/Link/Tree/Geography

28. http://deriocl.organik.uni-erlangen.de/public/world_project.html

29. http://www-nmd.usgs.gov/html/0nmdhome.html

30. http://www-nmd.usgs.gov/www/html/software.html

31. http://info.er.usgs.gov/research/gis/title.html

32. http://www.regis.berkeley.edu/analysis.html

33. http://www.regis.berkeley.edu/

34. http://online.anu.edu.au/Forestry/fire/firenet.html

35. http://www.cecer.army.mil/grass/GRASS.main.html

36. http://web.ngdc.noaa.gov/ngdc.html

37. http://www.usgs.gov/network/science/earth/usgs.html

38. http://www.odci.gov/94fact/fb94toc/fb94toc.html

39. http://sun1.cr.usgs.gov/eros-home.html

40. gopher://ashpool.micro.umn.edu:4324/7geo

41. http://sun1.cr.usgs.gov/glis/glis.html

42. http://internet.er.usgs.gov/reports/digital_data_series/index.html

43. http://h2o.er.usgs.gov:80/nsdi/

44. http://ncgia.geog.buffalo.edu//ncgia/NCGIA.html

45. http://bramble.er.usgs.gov:80/Harvest/brokers/usgs_web/query.html/

46. gopher://george.peabody.yale.edu:71/1

47. http://sun1.cr.usgs.gov/doc/edchome/ndcdb/ndcdb.html

48. http://esther.la.asu.edu/asu_tes/TES_Editor/SOLAR_SYST_TOUR/Earth.html

49. http://seds.lpl.arizona.edu/nineplanets/nineplanets/earth.html

50. http://www.c3.lanl.gov/~cjhamil/SolarSystem/earth.html

51. http://www.lib.utexas.edu/Libs/PCL/Map_collection/Map_collection.html

52. http://nsdi.usgs.gov/nsdi/products/aerial.html

53. http://sun1.cr.usgs.gov/dclass/dclass.html

54. http://www.soest.hawaii.edu/soest/about.ftp.html

55. http://pelican.cl.cam.ac.uk/people/qs101/coffee.html

14

Anthropology

CHAPTER PREVIEW

Anthropology is the study of human culture and how people have adapted to their environments. Many anthropologists study the development of culture and social patterns. Other anthropologists research human physical characteristics. Some anthropologists investigate the reasons for cultural differences and how those differences may be functional to survival. Anthropology is divided into several branches, including physical, biological, social, cultural, linguistic, applied, and theoretical anthropology. Archeology is a closely related field. Because anthropologists and archeologists use hard-to-describe artifacts in their work, many of the sites included in this chapter use graphical representation. Thus, you will need a Web browser that supports graphics to get the full effect from many of the sites listed below.

ANTHROPOLOGY AND THE INTERNET

Anthropology Internet sites are fewer in number than those of some other disciplines, but many anthropology sites are elegantly constructed and use graphics well. However, not all anthropologists see the Internet and multimedia as a panacea. For instance, Marcus Banks in an on-line article, Interactive Multimedia and Anthropology–a Sceptical View[1], argues that multimedia has shortcomings in the teaching of anthropology research. Not a complete skeptic, he intentionally overstates his arguments in order to stimulate discussion about the role of the Internet in anthropology. In fact, your own Internet exploring is similar to how anthropologists conduct research, except that you are looking at URLs while anthropologists are looking at artifacts. Both you and anthropologists then attempt to construct a coherent whole from the evidence collected—URLs or artifacts, respectively. In this chapter, we chose a slightly different structure and will start with a section on museums of anthropology and archeology.

MUSEUM HYPERLINKS

The Maxwell Anthropology Museum's <u>Maxwell Online</u>[2] is the home page of a museum located in New Mexico, and its page describes it as the only museum in the southwestern U.S. dedicated to the study of the entirety of human history. Another on-line museum tour is the <u>Kelsey Museum Exhibit Galleries</u>[3]. The <u>Canadian Museum of Civilization (CMC)</u>[4] is another museum Web site.

GENERAL ANTHROPOLOGY HYPERLINKS

Index Pages

We list some anthropology index pages and general URLs below. <u>Nicole's AnthroPage</u>[5] is a comprehensive Web index of anthropology. The page <u>Systematics in Prehistory</u>[6] is an on-line introductory text in archeology. The Galaxy search engine <u>Anthropology (Social Sciences)</u>[7] is another index page for anthropology and has links to collections, directories, and academic organizations and related sites. The World Wide Web Virtual Library page on anthropology, <u>The World-Wide Web Virtual Library: Anthropology</u>[8], is a comprehensive reference index page listing specialized fields, institutions, general resources, and other anthropology links. An archeology index page is <u>Archaeology (Anthropology)</u>[9]. Ethnology (the comparison and analysis of cultures) is the focus of the Web page <u>Ethnology Resources</u>[10]. The Center for Social Anthropology and Computing at the University of Kent at Canterbury maintains <u>Anthropology Resources at the University of Kent</u>[11], which both covers its own program and hyperlinks to others. You can use the Web page <u>anthro-l Home Page</u>[12] to find and join listservers (see Chapter 3) in anthropology.

On-Line Journals

Here are some anthropology on-line journals. The *Journal of World Anthropology* publishes articles on academic research, theory, and methodology that can be found at <u>*JWA*</u>[13]. You can also use this home page to subscribe to the print version of the journal. Articles from *Aboriginal History* can be obtained through its <u>gopher</u>[14]. A <u>Web page</u>[15] exists for the *Society for American Archaeology Bulletin*. The journal *Cultural Dynamics* has a <u>home page</u>[16] but no on-line articles yet.

Films

If you have decided that the best way to begin to learn about anthropology is not by reading journals but rather by reviewing films, then see the Web page <u>UCSB Anthropology Web Site–Archaeology on Film</u>[17]. It is a site for anthropology and archeology film reviews; you can add your own reviews as well. Sources for obtaining the films are also listed.

ANTHROPOLOGY DEPARTMENT HYPERLINKS

<u>ArchNet: Academic Departments & Programs</u>[18] is a worldwide listing of universities with anthropology and archeology departments. This page is a source of course offerings, faculty research interests, and hyperlinks to other universities. Some individual departments include the University of Virginia's <u>Department of Anthropology</u>[19], which tells how to send their faculty electronic mail directly from the page; UC-Santa Barbara's <u>UCSB Anthropology Web Site</u>[20]; UC-Irvine's <u>UC Irvine Department of Anthropology</u>[21]; American University's <u>Anthropology Web Page</u>[22]; the University of Nebraska's <u>UNL ANTHRO HOMEPAGE</u>[23]; and the University of Western Australia's <u>Department of Anthropology</u>[24].

ANTHROPOLOGY HISTORY HYPERLINKS

Other than references to films[25] (e.g., on Margaret Mead) and short excerpts from <u>historical works</u>[26] (Lévi-Strauss), we were unable to find many historical materials on anthropology on the Internet. Perhaps some anthropologists are now at work remedying this lack of historical context on the Internet.

ANTHROPOLOGY SUBFIELD HYPERLINKS

Cultural Antropology

The thrust of cultural anthropology is the study of human culture. Cultural anthropologists may study social institutions--religion, family structure, art, or music. They might also look at physical aspects of culture such as homes, architecture, and tools.

General Hyperlinks.   <u>Cultural Anthropology</u>[27] is a Galaxy index page that contains links to collections, periodicals, and nonprofit organizations and directories. <u>Ethnology Resources</u>[28] is another such site with links to studies in culture, papers, and cultural sites. To view many cultures at once, try Anthropology Exhibits on the WWW[29], which includes the Egyptian Artifacts Exhibit[30], Scrolls From the Dead Sea[31], and many others.

Hyperlinks to Specific Cultures.   Many of the cultural anthropology sites are about specific cultures. A home page dedicated to providing information about the people in the arctic regions of the world is Arctic Circle[32]. Chicano/Latino research conducted at UCLA is collected at the CLNET Home Page[33]. The University of Pennsylvania's Black Studies program Web page African Studies WWW (U. Penn)[34] has hyperlinks to an archive and to a searchable gopher. One gopher[35] archives excerpts from the postings of the Native American Usenet Group. Another Native American group is examined in the Web page Ethnographic Portraits: The Crees of Northern Québec[36], a photographic study from the James Bay area of Canada.

Paul Stirling of the Centre for Social Anthropology and Computing has put together a striking exhibit of culture in the Web page 45 years in the Turkish Village[37], which details his research in two villages in Turkey over a span of 45 years. For a look at ancient cultures see Hellenic Civilization[38], Egyptian Artifacts Exhibit[39], and Texts of Exploration[40]; the latter page contains prints made by De Bry between 1590 and1634. Contemporary culture can be explored via the Web page Yahoo - Society and Culture:Folklore[41]. An unusual page, The Panawina Expedition[42], allows you to follow an actual and on-going multidisciplinary research expedition as researchers attempt a 6000–mile sailing trip from Malta to Thailand. This page exploits the interactive nature of the Internet well.

Social Anthropology

Social anthropology examines the social relationships among members of a culture. Social development, kinship, and division of labor are commonly studied subjects. On the Internet, cultural and social anthropology are often treated as one and the same, and many of the cultural anthropology sites noted above also apply to the study of social anthropology. However, we did find some hyperlinks specific to social anthropology. For instance, the tutorial home page Kinship and Social Organization[43] includes discussions of how families develop in different cultures and what family means in terms of community and behavior. A similar Web page is Linkages[44], which provides tools for understanding the study of kinship, examples of kinship studies, and a discussion of the research process in kinship.

Many Usenet discussion groups (see Chapter 8) and mailing lists (see Chapter 3) exist in the area of cultural studies. One gopher[45] is an extensive index to such news groups and listservers in cultural anthropology.

Theoretical Anthropology

Theoretical anthropology is the subfield of anthropology that looks at our species' ability to adapt to the environment in the broadest possible ways. Theoretical anthropologists attempt to explain the functions of cultures and societies in general. The journal *Theoretical Anthropology* has a Web page Homepage for *Theoretical Anthropology*[46], an electronic journal linking various theoretical and methodological aspects of anthropology. The museums of anthropology listed above also contain materials of interest to theoretical anthropologists.

Linguistics

Linguists study language patterns to detect common links between different groups of people and their languages. Language used by different societies may reflect a common belief system or social status, both of interest to anthropologists. Anthropologists are concerned with the meaning of the words in the context of social settings, and this is studied through linguistics. Also, linguistic data can be used to support or refute data from physical anthropology. The Human-Languages Page[47] is a Web page devoted to amassing information about the languages of the world. The language resources listed here come from all around the world and include dictionaries, language tutorials, and spoken samples of languages. Another Web page[48] lists bulletin boards, listservers, and news groups for individual languages. Most of the major languages can be found on this site, and subscription information is given. Noun Classification in Swahili[49] is a Web page with a much narrower scope that includes audio samples. (You will need a computer with audio capability and appropriate software.) A current project in linguistic anthropology, the Dead Sea Scrolls, can be seen at the Library of Congress's Dead Sea–Intro[50].

The Usenet news group "sci.lang" is one place to find discussion of linguistics. Their FAQ file can be accessed via a Web page[51]. Another Web page source is the Linguist List[52], which bills itself as a place where academics can discuss language issues. Finally, the Web page LMBM: An Overview[53] is devoted to lexeme-morpheme base morphology, a kind of linguistic analysis.

Physical and Biological Anthropology

Physical and biological anthropologists deal with the study of human physical characteristics. Much of their work is centered on trying to understand how humans have changed physically over long periods of time. Galaxy's Web page Physical and Biological Anthropology[54] is an index page for physical and biological anthropology. Portions of the on-line text *The Ascent of Mind* can be found at the Web page W. H. Calvin's The Ascent of Mind[55]. The text is easy to navigate and makes extensive use of hyperlinks. It focuses on Calvin's work on the evolution of the brain and human intelligence. For a closer look at the study of skulls and brains, see Hominid Skulls[56] and Brain Evolution[57].

Paleontology is closely related to physical anthropology. Paleontologists study the prehistoric, fossilized remains of humans and other animals and plants. A University of California at Berkeley Museum of Paleontology gopher[58] offers hyperlinks to its exhibits, specimen catalogs, indices, mailing lists, and other, related gophers. Their dinosaur Web page Dinosaur Hall[59] is a very popular site and reflects one of the most common stereotypes about paleontologists—that they dig up bones and reconstruct those ancient beasts.

Archeology

Archeologists look for evidence of human culture. The large index page Archaeology (Anthropology)[60] will provide you with many hyperlinks to the study of archeology and to archeological finds. The University of Southern California's Mercury Project[61] was designed as another interactive use of the Internet. That Web page allowed people to control a real robot arm via the World Wide Web in order to "excavate" and interpret the meaning of a selection of objects from the 19th century. Although you can no longer control the robotic arm in real time, you can download video of other users doing so.

Historic Preservation

Although some people might not believe that historic preservation falls under the aegis of anthropology, we have included one Web site anyway. It is the Internet Resources for Heritage Conservation, Historic Preservation and Archaeology[62] home page, a clearinghouse of information on historic preservation. It also hyperlinks to more general anthropology sites.

APPLIED ANTHROPOLOGY HYPERLINKS

Anthropology is applied in many ways to help solve practical problems. For example, the Applied Anthropology Browser[63] is a Web browser specifically for applied anthropology. It has hyperlinks to resources in developmental anthropology, medical anthropology, environmental action, and other fields. Practice case studies in applied anthropology can be found at the gopher Anthropology Practice Case File[64]. The preservation of older knowledge traditions can be found at Iowa State University's Center for Indigenous Knowledge for Agriculture and Rural Development home page CIKARD[65]. The project's intent is to preserve and apply the knowledge of local farmers and other rural people around the globe. As you study the applications of anthropology, you will soon realize that there are many conflicting concepts about how to work with different societies and cultures. What is the best way to help them? One gopher[66] contains papers in applied anthropology that may help you answer this question. This gopher's on-line papers address such topics as aboriginal rights, anthropology practice case files, and East Timor language policy. One interesting paper, "Monogamy as a Prisoner's Dilemma[67]", attempts to approach monogamy via game theory.

Answers to questions about applied anthropology can be found on FAQ Web page[68]. Another place for discussion and answers about applied anthropology is The ANTHAP Home Page[69], the main access point for the Applied Anthropology Computer Network. Applied anthropology discussion groups can be found at the Web page Anthap Discussion Groups[70]. One gopher[71] has a similar list, and it reviews listservers in the area of anthropology and archeology by region or culture. An experimental Web server, the Devline Home Page[72], provides development information on-line from the Institute of Development Studies and the British Library for Development Studies.

RESEARCH HYPERLINKS

Anthropologists use very specialized forms of research. Much of their skill involves knowing how to enter a community in order to obtain data. Often, anthropologists will become members of the societies they study. The Internet can provide anthropology students with some of the tools they will need to understand the practice of anthropological field research.

The University of Southern California's Ethnographics Laboratory E-Lab Home Page[73] is a teaching, research, and archival facility for new media. It provides access to research archives and information on studying different cultures. Another site for general research data is

Anthropology Resources[74]. This anthropology site's hyperlinks include Aboriginal Studies Electronic Data Archive, Anthro-Gopher, Anthropology and Archaeology Corner, Anthropology Collection at the Yale Peabody Museum, and others. It can also be searched via its SOSIG search engine.

The Australian National University's Department of Anthropology maintains the Search of ANU-CanbAnthropology-Index[75], an anthropology WAIS server (see Chapter 7) that is searchable by key words. It makes quick data searches possible and provides data in anthropology, especially in the area of aboriginal studies. If you are particularly interested in aboriginal research, you could connect to the gopher *Aboriginal History Journal*[76]. This electronic journal can be read on-line.

The World-Wide Web Virtual Library: Anthropology[77] is an index page of general anthropology, information and it contains hyperlinks to data archives. If you select the hyperlink for the University of California, Berkeley, Library Anthropology Collection[78], you will find a gopher menu that links to a TELNET server and to the National Archeological Database. From this point you can find links to other electronic journals of anthropology.

Gopher Servers[79] is the name of a menu page of servers listing a wide range of gopher servers of interest to anthropologists. It contains hyperlinks to the Native American Net Server[80], Mayan Epigraphic Database Project[81], Primate Information[82], and many others.

Other data archives specific to anthropology include Anth[83], the anthropology archive at Rice University, with a searchable gopher and gopher hyperlinks to many other sites. You may search the archive by key words.

One site that allows the Web user to monitor research and that also explains the procedures of the research is The Leptiminus Archaeological Project[84], a report on Dr. John H. Humphrey's fieldwork from 1990 to1993 at the Leptiminus site. It includes text and images of the dig. Another such Internet site is the Shawnee Minisink Site[85], a home page for American University's archeological excavation of the Shawnee Minisink. The work at this site is used as a demonstration on how to conduct an excavation and how to catalog and interpret the artifacts found.

The Internet can actually assist you in your own research projects. For instance, the Integrated Archaeological Information System(IAIS)[86] home page is a computer-based system designed to provide research and instructional support for the archeology program at American University. It allows you to look at data analyses from this site. It also provides hyperlinks for downloading free software for anthropological research. Another source of such free software is the Centre for Social Anthropology and Computing's CSAC Ethnographics Gallery[87]. The University of Buffalo's Department of Anthropology Web page Software Resources[88] also has software for anthropology resources, including hyperlinks to the Bonn Archaeological Statistics Package, Software Resources for Archaeological Software, Sasha Force's list of commercially available software, and more.

CONCLUSION

Anthropology is a field with easily obtainable and useful Internet resources. We suspect that there will be many more such resources going on-line in anthropology in the near future. The work of anthropologists meshes nicely with the Internet because these scholars must travel the globe to perform that work. The Internet can help eliminate some of that travel. For example, field workers can now more easily communicate with their home laboratories. Also, some of the training necessary to become a successful anthropologist can now be done with less travel. Anthropologists work worldwide with many cultures, languages, and people, and strive to bring all these data together. The Internet makes their job much easier.

NOTES

1. http://www.rsl.ox.ac.uk/isca/marcus.banks.01.html

2. http://www.unm.edu/~mtsnmc/Maxwell/Maxon.html

3. http://classics.lsa.umich.edu/Kelsey/Galleries.html

4. http://www.cmcc.muse.digital.ca/cmc/cmceng/welcmeng.html

5. http://www.wsu.edu:8000/~i9248809/anthrop.html

6. http://weber.u.washington.edu/~anthro/BOOK/book.html

7. http://www.einet.net/galaxy/Social-Sciences/Anthropology.html

8. http://www.usc.edu/dept/v-lib/anthropology.html

9. http://www.einet.net/galaxy/Social-Sciences/Anthropology/Archaeology.html

10. http://sosig.ac.uk/Subjects/ethno.html

11. http://lucy.ukc.ac.uk/index.html

12. http://www.anatomy.su.oz.au/danny/anthropology/anthro-l/index.html

13. gopher://wings.buffalo.edu/11/academic/department/anthropology/jwa

14. gopher://cis.anu.edu.au:70/1ftp%3Acoombs.anu.edu.au@/coombspapers /coombsarchives/aboriginal-history-jrnl/

15. http://www.sscf.ucsb.edu:80/SAABulletin/

16. http://dynamics.rug.ac.be/

17. http://www.sscf.ucsb.edu:80/anth/videos/video.html

18. http://spirit.lib.uconn.edu/ArchNet/Depts/Univers.html

19. http://minerva.acc.Virginia.EDU:80/~anthro/

20. http://www.sscf.ucsb.edu:80/anth/index.html

21. http://www.socsci.uci.edu/anthro/anthro.html

22. http://www.american.edu:70/0/academic.depts/cas/anthro/antmain.html

23. http://www.unl.edu/anthro/Homepage.html

24. http://www.arts.uwa.edu.au/AnthropWWW/overview.htm

25. http://cs.wpi.edu/~ptbast/der/filmmakers/films/margaret.html

26. http://www.slip.net/~jwithers/indexbc.html

27. http://www.einet.net/galaxy/Social-Sciences/Anthropology/Cultural-Anthropology.html

28. http://sosig.ac.uk/Subjects/ethno.html

29. http://lucy.ukc.ac.uk/exhibits.html

30. http://www.memphis.edu/egypt/artifact.html

31. http://sunsite.unc.edu/expo/deadsea.scrolls.exhibit/intro.html

32. http://www.lib.uconn.edu/ArcticCircle/

33. http://latino.sscnet.ucla.edu/

34. http://www.sas.upenn.edu/African_Studies/AS.html

35. ftp://ftp.cit.cornell.edu/pub/special/NativeProfs/usenet/

36. http://www.lib.uconn.edu/ArcticCircle/CulturalViability/Cree/creeexhibit.html

37. http://lucy.ukc.ac.uk/stirling.html

38. gopher://ithaki.servicenet.ariadne-t.gr/11/HELLENIC_CIVILIZATION

39. http://www.memphis.edu/egypt/artifact.html

40. http://bateson.ukc.ac.uk/Gallery/Explore/Images/Frontpiece1.html

41. http://www.yahoo.com/Society_and_Culture/Folklore/

42. http://lucy.ukc.ac.uk/Panawina/Contents.html

43. http://www.umanitoba.ca/anthropology/kintitle.html

44. http://eclectic.ss.uci.edu/linkages/linkages.html

45. gopher://gopher.mid.net:7002/11/07menu/03menu

46. http://www.univie.ac.at/voelkerkunde/theoretical-anthropology/

47. http://www.willamette.edu/~tjones/Language-Page.html

48. http://condor.stcloud.msus.edu:20020/docs/lnglst1a.txt

49. http://jefferson.village.virginia.edu/swahili/swahili.html

50. http://sunsite.unc.edu/expo/deadsea.scrolls.exhibit/intro.html

51. http://atd.let.kun.nl/ATD/Studiegids/sci.lang-FAQ.html

52. http://www.ling.rochester.edu/linguist/contents.html

53. http://www.bucknell.edu/~rbeard/homepage.html

54. http://www.einet.net/galaxy/Social-Sciences/Anthropology/Physical- and-Biological-Anthropology.html

55. http://weber.u.washington.edu/wcalvin/bk5.html

56. http://www.wsu.edu:8000/~walters/skull.html

57. http://comp9.psych.cornell.edu/Psychology/News/Brain_Evolution

58. gopher://ucmp1.berkeley.edu/

59. http://ucmp1.berkeley.edu/exhibittext/dinosaur.html

60. http://www.einet.net/galaxy/Social-Sciences/Anthropology/Archaeology.html

61. http://www.usc.edu/dept/raiders/

62. http://hpb1.hwc.ca:10002/Internet_Resource_Guide.html

63. http://www.acs.oakland.edu/%7Edow/browse.htm

64. gopher://gopher.acs.oakland.edu:70/0ftp%3Avela.acs.oakland.edu@/pub/anthap/Anthropology_practice_case_files

65. http://www.physics.iastate.edu/cikard/cikard.html

66. gopher://gopher.acs.oakland.edu:70/1ftp%3avela.acs.oakland.edu%40/pub
     /anthap/

67. http://ccme-mac4.bsd.uchicago.edu/JCV/JMono.html

68. http://www.acs.oakland.edu/%7Edow/napafaq.htm

69. http://www.acs.oakland.edu/%7Edow/anthap.html

70. http://www.acs.oakland.edu/%7Edow/discuss.htm

71. gopher://gopher.mid.net:7002/11/07menu/01menu

72. http://www.ids.ac.uk/

73. http://www.usc.edu/dept/elab/welcome/

74. http://sosig.esrc.bris.ac.uk/Subjects/anthro.html

75. http://server.wais.com/wais-dbs/ANU-CanbAnthropology-Index.html

76. gopher://cis.anu.edu.au:70/1ftp%3Acoombs.anu.edu.au@/coombspapers
     /coombsarchives/aboriginal-history-jrnl/

77. http://www.usc.edu/dept/v-lib/anthropology.html

78. gopher://infolib.lib.berkeley.edu/11/resdbs/anth

79. http://lucy.ukc.ac.uk/Afaq_tools/gopher.html

80. gopher://alpha1.csd.uwm.edu/

81. gopher://alpha1.csd.uwm.edu/

82. gopher://saimiri.primate.wisc.edu

83. gopher://riceinfo.rice.edu/11/Subject/Anth

84. http://rome.classics.lsa.umich.edu/projects/lepti/lepti.html

85. http://www.american.edu:70/I/academic.depts/cas/anthro/sms/sms.html

86. http://www.american.edu:70/I/academic.depts/cas/anthro/sms/iais.html

87. http://lucy.ukc.ac.uk/archives.html

88. http://wings.buffalo.edu/academic/department/anthropology/software

15

History

CHAPTER PREVIEW

History is the study of the human past and the relationships between historical events. The use of computers in researching and teaching history is an old topic because historians were among the early users of computers and the Internet. The <u>New Home Page Association for History and Computing</u>[1] is the World Wide Web home page for the Association for History and Computing. It is an international organization that aims to promote and develop interest in the use of computers in all types of historical study at every level, in both teaching and research. We have pointed out in other chapters that, with the right tools, you can use the Internet to access information in a multimedia format. The Internet can provide historical information as text, photographs, graphics, sound, and movies. In the study of history, this can make a networked computer a type of time machine. The Internet has the potential to bring history to life.

Hyperlinks to history are so extensive that the unacquainted student may find locating information on specific historical events difficult. In this chapter, we identify only a fraction of the specific historical sites available. We decided that with so much material available, we would focus less on specific historical events and more on lists hyperlinking to specific events. We have tried to arrange the hyperlinks in a format that will allow you to quickly locate the longer lists of hyperlinks and then find the more specific sites.

Beginning history students may visit a <u>gopher site</u>[2] from Tennessee Tech's history department. This gopher provides hyperlinks to the question, "Why study history?" Other hyperlinks include studying and teaching history, Internet resources in history, and computers, audiovisual resources, and history. Another site you may wish to consider early on is the <u>ISHA-Homepage</u>[3] Web page. This site is the home page for the International Students of History Association (ISHA) and provides information about the organization and how to become a member.

GENERAL HISTORY HYPERLINKS

Some Web pages that contain lists of history hyperlinks include General History Sources/Sites[4], Yahoo–SocialScience:History[5], and Hum anities:History[6]. Each of these sites is easy to use and provides either descriptive names or brief explanations of the hyperlink to help in navigating. Of the many gopher menus that list hyperlinks to history, History[7] and another gopher[8] are good places to begin looking at history sites using gopher.

The Regional History Center of the University of Southern California and the Los Angeles City Historical Society maintain the Web site History Computerization Project[9]. This site is comprehensive and can direct you to many of history's Internet resources. The long listings are subdivided by topics and issues, with brief descriptions of each hyperlink. Gateway to World History[10] is a general index Web page of Internet resources for the study of world history in support of "the struggle for social progress." It contains hyperlinks to documentary archives, world history on-line resources, a list of history departments, and more.

HISTORY DEPARTMENT HYPERLINKS

University departments of history are the source of much of the historical information on the Internet. Locating a history department on the World Wide Web is simple, thanks to WWW-pages of History Departments[11]. You can do the same using a gopher[12]. These two routes will take you to specific departments of history at the different universities. Two such sites are the Web page Tennessee Technological University History Home Page[13] and an Indiana University gopher[14].

MUSEUM HYPERLINKS

An interesting segment of history's Internet resources are the on-line museums or exhibits. There are many historical exhibits available through the Internet, and those on the World Wide Web take full advantage of its multimedia capabilities. To locate a museum, begin with Galaxy's general listing of historical on-line museums, Museums- Exhibits and Special Collections[15]. Scholarship: Museums and Special Exhibits[16] is another list of museums where you may start a review. Both the World Wide Web Virtual Library's Museums[17] and the WWW Virtual Library: Museums Around the World[18] can be jumping–off points for museums, too. Another example of a site to hyperlink is The Smithsonian Institution Home Page[19], which will direct you to the different areas within the museum.

Some areas have on-line exhibits, and others simply provide information. Other possible on-line museums that may be of interest are the National Archives Online Exhibit Hall[20] and the PARIS.MUSEES.LOU-VRE[21]. The Carlos homepage[22] is the home page for the Michael C. Carlos Museum of Emory University. This museum covers a wide span of history and has historical photographic displays. The Israel Museum, Jerusalem - Main Entrance[23] leads you to the history of Jerusalem. An interesting on-line exhibit is the National Park Service Links to the Past[24]. From the home page you can visit historical places throughout the United States.

HYPERLINKS TO AREAS OF HISTORY

Historians typically break the study of history into three classifications. The first is period history—or those events that relate to a particular time span. In European history, for example, these eras might be ancient history, medieval history, and modern history. The second classification is national history—the history of specific nations or peoples. The third classification is topical history—the study of specific subjects. All three classifications can be found within the framework of the Internet.

Period History

Students investigating ancient history may begin with the hyperlinks provided in the Web page Exploring Ancient World Cultures[25], which includes the on-line article "Why Study Ancient World Cultures?" by Bill Hemminger and sites related to particular cultures. General[26] is also a listing of ancient history links that will lead to different ancient cultures. Sites of specific interest are Egyptology Resources[27], a large list of resource hyperlinks on Egyptology. Egypt Interactive–Egyptian Internet Resources[28] is another set of Egyptology hyperlinks.

The WebAcropol : Welcome !![29] will take you on a virtual tour of the Acropolis in Greece. Rome Resources[30] is a site dedicated to the study of the Roman Empire. The home page will connect you to a map of the Roman Empire. From there you click on the map area of interest, and it will hyperlink you to detailed information. The home page The Mayas[31] explores these ancient people, and further information can be found at CMC–Mystery of the Maya[32].

National History

Students will often study history within the context of the development of a nation. Many national histories exist in various levels of completeness on the Internet. Those nations that have the greater presence on the Internet also seem to have more of a historical presence. This section will emphasize hyperlinks to United States history.

International History.   There are lists on Web pages that will connect you to countries throughout the world. A broad list on the World Wide Web is World History Archives[33], a repository for documents that support an understanding of world history through the struggle for social progress. The hyperlinks from this Web page are listed by area of the world. You can hyperlink from continents to specific countries. The World Wide Web Virtual Library will also connect you to many histories of countries. An example would be CERN/ANU - Asian Studies WWW VL[34], a Web list of studies by national categories in Asia. East Asia History Archives[35] provides access to the history of the nations of East Asia. In the same manner, Russian and East European Studies Internet History, Geography andSociology Resources[36] and soviet.archives.dir[37] can provide data on Russian and Eastern European history. After reviewing the hyperlinks in this chapter, it will not be difficult to locate information on a specific nation for study.

United States History.   The history of the United States is represented within many Internet sites. As with world history, the easiest way to navigate is to review a long list of hyperlinks. From that point you can jump to the specific site. Yahoo - Social Science:History:American History[38] is the subdivision for American history on the Yahoo history list. Two other general U.S. history lists of hyperlinks are US-History[39] and American and British History Resources[40]. Together, these constitute a very large collection of historical hyperlinks that include many historical texts. A very interesting electronic history project under construction at the Library of Congress is the Home Page: American Memory From the Library of Congress[41]. The American Memory Project is an extensive collection of text, pictures, and audio recordings from the American past. Eventually, the entire project will be on-line. Students can now use their Web browsers to look at events of the American past.

Topical History

Historians may wish to study the history of a particular subject such as medicine or science. The Internet contains much information on the history of many subjects. Some subjects have a greater Internet presence than others.

Military.   Military history is a subject with an extensive presence on the World Wide Web. Yahoo - Social Science:History:Military History[42] is a list of military history sites. The American Revolution and the Struggle for Independence[43] is an on-line text on the colonial period and the Revolutionary War. Information on the Civil War can be obtained from several sites. For instance, The American Civil War Homepage[44] contains a great deal of Civil War data.

World War II is the subject of many historical Internet sites. WORLD WAR II[45], a Web page maintained by Mississippi State University, hyperlinks WWII sites to servers at international sites. Yahoo - Social Science:History:Military History:World War II[46] is a hyperlink from the Yahoo history list with many WWII URLs. World War II Archive[47] is another archive of WWII information. Some of these hyperlinks include text, sound recordings, and QuickTime movies, but you will need the appropriate software to take advantage of the sound and movies. One FTP site[48] contains WWII archives including daily reports, maps, battles and other information. Another FTP site[49], from the Patch High School WWII archive is part of their WWII Web pages and reviews the events surrounding the Normandy invasion. Other unique World War II Web pages are the Nanjing Massacre[50] and The Warsaw Uprising[51].

The Korean War Project Home page[52] hyperlinks to sites of interest regarding the Korean War. Vietnam Memoirs[53] is a Web page that looks at the events surrounding the Vietnam War.

Other Topics.   Another example of a topical site in history that may be of interest is the 1492 Exhibit[54] entitled "1492: An Ongoing Voyage." This Web page hyperlinks to Web pages addressing questions like, "What was life like in America before 1492?" "What spurred European expansion?" "How did European, African and American peoples react to each other?" "What were some of the immediate results of these contacts?" Still other histories that are on-line include the Società Italiana degli Storici dell'Economia[55] economic histories. This site originates in Italy and contains hyperlinks to economic history. This page can be accessed in both Italian and English. HyperDOC: NLM History of Medicine Division[56] is a Web page dedicated to the study of the history of medicine. The historical study of sacred texts has a Web site, World Scripture[57]. This page describes the contents as "A Comparative Anthology of Sacred Texts" and contains on-line versions of sacred writings.

One last example of topical historical Internet sites is the Holocaust. This subject has many on-line sites, starting with the on-line museum United States Holocaust Memorial Museum[58], which contains a searchable data archive. Other Web pages related to this subject are the Cybrary of the Holocaust[59] and the I*EARN Holocaust/Genocide Project[60]

RESEARCH HYPERLINKS

Most of the sites listed below are archives with collections of historical writings and documents. Other sites include electronic libraries and journals that provide electronic means of researching history.

Archives

History[61] is a large index of historical archives. The subject listings are done by place, time, and subject, making the locating of information easier. The site Archives[62] is a listing of archives of historical data via a gopher server and can be accessed using that tool. Another Web page is the American Studies Web: Historical Essays and Archival Resources[63], an archive of historical American writings and other data. One URL[64] links to a directory of archives, historical associations, and institutes—all possible areas to gather data on topics of interest.

Electronic Libraries and Journals

Reference Works for History[65] provides access to a wide range of reference tools for historical study. Many traditional reference works are now included within virtual libraries. For instance, Presidential Libraries IDEA Network[66] is a single Web page that hyperlinks to many presidential libraries, thus providing access to all from one page. The Library of Congress World Wide Web Home Page[67] is the place to find their extensive on-line collection of resources. CARRIE: An Electronic Library[68] specializes in hyperlinking to full–text on–line documents and books. Many of these are historical in nature. The Gutenberg Master Index in Order of Release[69] page is not an electronic library. Rather, the Gutenberg Project aims to bring a large collection of writings of all types on-line. Many of those that can currently be found on-line are of a historical nature. You can hyperlink from the listing to the full on-line text.

A source of information on historical collections is General Information[70], an electronic journal devoted to reviewing books in all fields of history. It is supported by the University of Cincinnati and is issued quarterly. History and Theory Home Page[71] is an electronic journal that is available on-line. The Web page gives subscription information and an overview of the contents.

Other Resources

<u>Discussion Threads</u>[72] is a listing of the electronic mail addresses for discussion groups on medieval history. This site also contains hyperlinks to other medieval history hyperlinks. <u>WWW Services for Historians</u>[73] enables full-text searches of the AHC bibliography. This is a hyperlink history students will find helpful. <u>Scholarly Groups, Grants, and Travel</u>[74] is a Web page from Tennessee Tech that provides information on opportunities and resources for study and research.

CONCLUSION

History resources are plentiful and varied. You may spend many hours searching them. In the future, history's portion of the Internet is sure to grow even more than it already has.

NOTES

1. http://grid.let.rug.nl/ahc/welcome

2. gopher://gopher.tntech.edu:70/00gopher_root%3A%5Bcampusas.hist%5Dwh-ystudy.hst

3. http://hagar.arts.kuleuven.ac.be/org/isha/

4. http://execpc.com/~dboals/hist-gen.html

5. http://www.yahoo.com/text/Social_Science/History/

6. gopher://akebono.stanford.edu:80/hGET%20/yahoo/Humanities/History/

7. gopher://riceinfo.rice.edu/11/Subject/History

8. gopher://gopher.tntech.edu:70/11gopher_root%3a%5bcampus.as.hist%5d

9. http://www.wesleyan.edu:80/histjrnl/hthome.htm

10. http://neal.ctstateu.edu/history/world_history/world_history.html

11. http://grid.let.rug.nl/ahc/history.html

12. gopher://gopher.tntech.edu:70/11gopher_root%3A%5Bcampus.as.hist%5D

13. http://www.tntech.edu/www/acad/hist/history.html

14. http://www.indiana.edu:80/~amhrev/

15. http://galaxy.einet.net/GJ/museums.html

16. http://scholar.cc.emory.edu/scripts/schol/schol-museums.html

17. http://www.comlab.ox.ac.uk/archive/other/museums.html

18. http://www.comlab.ox.ac.uk/archive/other/museums/world.html

19. http://www.si.edu/

20. http://clio.nara.gov/exhall/exhibits.html

21. http://meteora.ucsd.edu:80/~norman/paris/Musees/Louvre/

22. http://www.gatech.edu/CARLOS/carlos.html

23. http://www.imj.org.il/

24. http://www.cr.nps.gov/

25. http://www.evansville.edu/~wcweb/wc101/

26. http://www.urz.uni-heidelberg.de/subject/hd/fak7/hist/e2/gen/

27. http://www.newton.cam.ac.uk/egypt/

28. http://www.channel1.com/users/mansoorm/eir.html

29. http://atlas.central.ntua.gr:8080/webacropol/

30. http://www.nltl.columbia.edu/groups2/rome/rome.html

31. http://ukanaix.cc.ukans.edu/~marc/geography/latinam/mexico/mayamenu.html

32. http://www.cmcc.muse.digital.ca/cmc/cmceng/mminteng.html

33. http://neal.ctstateu.edu/history/world_history/archives/archives.html

34. http://coombs.anu.edu.au/WWWVL-AsianStudies.html

35. http://neal.ctstateu.edu/history/world_history/archives/archive56.html

36. http://www.pitt.edu/~cjp/rshist.html

37. gopher://gopher.tamu.edu:70/11/.dir/soviet.archives.dir

38. http://www.yahoo.com/Humanities/History/American_History/

39. gopher://wiretap.spies.com/11/Gov/US-History

40. http://info.rutgers.edu/rulib/artshum/amhist.html

41. http://rs6.loc.gov/amhome.html

42. http://www.yahoo.com/Social_Science/History/Military_History/

43. http://grid.let.rug.nl/~welling/usa/revolution.html

44. http://cobweb.utcc.utk.edu/~hoemann/cwarhp.html

45. http://www.msstate.edu/Archives/History/USA/WWII/ww2.html

46. http://www.yahoo.com/Social_Science/History/Military_History/World_War-_II/

47. http://192.253.114.31/D-Day/GVPT_stuff/new.html

48. ftp://byrd.mu.wvnet.edu/pub/history/military/wwii/

49. ftp://192.253.114.3/pub/D-Day/

50. http://www.arts.cuhk.hk/NanjingMassacre/NM.html

51. http://www.princeton.edu/~mkporwit/uprising/top.html

52. http://www.onramp.net/~hbarker/

53. http://marlowe.wimsey.com/rshand/reflections/vietnam/vietnam.html

54. http://sunsite.unc.edu/expo/1492.exhibit/Intro.html

55. http://www.unifi.it/centri/sise/ewelcome.htm

56. http://www.nlm.nih.gov/hmd.dir/hmd.html

57. http://www.silcom.com/~origin/wscon.html

58. http://www.ushmm.org/

59. http://www.best.com/~mddunn/cybrary/

60. http://www.peg.apc.org/~iearn/hgpproject.html

61. http://www.arts.cuhk.hk/His.html

62. gopher://musicbox.mse.jhu.edu/11/others/archives

63. http://pantheon.cis.yale.edu/~davidp/archives.html

64. gopher://gopher.tntech.edu/00/gopher_root%3a%5bcampus.as.his
     t.res%5dhistorgs.dir

65. http://neal.ctstateu.edu/history/world_history/gate06.html

66. http://sunsite.unc.edu/lia/president/pres.html

67. http://lcweb.loc.gov/homepage/lchp.html

68. http://kuhttp.cc.ukans.edu/carrie/carrie_main.html

69. http://www.w3.org/hypertext/DataSources/bySubject/Literature/Gutenberg
     /Order.html

70. http://www.uc.edu/www/history/general.html

71. http://www.wesleyan.edu:80/histjrnl/hthome.htm

72. http://history.cc.ukans.edu/history/deremil/w_disc.html

73. http://grid.let.rug.nl/ahc/biblio2.html

74. http://www.tntech.edu/www/acad/hist/research.html

References

Aboba, Bernard, (1992). *The online user's encyclopedia: Bulletin boards and beyond,* Addison-Wesley: Reading, MA.

Angell, D., & Heslop, B. (1994). *The elements of e-mail style: Communicate effectively via electronic mail.* Addison-Wesley: Reading, MA.

Oatley, K. G. (1977). Inference, navigation, and cognitive maps. In Johnson-Laird, P.N., and Wason, P.C. (Eds), *Thinking: Readings in cognitive science* (pp. 537-547). Cambridge: Cambridge University Press.

Seabrook, J. (1994). My first flame. *New Yorker, 70*(16), 70–79.

Appendix A

Archives

alt.memetics resources page
http://www.xs4all.nl/~hingh/
alt.memetics/index.html#archives

Internet Crime Archives
http://underground.net/Art/Crime
/archives.html

OTHER DATA ARCHIVES
http://ssda.anu.edu.au/foreign.html

POLS Guide: On-line Documents
http://www.trincoll.edu/pols
/research/documents.html

Archives-Envtecsoc
gopher://csf.colorado.edu/11
/environment/Archives-Envtecsoc

CLIO -- The National Archives
Information Server
http://www.nara.gov/

National Archives Online Exhibit Hall
http://gopher.nara.gov:70/0/exhall
/exhibits.html

//cis.anu.edu.au•70/1ftp%3Acoom
gopher://cis.anu.edu.au:70
/1ftp%3Acoombs.anu.edu.au
@/coombspapers/coombsarchives
/aboriginal-history-jrnl/

WORLD WAR II
http://www.msstate.edu/Archives
/History/USA/WWII/ww2.html

soviet.archives.dir
gopher://gopher.tamu.edu:70/11/.dir
/soviet.archives.dir

World History Archives
http://neal.ctstateu.edu/history
/world_history/archives/archives.html

archives
gopher://musicbox.mse.jhu.edu/11
/others/archives

JPL image/information archives
http://www.jpl.nasa.gov/archive/

East Asia History Archives
http://neal.ctstateu.edu/history
/world_history/archives/archive56.html

The Archives
http://www.cityscape.co.uk/users
/ad88/arch.htm

EDUCATION POLICY ANALYSIS
ARCHIVES
http://info.asu.edu/asu-
cwis/epaa/welcome.html

Children
Children's Research Laboratory
http://www.psy.utexas.edu/psy/crl.html

Infants and babies
http://www.efn.org/~djz/birth
/babylist.html

Index of
/group/dss/Info.by.disability
/Attention.Deficit.Disorder/
http://www-
leland.stanford.edu:80/group/dss/
Info.by.disability/Attention.D
eficit.Disorder/

Kids_Count
gopher://cyfer.esusda.gov:70/11
/CYFER-net/statistics/Kids_Count

ChildCare
gopher://gopher-
cyfernet.mes.umn.edu:4242/11/ChildCare

ChildDevel
gopher://tinman.mes.umn.edu.:4242/11
/ChildCare/ChildDevel

SAFE-T-CHILD Online
http://yellodino.safe-t-child.com/

Panic Disorders in Children and
Adolescents
http://www.med.umich.edu/aacap
/panic.disorders.html

childrens-health.unicef-94
gopher://csf.Colorado.EDU:70/00/psn

/ppn-archives/childrens-health.unicef-94

National Child Rights Alliance
http://www.ai.mit.edu/people/ellens
/NCRA/ncra.html

CHILD QUEST INTERNATIONAL - Finds
missing children
http://www.omega.com/adima/bands
/child_quest/cqmain.html

Kempe National Center for the Prevention
and Treatment of Child Abuse and Neglect
http://nhic-
nt.health.org/htmlgen/htmlgen.exe
/Entry?HRCode='HR1106'

ChildCare
gopher://tinman.mes.umn.edu.:4242/11
/ChildCare

Child Welfare League of America
http://nhic-
nt.health.org/htmlgen/htmlgen.exe
/Entry?HRCode='HR0287'

Administration for Children and Families
http://www.acf.dhhs.gov/

Laboratory of Developmental
Neuropsychology
http://grafi.oulu.fi/lab/

European Society for Developmental
Psychology WWW server
http://fnord.dur.ac.uk/eurodev/
index.html

Community
The City of Philadelphia: Neighborhoods
Online
http://www.libertynet.org/community
/phila/nol.html

The USA CityLink Project
http://www.neosoft.com/citylink
/default.html

Community Development Society
International
http://www.infoanalytic.com/cds/

Community Economic Development
Network
http://titsoc.soc.titech.ac.jp/titsoc
/higuchi-lab/icm/ced-net.html

PlanetKeepers Home Page
http://galaxy.einet.net/galaxy

/Community/Environment
/Environmental-Activism/wayne-
pendley/plankeep.html

Neighborhoods Online: National
http://www.libertynet.org/community
/phila/natl.html

Maryland Community Crime Prevention
Institute
http://midget.towson.edu:8001/
MDCP.HTML

Community and Urban Development
Descriptions
http://asa.ugl.lib.umich.edu/chdocs
/nonprofits/urbandev.html#cednet

Computers and Computing
Society for Computers in Psychology
http://www.lafayette.edu/allanr/
scip.html

Academic Computing Center
http://albie.wcupa.edu/

Social Science Computing
http://www.ssc.upenn.edu/

New Home Page Association for History
and Computing
http://grid.let.rug.nl/ahc/welcome

QMW HCI Research Group Home Page
http://www.dcs.qmw.ac.uk/research
/hci/

The HCI Group at QMW
http://www.dcs.qmw.ac.uk/research
/hci/Introduction.html

Human-Computer Interaction Resources
http://www.ida.liu.se/labs/aslab
/groups/um/hci/

Netscape: The HCI Bibliography
ftp://archive.cis.ohio-
state.edu/pub/hcibib/README.
html#books

Conflict
ConflictNet Home Page
http://www.igc.apc.org/igc/cn.html

conflict
gopher://gopher.igc.apc.org/11/conflict

ConflictNet Home Page

http://www.igc.apc.org/conflictnet/

Yahoo - Social Science:History:Military
History:World War II
http://www.yahoo.com
/Social_Science/History
/Military_History/World_War_II/

World War II Archive
http://192.253.114.31/D-
Day/GVPT_stuff/new.html

WORLD WAR II
http://www.msstate.edu/Archives
/History/USA/WWII/ww2.html

KOREAN WAR PROJECT HOME PAGE
http://www.onramp.net/~hbarker/

The American Civil War Homepage
http://cobweb.utcc.utk.edu/~hoemann
/cwarhp.html

Databases
Rat Atlas Image Database
http://www.loni.ucla.edu/ratdata/
Rat.html

Trends in Developing Economies Database
Search
http://quasar.poly.edu:9090
/WorldBank/tides.html

1990 Census LOOKUP
http://cedr.lbl.gov/cdrom/doc
/lookup_doc.html

U. S. Bureau of the Census Home Page
http://www.census.gov/

U.S. Gazetteer
http://tiger.census.gov/cgi-bin/gazetteer

Housing and Household Economic
Statistics Division
http://www.census.gov/org/hhes
/index.html

statistics
gopher://cyfer.esusda.gov:70/11
/CYFER-net/statistics

Kids_Count
gopher://cyfer.esusda.gov:70/11
/CYFER-net/statistics/Kids_Count

1994 Green Book
http://www.os.dhhs.gov/0/aspe
/green_book/gbpage.html

USGS Node of National Geospatial Data
Clearinghouse
http://h2o.er.usgs.gov:80/nsdi/

USGS NSDI Clearinghouse - Aerial
Photographs and Satellite Photographs
http://nsdi.usgs.gov/nsdi/products
/aerial.html

ESRC Data Archive
http://www.ciesin.org/IC/esrc/ESRC-
home.html

Norwegian Social Science Data Services
(NSD)
http://www.uib.no/nsd/nsd-eng.html

Socioeconomic Data and Applications
Center - Home Page
http://www.ciesin.org/IC/SEDAC
/SEDAC-home.html

EURODATA Research Archive
http://www.sowi.uni-
mannheim.de/eurodata/eurodata.html

Environment
Humans and the Environment
http://kaos.erin.gov.au/human_env
/human_env.html

1994 National Environmental Scorecard
http://www.econet.apc.org/lcv
/scorecard.html

Environmental Protection Agency WWW
Server.
http://www.epa.gov/

Landscapes
http://life.anu.edu.au:80
/landscape_ecology/landscape.html

EcoNet Home Page
http://www.econet.apc.org/econet/

Eco-Hab Home Page
http://www.panix.com/~urbanomi
/ecohab.html

//ecosys.drdr.virginia.edu/
gopher://ecosys.drdr.virginia.edu/

League of Conservation Voters
http://www.econet.apc.org/lcv
/scorecard.html

The House of Representatives - Internet

Law Library - Environmental, natural
resource and energy law
http://www.pls.com:8001/d2/kelli
/httpd/htdocs/his/101.GBM

Environmental Protection Agency WWW
Server.
http://www.epa.gov/

REGIS: Environmental Planning GIS at
Berkeley
http://www.regis.berkeley.edu/

Integrating Environment and Development
http://kaos.erin.gov.au/portfolio/esd
/integ.html

PlanetKeepers Home Page
http://galaxy.einet.net/galaxy
/Community/Environment
/Environmental-Activism/wayne-pendle

Families
Three Essential Elements of Biblical
Charity: Faith, Family, and Work
http://www.usit.net/public/capo
/premise/95/feb/grnt1.html

Family
gopher://tinman.mes.umn.edu.:4242/11
/Family

famnet
gopher://tinman.mes.umn.edu.:4242/00
/Family/famnet

Sociology Resources
http://sosig.esrc.bris.ac.uk/Subjects
/sociol.html#family

Family World HomePage
http://www.family.com/

Family World Home Page
http://family.com/indexGX.html

Youth Indicators 1993 - HOME :
Demographics and Family Composition
http://www.ed.gov/pubs
/YouthIndicators/Demographics.html

Family
gopher://gopher-
cyfernet.mes.umn.edu:4242/11/Family

Administration for Children and Families
http://www.acf.dhhs.gov/

Parents Helping Parents

http://www.portal.com/~cbntmkr/
php.html

Baby Web: The Internet Parenting Resource
http://www.netaxs.com:80/~iris
/infoweb/baby.html

Facts for Families
http://www.psych.med.umich.edu/web
/aacap/factsFam/

Facts for Families
http://www.med.umich.edu/aacap
/facts.index.html

Fatherhood and Fatherlessness
http://www.vix.com/pub/men
/nofather/nodad.html

WORLDWIDE MARRIAGE
ENCOUNTER (Menu=wwme)
http://freenet3.scri.fsu.edu:81/ht-
free/wwme.html

Housing

Virginia Center for Housing Research
http://www.arch.vt.edu/vchr/vchr.html

Housing and Household Economic
Statistics Division
http://www.census.gov/org/hhes
/index.html

Housing and Urban Development
http://www.whitehouse.gov
/White_House/Cabinet/html/HUD.html

Overview of 54 Ways You Can Help The
Homeless
http://ecosys.drdr.virginia.edu/ways
/54.html

//csf.colorado.edu/11/psn/homel
gopher://csf.colorado.edu/11/psn
/homeless/

Cohousing
http://everest.cs.ucdavis.edu/~stanifor
/cohousing.html

Journals / Texts / Books
Netscape: OTHER RESOURCES
http://www.ucm.es/OTROS/Psyap
/resources/index.html#journals

etextcenters
http://ccat.sas.upenn.edu/jod
/etextcenters

Welcome to JEAB & JABA
http://www.envmed.rochester.edu
/wwwrap/behavior/jeabjaba.htm

APA Science Journals
http://www.apa.org/journals/
scjnlind.html

Psycoloquy Journal, Behavioral
& Brain Sciences (BBS), and Harnad E-
Print Archive
http://www.princeton.edu/~harnad/

Journal of World-Systems Research
http://csf.Colorado.EDU:80/wsystems
/jwsr.html

Meanderings - An African American
Journal of Politics, Art and Culture
http://www.webcom.com/~sppg
/meanderings/me.shtml

_INTERNET RESOURCES _ Newsletter
Issue 6
http://www.hw.ac.uk/libWWW/irn
/irne6.html

interNEWS Headlines
http://www.gold.net/info-
highway/internews/news18/news18.htm

Alex: A Catalogue of Electronic Texts on
the Internet
http://www.lib.ncsu.edu/stacks/alex-
index.html

Texts of Exploration
http://bateson.ukc.ac.uk/Gallery
/Explore/Images/Frontpiece1.html

Gutenberg Master Index in Order of
Release
http://www.w3.org/hypertext
/DataSources/bySubject/Literature
/Gutenberg/Order.html

On-line Documents & Texts
http://www.trincoll.edu/pols
/research/documents.html

Netscape: The HCI Bibliography
ftp://archive.cis.ohio-
state.edu/pub/hcibib/README.
html#books

Welcome to the Internet Book Shop
http://www.bookshop.co.uk/

Hoover Institution Newsletter Winter
1995
http://hoover.stanford.edu/www
/newsWin1995.html

Ethnomethodology Newsletter Index
http://www.comp.lancs.ac.uk
/sociology/research/ethnonews
/ethnonewsindex.html

The Cyber Herald: Poverty News
http://www2.ari.net/home/poverty
/news.html

Self-Help & Psychology Magazine
http://www.well.com/user/selfhelp/

Mental Health
Texas Department of Mental Health and
Mental Retardation
http://www.mhmr.texas.gov/

Florida Mental Health Institute Home Page
http://hal.fmhi.usf.edu/

Mental Health
http://baby.indstate.edu:80/msattler/sci-
tech/med/psych/index.html

Mental Health Risk Factors for
Adolescents
http://education.indiana.edu/cas/adol
/mental.html

The GROHOL Mental Health Page - Main
Menu
http://www1.mhv.net/~grohol/

STAR (Stress and Anxiety Research)
Society
http://www.uib.no/STAR/

Mental Health Resources
http://www.cityscape.co.uk/users
/ad88/resuk.htm

The Arc, a national organization on mental
retardation
http://fohnix.metronet.com/~thearc
/welcome.html

Mood Disorders
http://avocado.pc.helsinki.fi/~janne
/mood/mood.html

Poverty
gopher://garnet.berkeley.edu:1250/11
/.welfare/.poverty

The Cyber Herald: Poverty News
http://www2.ari.net/home/poverty
/news.html

c.pov
gopher://poverty.sass.cwru.edu:70/11
/centers/c.pov

Overview of 54 Ways You Can Help The
Homeless
http://ecosys.drdr.virginia.edu/ways
/54.html

//csf.colorado.edu/11/psn/homel
gopher://csf.colorado.edu/11/psn
/homeless/

Housing and Household Economic
Statistics Division
http://www.census.gov/org/hhes
/index.html

Economics
gopher://cesar.unicamp.br/11/Papers
/Economics

Welcome to helpwanted.com
http://helpwanted.com/welcome.html

1994 Green Book
http://www.os.dhhs.gov/0/aspe
/green_book/gbpage.html

Research Centers
POLS Guide: Research Institutions
http://www.trincoll.edu/pols
/research/institutions.html

The Cato Institute
http://w3.ag.uiuc.edu/liberty/cato
/index.html

RAND Home Page
http://www.rand.org/

Hubert H. Humphrey Institute of Public
Affairs
http://www.hhh.umn.edu/

The Cascade Center for Public Service
http://cases.pubaf.washington.edu/0c:
/center.htm l /

Hoover Institution
http://hoover.stanford.edu/www
/Welcome.html

Brookings Institute
gopher://gopher.brook.edu/

AusWeb95-WWW, Researchers and
Research Services- Collaborative Use of
the Web-sociology of the Web
http://www.scu.edu.au/ausweb95
/papers/sociology/dawe/

Children's Research Laboratory
http://www.psy.utexas.edu/psy/crl.html

Office of Research - Funding Resources
http://johnson.bcm.tmc.edu/resource.html

Survey Research Center
http://www.princeton.edu/~abelson
/index.html

The ERaM (Ethnicity, Racism and the
Media) Programme
http://www.brad.ac.uk/bradinfo
/research/eram/eram.html#eramtop

QMW HCI Research Group Home Page
http://www.dcs.qmw.ac.uk/research
/hci/

National Center for Research on Cultural
Diversity and Second Language Learning
http://zzyx.ucsc.edu/Cntr/cntr.html

Craig McKie's Social Science Research
Engines
http://www.uakron.edu/hefe/mckie.html

Penn State Population Research Institute
http://www.pop.psu.edu/

Center for Social Science Computation and
Research
http://augustus.csscr.washington.edu/

Social Science Software
USGS Mapping Information: Mapping
Science Software
http://www-
nmd.usgs.gov/www/html/software.html

OAK Software Repository
http://www.acs.oakland.edu/oak/
oak.html

CSAC Software Archives
http://lucy.ukc.ac.uk/archives.html

UB Anthropology - Software Resources
http://wings.buffalo.edu/academic
/department/anthropology/software

Appendix B

A Primer on How to Work With the Usenet Community

by Chuq Von Rospach

Archive-name: usenet/primer/part1
Original-author: chuq@apple.COM (Chuq Von Rospach)
Comment: enhanced & edited until 5/93 by spaf@cs.purdue.edu (Gene
Spafford) Last-change: 29 Jan 1995 by netannounce@deshaw.com (Mark
Moraes)
Changes-posted-to: news.misc,news.answers

This message describes the Usenet culture and customs that have
developed over time. Other documents in this newsgroup describe what
Usenet is and manuals or on-line help on your system should provide
detailed technical documentation. All new users should read this
message to acclimate themselves to Usenet. (Old users could read it, too,
to refresh their memories.)

It is the people participating in Usenet that make it worth the
effort to read and maintain; for Usenet to function properly those people
must be able to interact in productive ways. This document is intended
as a guide to using the net in ways that will be pleasant and productive
for everyone. This document is not intended to teach you how to use
Usenet. Instead, it is a guide to using it politely, effectively and
efficiently. Communication by computer is new to almost everybody,
and there are certain aspects that can make it a frustrating experience
until you get used to them. This document should help you avoid the
worst traps. The easiest way to learn how to use Usenet is to watch how
others use it. Start reading the news and try to figure out what people
are doing and why. After a couple of weeks you will start understanding
why certain things are done and what things shouldn't be done. There
are documents available describing the technical details of how to use the
software. These are different depending on which programs you use to
access the news. You can get copies of these from your system administrator. If you do not know who that person is, they can be contacted on
most systems by mailing to account "news", "usenet" or "postmaster".

213

NEVER FORGET THAT THE PERSON ON THE OTHER SIDE IS HUMAN

Because your interaction with the network is through a computer it is easy to forget that there are people "out there." Situations arise where emotions erupt into a verbal free-for-all that can lead to hurt feelings. Please remember that people all over the world are reading your words. Do not attack people if you cannot persuade them with your presentation of the facts. Screaming, cursing, and abusing others only serves to make people think less of you and less willing to help you when you need it. If you are upset at something or someone, wait until you have had a chance to calm down and think about it. A cup of (decaf!) coffee or a good night's sleep works wonders on your perspective. Hasty words create more problems than they solve. Try not to say anything to others you would not say to them in person in a room full of people.
Don't Blame System Admins for their Users' Behavior. Sometimes, you may find it necessary to write to a system administrator about something concerning his or her site. Maybe it is a case of the software not working, or a control message escaped, or maybe one of the users at that site has done something you feel requires comment. No matter how steamed you may be, be polite to the sysadmin -- he or she may not have any idea of what you are going to say, and may not have any part in the incidents involved. By being civil and temperate, you are more likely to obtain their courteous attention and assistance.

NEVER ASSUME THAT A PERSON IS SPEAKING FOR THEIR ORGANIZATION

Many people who post to Usenet do so from machines at their office or school. Despite that, never assume that the person is speaking for the organization that they are posting their articles from (unless the person explicitly says so). Some people put explicit disclaimers to this effect in their messages, but this is a good general rule. If you find an article offensive, consider taking it up with the person directly, or ignoring it. Learn about "kill files" in your newsreader, and other techniques for ignoring people whose postings you find offensive.

BE CAREFUL WHAT YOU SAY ABOUT OTHERS

Please remember -- you read netnews; so do as many as 3,000,000 other people. This group quite possibly includes your boss, your friend's boss, your girl friend's brother's best friend and one of your father's beer buddies. Information posted on the net can come back to haunt you or the person you are talking about. Think twice before you post personal information about yourself or others. This applies especially strongly to groups like soc.singles and alt.sex but even postings in groups like talk.politics.misc have included information about the personal life of third parties that could get them into serious trouble if it got into the wrong hands.

BE BRIEF

Never say in ten words what you can say in fewer. Say it succinctly and it will have a greater impact. Remember that the longer you make your article, the fewer people will bother to read it.

YOUR POSTINGS REFLECT UPON YOU—BE PROUD OF THEM

Most people on Usenet will know you only by what you say and how well you say it. They may someday be your co-workers or friends. Take some time to make sure each posting is something that will not embarrass you later. Minimize your spelling errors and make sure that the article is easy to read and understand. Writing is an art and to do it well requires practice. Since much of how people judge you on the net is based on your writing, such time is well spent.

USE DESCRIPTIVE TITLES

The subject line of an article is there to enable a person with a limited amount of time to decide whether or not to read your article. Tell people what the article is about before they read it. A title like "Car for Sale" to rec.autos does not help as much as "66 MG Midget for sale: Beaverton OR." Don't expect people to read your article to find out what it is about because many of them won't bother. Some sites truncate the length of the subject line to 40 characters so keep your subjects short and to the point.

THINK ABOUT YOUR AUDIENCE

When you post an article, think about the people you are trying to reach. Asking UNIX(*) questions on rec.autos will not reach as many of the people you want to reach as if you asked them on comp.unix.questions or comp.unix.internals. Try to get the most appropriate audience for your message, not the widest. It is considered bad form to post both to misc.misc, soc.net-people, or misc.wanted and to some other newsgroup. If it belongs in that other newsgroup, it does not belong in misc.misc, soc.net-people, or misc.wanted. If your message is of interest to a limited geographic area (apartments, car sales, meetings, concerts, etc...), restrict the distribution of the message to your local area. Some areas have special newsgroups with geographical limitations, and the recent versions of the news software allow you to limit the distribution of material sent to world-wide newsgroups. Check with your system administrator to see what newsgroups are available and how to use them. If you want to try a test of something, do not use a world-wide newsgroup! Messages in misc.misc that say "This is a test" are likely to cause large numbers of caustic messages to flow into your mailbox. There are newsgroups that are local to your computer or area that should be used. Your system administrator can tell you what they are. Be familiar with the group you are posting to before you post! You shouldn't post to groups you do not read, or post to groups you've only read a few articles from -- you may not be familiar with the on-going conventions and themes of the group. One normally does not join a conversation by just walking up and talking. Instead, you listen first and then join in if you have something pertinent to contribute.

BE CAREFUL WITH HUMOR AND SARCASM

Without the voice inflections and body language of personal communications, it is easy for a remark meant to be funny to be misinterpreted. Subtle humor tends to get lost, so take steps to make sure that people realize you are trying to be funny. The net has developed a symbol called the smiley face. It looks like ":-)" and points out sections of articles with humorous intent. No matter how broad the humor or satire, it is safer to remind people that you are being funny. But also be aware that quite frequently satire is posted without any explicit indications. If an article outrages you strongly, you should ask yourself if it just may have been unmarked satire. Several self-proclaimed connoisseurs refuse to use smiley faces, so take heed or you may make a temporary fool of yourself.

ONLY POST A MESSAGE ONCE

Avoid posting messages to more than one newsgroup unless you are sure it is appropriate. If you do post to multiple newsgroups, do not post to each group separately. Instead, specify all the groups on a single copy of the message. This reduces network overhead and lets people who subscribe to more than one of those groups see the message once instead of having to wade through each copy.

PLEASE ROTATE MESSAGES WITH QUESTIONABLE CONTENT

Certain newsgroups (such as rec.humor) have messages in them that may be offensive to some people. To make sure that these messages are not read unless they are explicitly requested, these messages should be encrypted. The standard encryption method is to rotate each letter by thirteen characters so that an "a" becomes an "n". This is known on the network as "rot13" and when you rotate a message the word "rot13" should be in the "Subject:" line. Most of the software used to read Usenet articles have some way of encrypting and decrypting messages. Your system administrator can tell you how the software on your system works, or you can use the Unix command
        tr '[a-m][n-z][A-M][N-Z]' '[n-z][a-m][N-Z][A-M]'
Don't forget the single quotes!)

SUMMARIZE WHAT YOU ARE FOLLOWING UP

When you are following up someone's article, please summarize the parts of the article to which you are responding. This allows readers to appreciate your comments rather than trying to remember what the original article said. It is also possible for your response to get to some sites before the original article. Summarization is best done by including appropriate quotes from the original article. Do not include the entire article since it will irritate the people who have already seen it. Even if you are responding to the entire article, summarize only the major points you are discussing.

WHEN SUMMARIZING, SUMMARIZE!

When you request information from the network, it is common courtesy to report your findings so that others can benefit as well. The best way of doing this is to take all the responses that you received and edit them into a single article that is posted to the places where you originally posted your question. Take the time to strip headers, combine duplicate information, and write a short summary. Try to credit the information to the people that sent it to you, where possible.

USE MAIL, DON'T POST A FOLLOW-UP

One of the biggest problems we have on the network is that when someone asks a question, many people send out identical answers. When this happens, dozens of identical answers pour through the net.

Mail your answer to the person and suggest that they summarize to the network. This way the net will only see a single copy of the answers, no matter how many people answer the question. If you post a question, please remind people to send you the answers by mail and at least offer to summarize them to the network.

READ ALL FOLLOW-UPS AND DON'T REPEAT WHAT HAS ALREADY BEEN SAID

Before you submit a follow-up to a message, read the rest of the messages in the newsgroup to see whether someone has already said what you want to say. If someone has, don't repeat it.

CHECK THE HEADERS WHEN FOLLOWING UP

The news software has provisions to specify that follow-ups to an article should go to a specific set of newsgroups -- possibly different from the newsgroups to which the original article was posted. Sometimes the groups chosen for follow-ups are totally inappropriate, especially as a thread of discussion changes with repeated postings. You should carefully check the groups and distributions given in the header and edit them as appropriate. If you change the groups named in the header, or if you direct follow-ups to a particular group, say so in the body of the message -- not everyone reads the headers of postings.

BE CAREFUL ABOUT COPYRIGHTS AND LICENSES

Once something is posted onto the network, it is *probably* in the public domain unless you own the appropriate rights (most notably, if you wrote the thing yourself) and you post it with a valid copyright notice; a court would have to decide the specifics and there are arguments for both sides of the issue. Now that the US has ratified the Berne convention, the issue is even murkier (if you are a poster in the US). For all practical purposes, though, assume that you effectively give up the copyright if you don't put in a notice. Of course, the *information* becomes public, so you mustn't post trade secrets that way. When posting material to the network, keep in mind that material that is UNIX-related may be restricted by the license you or your company signed with AT&T and be careful not to violate it. You should also be aware that posting movie reviews, song lyrics, or anything else published under a copyright could cause you, your company, or members of the net community to be held liable for damages, so we highly recommend caution in using this material.

CITE APPROPRIATE REFERENCES

If you are using facts to support a cause, state where they came from. Don't take someone else's ideas and use them as your own. You don't want someone pretending that your ideas are theirs; show them the same respect.

MARK OR ROTATE ANSWERS AND SPOILERS

When you post something (like a movie review that discusses a detail of the plot) which might spoil a surprise for other people, please mark your message with a warning so that they can skip the message. Another alternative would be to use the "rot13" protocol to encrypt the message so it cannot be read accidentally. When you post a message with a spoiler in it make sure the word "spoiler" is part of the "Subject:" line.

SPELLING FLAMES CONSIDERED HARMFUL

Every few months a plague descends on Usenet called the spelling flame. It starts out when someone posts an article correcting the spelling or grammar in some article. The immediate result seems to be for everyone on the net to turn into a 6th grade English teacher and pick apart each other's postings for a few weeks. This is not productive and tends to cause people who used to be friends to get angry with each other. It is important to remember that we all make mistakes, and that there are many users on the net who use English as a second language. There are also a number of people who suffer from dyslexia and who have difficulty noticing their spelling mistakes. If you feel that you must make a comment on the quality of a posting, please do so by mail, not on the network.

DON'T OVERDO SIGNATURES

Signatures are nice, and many people can have a signature added to their postings automatically by placing it in a file called "$HOME/.signature". Don't overdo it. Signatures can tell the world something about you, but keep them short. A signature that is longer than the message itself is considered to be in bad taste. The main purpose of a signature is to help people locate you, not to tell your life story. Every signature should

include at least your return address relative to a major, known site on the
network and a proper domain-format address. Your system administrator can give this to you. Some news posters attempt to enforce a 4 line
limit on signature files -- an amount that should be more than sufficient
to provide a return address and attribution.

LIMIT LINE LENGTH AND AVOID CONTROL CHARACTERS

Try to keep your text in a generic format. Many (if not most) of the
people reading Usenet do so from 80 column terminals or from
workstations with 80 column terminal windows. Try to keep your lines
of text to less than 80 characters for optimal readability. If people quote
part of your article in a followup, short lines will probably show up
better, too. Also realize that there are many, many different forms of
terminals in use. If you enter special control characters in your message,
it may result in your message being unreadable on some terminal types; a
character sequence that causes reverse video on your screen may result in
a keyboard lock and graphics mode on someone else's terminal. You
should also try to avoid the use of tabs, too, since they may also be
interpreted differently on terminals other than your own.
      Please do not use Usenet as a resource for homework assignments.
Usenet is not a resource for homework or class assignments. A common
new user reaction to learning of all these people out there holding
discussions is to view them as a great resource for gathering information
for reports and papers. Trouble is, after seeing a few hundred such
requests, most people get tired of them, and won't reply anyway.
Certainly not in the expected or hoped-for numbers. Posting student
questionnaires automatically brands you a "newbie" and does not usually
garner much more than a tiny number of replies. Further, some of those
replies are likely to be incorrect. Instead, read the group of interest for a
while, and find out what the main "threads" are - what are people
discussing? Are there any themes you can discover? Are there different
schools of thought? Only post something after you've followed the group
for a few weeks, after you have read the Frequently Asked Questions
posting if the group has one, and if you still have a question or opinion
that others will probably find interesting. If you have something
interesting to contribute, you'll find that you gain almost instant
acceptance, and your posting will generate a large number of follow-up
postings. Use these in your research; it is a far more efficient (and
accepted) way to learn about the group than to follow that first instinct
and post a simple questionnaire.

PLEASE DO NOT USE USENET AS AN ADVERTISING MEDIUM

Advertisements on Usenet are rarely appreciated. In general, the louder or more inappropriate the ad is, the more antagonism it will stir up. The accompanying posting "Rules for posting to Usenet" has more on this in the section about "Announcement of professional products or services". Try the biz.* hierarchies instead.

AVOID POSTING TO MULTIPLE NEWSGROUPS

Few things annoy Usenet readers as much as multiple copies of a posting appearing in multiple newsgroups. (called 'spamming' for historical reasons) A posting that is cross-posted (i.e lists multiple newsgroups on the Newsgroups: header line) to a few appropriate newsgroups is fine, but even with cross-posts, restraint is advised. For a cross-post, you may want to set the Followup-To: header line to the most suitable group for the rest of the discussion.

(*)UNIX is a registered trademark of X/Open.

This document is in the public domain (Appendix B) and may be reproduced or excerpted by anyone wishing to do so.

Dear Student:

Thank you for buying *Using the Internet for Social Science Research and Practice* by Edward Kardas and Tommy Milford. **As a complimentary bonus, and to demonstrate the value of online information, OCLC Online Computer Library Center, Inc., and Wadsworth Publishing Company are pleased to provide access to the world's fastest growing online reference service–OCLC's FirstSearch® service.** Your access to this service is free with the purchase of this book. The authorization will expire in December 1997.

FirstSearch is comprehensive and easy to use
Available via the Internet, FirstSearch is comprehensive and easy to use, providing seamless access to bibliographic and abstract information. You simply select a topic area and a database from the menu and follow the online instructions and examples. Additional searching hints are given on each screen. Use FirstSearch to:
- access popular and unique databases in a variety of topic areas
- research current and accurate information
- identify references to articles, books, sound recordings, videocassettes, etc.
- find location information for the items you need

Search unique and popular databases
Your FirstSearch account gives you virtually 24-hour access from your home, dorm, or office to a base package* of unique and popular FirstSearch databases, including:
- **NetFirst™**–OCLC's new authoritative directory for Internet resources containing citations, complete with summary descriptions and subject headings, describing World Wide Web pages, interest groups, library catalogs, FTP sites, Internet services, Gopher servers, electronic journals and newsletters, and more
- **WorldCat®**–the holdings of 21,000 libraries around the world, including books, serials, videocassettes, maps, musical scores, etc.
- **ArticleFirst®**–citations to table of contents items from 13,000 journals in science, technology, medicine, social science, business, etc.
- **ContentsFirst®**–complete tables of contents from the 13,000 ArticleFirst journals
- **FastDoc™**–citations to articles available for fast online ASCII full-text delivery, covering title lists from 800 ABI/INFORM and Periodical Abstracts journals
- **ERIC**–a guide to published and unpublished educational sources
- **GPO Monthly Catalog**–a catalog of U.S. Government publications since July 1976
- **MEDLINE**–3,500 journals covering all areas of medicine
- **PapersFirst™**–over 580,000 records of papers presented at conferences worldwide
- **ProceedingsFirst™**–list of papers presented at each conference covered in PapersFirst

* OCLC reserves the right to add or delete databases from this complimentary offer

Access is available using various methods

It's easy to access FirstSearch using one of the following methods. Your authorization and password are included in the following directions.

- **From the OCLC Reference Services Home Page on the WWW:**
    Type **http://ref.oclc.org:2000**
    From the Logon Prompt type your FirstSearch authorization:
    100-123-141 and press <Tab>
    Type your user password: **Wadsworth**
    Click on <Start>
- **From the OCLC Home Page on the WWW:**
    Type **http://www.oclc.org**
    From the On Ramp to OCLC Services choose FirstSearch
    Type your FirstSearch authorization: **100-123-141** and press <Enter>
    Type your FirstSearch user password: **Wadsworth** and press <Enter>
- **Using telnet:**
    Type **telnet fscat.oclc.org** and press <Enter>
    Type your FirstSearch authorization: **100-123-141** and press <Enter>
    Type your FirstSearch user password: **Wadsworth** and press <Enter>

Look for FirstSearch Web access, available December 1995, so you can use Netscape or Mosaic to point, click, and find what you need.

For more information

Once you've tried FirstSearch, we're sure you'll want access to the full range of over 55 databases, including a growing number of databases with full-text options. Contact your local public or academic library and ask for FirstSearch. If it's not available, ask them to contact OCLC's National Sales Division at (800) 848-5878, ext. 6251. Information about OCLC's products and services is also available from OCLC's Home Page on the World Wide Web: http://www.oclc.org.

OCLC is a nonprofit computer library service and research organization whose computer networks and services link more than 21,000 libraries in 63 countries and territories.